Instruments of Devotion

INSTRUMENTS OF DEVOTION

The Practices and Objects of Religious Piety
from the Late Middle Ages to the 20th Century

Henning Laugerud & Laura Katrine Skinnebach (eds.)

Instruments of Devotion
The Practices and Objects of Religious Piety from
the Late Middle Ages to the 20th Century
© Aarhus University Press and the authors 2007

Design, typesetting and cover: Anne Marie Kaad
Typeface: Giovanni 9/14 and Antiqua
Printed by Narayana Press, Gylling
Printed in Denmark 2007

ISBN 978 87 7934 200 2

Published with the financial support of
The Norwegian Research Council
The Meltzerfoundation, University of Bergen
Bergen Museum, University of Bergen

Aarhus University Press
Langelandsgade 177
DK-8200 Aarhus N
www.unipress.dk

White Cross Mills
Hightown, Lancaster, LA1 4XS
United Kingdom
www.gazellebookservices.co.uk

PO Box 511
Oakville, CT 06779
USA
www.oxbowbooks.com

European Network on the Instruments of Devotion, ENID
Publication no. 1

www.enid.uib.no

Table of Contents

Preface   7

HENNING LAUGERUD · LAURA KATRINE SKINNEBACH
'Introduction'   9

1ST SECTION

HENRIK VON ACHEN
'Piety, Practise and Process'   23

MARIO PERNIOLA
'The Cultural Turn of Catholicism'   45

METTE BIRKEDAL BRUUN
'Manual Labour as *praxis pietatis*:
Sketch of a Motif in the
17th Century Cistercian Reform at La Trappe'   61

ROB FAESEN
'The Great Silence of Saint Joseph:
Devotion to Saint Joseph and the 17th Century Crisis
of Mysticism in the Jesuit Order'   73

FRED VAN LIEBURG
'The Medical Market Compared with the Pastoral Market:
A Perspective from Early Modern Dutch History'   93

2ND SECTION

SALVADOR RYAN
'Weapons of Redemption:
Piety, Poetry and the Instruments of
the Passion in Late Medieval Ireland'   111

PETER DE MEY
'Looking at the Mystery of the Incarnated God:
Eastern and Western Iconography as a Source
of Theological Reflection'   125

NILS HOLGER PETERSEN
'Sepolcro:
Musical Devotion of the Passion in 17th-18th Century Austria'   145

ELI HELDAAS SELAND
'19th Century Devotional Medals'   157

HENNING LAUGERUD
'Visuality and Devotion in the Middle Ages'   173

LAURA KATRINE SKINNEBACH
'"the solace of his image":
Images and Presence in Late Medieval Devotional Practice'   189

Bibliography   209

Notes on contributors   221

Preface

The editors would like to thank Henrik von Achen and Eli Heldaas Seland for all their help in preparing this anthology. Warmly felt thanks goes to The Norwegian Research Council, Bergen Museum, University of Bergen and the Meltzer Foundation, also University of Bergen, for their generous financial support. Many thanks goes to Arthur Sand, University of Oslo, for helping out with the illustrations. We would also like to thank Aarhus University Press for their cooperation and professional help in preparing this book for publication.

Henning Laugerud & Laura Katrine Skinnebach

Introduction

Henning Laugerud and Laura Katrine Skinnebach

The so-called 'return of religion' in world-affairs has by now become rather obvious. At universities special courses, even at undergraduate level, are dedicated to this topic. Peter Berger's maxim of 'the desecularization of the World' has in a surprisingly short time become something of a commonplace.[1] The secularization process in Western culture has proven, if not a myth, at least grossly overrated, and as Berger points out: 'secularization on the societal level is not necessarily linked to secularization on the level of individual consciousness.'[2] Peter Berger sees the assumption that we live in a secularized world as false. Perhaps even the supposedly 'secular' political theory from the 18th and 19th centuries is really 'theology in disguise', as William Cavanaugh argues.[3] The weberian claim of 'die Entzauberung der Welt' is perhaps nothing more than a wishful myth of the High Priests of Modernity.

Belief and religion are certainly returning as focal concerns in modern philosophical debate. Interestingly, this religious turn is most clearly seen in so-called post-modern or post-structuralist thinking.[4] As Santiago Zabala states in his introduction to the discussion between Richard Rorty and Gianni Vattimo on the future of religion: 'Today, [...], we are witnessing the dissolution of philosophical

---

1 See Berger, Peter L. (ed.): *The Desecularization of the World. Resurgent Religion and World Politics*. Washington D.C. 1995.

2 Berger 1995, p. 3.

3 Cavanaugh, William T.: *Theopolitical Imagination*. London 2002, p. 2.

4 An important contribution to this debate is the Italian philosopher Mario Perniola's book: *Del sentire cattolico. La forma culturale di una religione universale*, from 2001. See also his contribution in the present anthology.

theories such as positivist scientism and marxism that thought they had definitively liquidated religion. After modernity, there are no more strong philosophical reasons either to be an atheist refusing religion or to be a theist refuting science'.[5]

This, or similar attitudes, form a common point of departure for all the contributors to this anthology, being the reason why we all feel that the studies of matters concerning religion in all aspects of life are of utmost importance. Today's situation in Europe illustrates the need for historical knowledge and perspective on culture and religion, particularly Christianity and all its denominational varieties. Christianity's influence *on* and *in* European culture cannot be overestimated, particularly understood as a dynamic and multifaceted force.

The outwardness of belief

An important element in Christian cultures is devotion, a phenomenon that articulates itself as practices expressed through instruments. Instruments can be broadly defined as all actions, rituals, gestures, and material devices such as books, images, music etc. that are articulated in and by devotional practice. The contributions in this anthology have their main focus on such religious practices and devotional instruments – that which we could call the material or physical and expressive aspects of religion. This active or external aspect of religion, which religious practices and artefacts represent, is what creates religious communities and makes it possible for humans to act as social beings by making things memorable. Through actions, objects and places one creates a cultural memory that passes on values, ideas, and insights to coming generations. This is clearly seen in the core ritual of Christianity – the eucharistic celebration – as formulated in St. Paul: 'This is my body which is for you. Do this in remembrance of me'.[6] This is no mere reminder of a past event: Strictly speaking, *anamnesis* is much more than the simple sign of a fact distant (in time) from itself; it is rather the actual 're-collection' of a truth which eternally *is*, so that to recollect the sacrifice of Christ is to make it really and effectively present.[7] This is a memory that is retrospective, present and prospective. In this sense Christianity can be seen as a memory-religion or a religion of remembrance: '[…] weil das Gedenken der Heilstaten Gottes Hauptinhalt des Glaubens ist. Deshalb entscheidet auch das Gedenken Gottes an

---

5   Zabala, Santiago (ed.): *The Future of Religion*. New York 2005, p. 1. One of the foremost representatives of this philosophical attitude, in addition to Mario Perniola, is Gianni Vattimo. For references see Zabala's introduction.

6   1 Cor. 11.24.

7   Watts, Alan: *Myth and Ritual in Christianity*. London 1983 (1954), p. 95.

die Menschen (wie sein vergessen) über Heil oder Verdammnis. Durch Erinner-ung (Anamnesis) wird die Gemeinschaft der Gläubigen konstituiert.'[8]

The idea that religion is fundamentally an interior disposition of the individual toward the Transcendent is after all an invention of fairly recent historical origin. There is no *homo interior* without the *homo exterior* as Henrik von Achen states in his contribution to the present anthology. The external aspects of religion, its instru-ments, have played their part in the cultural construction of society and may be studied to understand the beliefs, attitudes and practices they manifest. Therefore, studies of devotional instruments may lead us to an understanding of piety. Such studies are by necessity intrinsically and irreducibly interdisciplinary, since the objects in question express themselves as such multifaceted phenomena.

Faith or religion necessarily has 'horizontal aspects', in terms of sociological and organisational structures and attitudes within mankind, as well as a 'horizon-tal practice' in and towards society, but no religion can survive without a 'vertical aspect': cults and rituals. In Christianity, where rituals do not serve magical pur-poses of control or protection, the religion cannot survive if this vertical practice does not engage the hearts of the faithful. Therefore, in a Christian context, all ritual practices must to some extent become devotional practices. Integral to any *praxis pietatis* is a certain order, a structure of this particular devotion, its process and apparatus being not merely a question of form, but of substance. Most such practices have a clear instrumental (material) component, be it a book, a pattern of prayers, a structuring of the day, the use of devotional objects, pictures or songs etc. It belongs to the nature of practical piety that it is not just a question of pi-ous thoughts, but also of something done in a certain way to evoke and structure such thoughts. A living religion then, must express itself in devotional practices. Fundamental to such practices are order and instrumentality, which create a sig-nificant relationship with the more generic concept of collective ritual, and thus memory, culture and the sense of a dynamic tradition.

What is the European Network on the Instruments of Devotion?

The above stated ideas about religion, devotional practice and culture form the basis of a network formed in 2003 called *European Network on the Instruments of Devotion* or ENID, an international research network coordinated from the Uni-

---

8   Oexle, Otto G.: 'Memoria, Memorialüberliefung, in *Lexikon des Mittelalters, vol. VI*. München 2002, col. 510-512. For a more in depth discussion of this see also his article: 'Memoria in der Gesellschaft und in der Kultur des Mittelalters'. Heinzle J. (ed.): *Modernes Mittelalter. Neue Bilder einer populären Epoche*. Frankfurt am Main 1999, pp. 297-323.

versity of Bergen, Norway.[9] It focuses on the instrumentality of Christian piety and devotional practices, from 14th century *devotio moderna* to Vatican II in the 20th century.[10] Scholars from aesthetics, history, art history, literature, musicology, philosophy and theology form a cross disciplinary group. Through interchange of ideas, sharing of knowledge and critical discourse, the interdisciplinary research of ENID aims at gaining a deeper insight into the mechanisms of piety and devotion. The phenomena and their instruments, the relation between which must be seen as dialectical, since the instrumentality of devotions both expresses and forms piety, are seen and sought explained as essential features in the religious and cultural development of Europe. At least after the Reformation one cannot understand the religious culture of Europe without studying the entire denominational pattern. Thus ENID focuses on both denominational and interdenominational features of Christian piety.

The broad time frame allows the network to focus on a variety of themes, ranging from the roots of late medieval piety to the explosion of devotional items in the 19th and 20th centuries. It further provides opportunities for diachronic approaches, in studies for instance of the dialectics between monastic and lay piety, the relationship between theology and piety, the phenomenon of secularization or, indeed, iconographical, musicological or literary developments.

The historical perspective is seen as crucial for the understanding of religion in its cultural contexts and varieties, and therefore central to the research conducted by the ENID-members. Religion is culture, and culture and religion are closely knit together. One cannot understand Europe without understanding its history and culture, and this history is incomprehensible unless one understands the religious components which have been, and still are, such important characteristics of European culture. But this understanding, and this necessary knowledge of Christianity in Europe, both past and present, is about to disappear, particularly perhaps among the younger generations.[11]

---

9   ENID was established in Bergen on 16th November 2003. The network is coordinated by Professor Henrik von Achen, and its host institution is the University of Bergen through its museum, Bergen Museum.

10   See the ENID charter on the network website: www.enid.uib.no. The charter is a basic document, defining what ENID is, what the network wants to do, and briefly outlining how it intends to do it. The present version is the first, accepted by the members in January 2004.

11   See Grace Davies article: 'Europe: The Exception That Proves the Rule?' in Berger 1995, pp. 65-83. Her conclusion is that there today seems to be a generation-by-generation drop in religious knowledge, and an ignorance of even the most basic understandings of Christian teaching especially among young people. If this really is so, it will have heavy cultural and historical consequences, and is something that underlines the need for a broad scholarly interest and research on the importance of religion in the European culture(s). See also her book *Religion in Modern Europe. A Memory Mutates*. Oxford 2000.

Traditions of Devotion

Questions concerning cultural and religious continuity, change, and interchange between denominational preferences are shown great interest within the research conducted by the members of ENID. A piety expressed in devotional practices obviously is an important ingredient in understanding medieval, particularly late medieval, Christianity. To the *devotio moderna* of the 14th century and to the entire late medieval piety, the devotional image (Andachtsbild) was a vital instrument serving as a point of focus. It gave each devotion its particular character derived from the motif depicted or practice involved, and this instrumentality distinguished it from any other pious practice. Thus the instrument played a constitutive role in creating that special, intense, spiritual, and fundamental or existential meeting between God and the individual believer which we call 'devotion'.

Lutherans, in the post-reformation period, were by no means without pious practices. Among the most prominent were perhaps the 'house service' and the use of edifying books containing prayers for every day or time of day, imposing a religious structure on the every day life of the individual – not unlike the late medieval book of hours. In this respect something done, 'actions' as it were, still had a role to play as a Lutheran *praxis pietatis*, and they were defined precisely as spiritual actions, something pertaining to the spiritual life and hence belonging to the life of prayer.

Following the controversialist theology of the 16th century, a new interest in 'homo interior', the inner man, developed in as well Lutheran as Catholic areas. Intense practiced devotions rooted in late medieval spirituality emerged, heavily influencing the mentality of 17th and to a certain extent even 18th century Europe. This development can be observed on both sides of the denominational border, on the Catholic side for instance with the École française, on the Lutheran side with the devotional piety of Johann Arndt and his followers, and the Pietist continuation of this tradition in the 18th century. Such devotions were meant not just for the religious elite, but also for lay people. In varying degrees Christian piety, expressed as devotional practices with corresponding instrumental dimensions or aspects, thus engaged large parts of the European population.

The Enlightenment of the 18th century might have accelerated a process of secularization[12], and even if it does not seem to have had great influence on popular piety, it might have widened the gap between the theological-intellectual reflection on faith on the one hand, and the devotion (piety, spirituality) on the other

12 The idea of secularization is, as we have stated earlier, a rather dubious concept. Secularization can of course not be understood without being related to religion, as a response to or protest against it. But secularization can also be understood in some sense as a product of the Christian religious tradition(s) of Europe. Here again see Berger 1995 and Cavanaugh 2002. See also Zabala's introduction in: Zabala 2005, pp. 1-27.

hand. How are we, then, to understand the revitalization of many, often collectively expressed, devotions, or the creation of new ones, in the 19th century? This epoch, with such a great variety of new mass produced devotional instruments, drew inspiration from the history of Christianity, its religion heavily influenced by middle class ideals, yet marked by a certain ambivalence in its relations with secular society.

When studying piety or devotion, it is important not to sever such phenomena from official Christianity with its churches and theologies. There is a dialectical relationship between piety and theology, between devotional practice and the rituals of a church. Piety of course both influences and is influenced by official church teachings and liturgies.

The anthology

The present anthology aims at giving a presentation of the work of ENID and its individual members. The scope of the anthology is rather broad; spanning in time from the medieval times to the present. The topics range from medieval visual theories to post-modern perspectives on the idea of Catholicism. In this respect the book reflects the wide range of scholarly interests and research activities of the ENID members, even though the whole network is not represented here.

The anthology has no intention of giving a coherent, comprehensive or chronological account of the history of instruments of devotion in European culture. A project like this, with such a wide topic and involving so many different scholarly contributions, inevitably results in different constructions of meaning. Recognizing this fact, the anthology represents a way of writing history which adheres to collaboration of specialized scholarly forces rather than synthesizing efforts. Thus, the scope of this anthology and of ENID as such, is to present a variety of studies which often take very different approaches and make use of different theoretical perspectives and methods.

The contributions to the anthology have been divided into two different sections. The articles in the first section deal with continuities and discontinuities of devotional practises related to instruments, while the second section contains articles dealing with specific instruments and the devotional practices related to them. Since none of the articles have been written with the others in mind, the division into sections is merely an editorial construct which highlights the main topical interests of ENID as a network, rather than the specific methodological or scholarly interests of the individual contributors. The aim of such a juxtaposition of articles and their different ideas is of course to foreground specific topical issues which, then, also becomes the aim and justification of the book; to illustrate how cultural history can be approached by way of its instruments and to give some examples of the kind of answers such an approach produces.

The first section begins with Henrik von Achen's contribution 'Piety, Practise and Process'. From an introductory definition of two central terms, piety and practice, von Achen continues to investigate the process of conversion as it was described and articulated in some early 17th century illustrated devotional books and how they relate to the late 14th century devotional treatise, *The Scale of Perfection* by the Augustinian canon Walter Hilton. The article argues that there are substantial affinities between Catholic and Protestant spirituality converging in the symbol of the human heart and advocating 'a sincere, heartfelt, emotional Christianity, expressing itself in a life of prayer following certain patterns and structures thought to be expedient in terms of sustaining the *nova oboedientia* of the order of salvation, to stay in Grace as long as possible or successfully to convert again.' He points out that in spite of changes in theological ideas and ideals introduced by the Protestants, relations can be traced in the devotional patterns and their instruments. Daniel Cramer has the last word: in 1623 he simply exclaimed 'St. Bernhard is ours too.'

While Henrik von Achen focuses on continuity and likenesses between Catholic and Protestant devotional instruments and practices, Mario Perniola's philosophical contribution 'The Cultural Turn of Catholicism' focuses on the specificities of Catholic cultural identity. He argues that 'ritual feeling' is the one aspect that particularly determines Catholicism even though it dwells in the Catholic unconscious. This is due to an ongoing engagement in a 'relation of mimetic rivalry with Protestantism and Enlightenment, instead of reflecting independently on the specificity of its own feeling.' Modern Catholicism seems to be caught between institutional dogmas and norms on one side and Catholic identity on the other. This bad integration of moral and cognitive aspects of religion results in a discrepancy which, from the outside, is 'generally considered a sign of superficiality and opportunism, if not of bad faith and hypocrisy.' With his article Perniola aims at unveiling the *intrasystematic consistency* of Catholic feeling, and making way for a Catholicism without orthodoxy.

In a certain respect the attempt made by Mario Perniola in arguing for a more 'true' Catholicism has parallels in earlier attempts to reform or revitalize religious practices, such as the one described in Mette Birkedal Bruuns article on 'Manual Labour as *praxis pietatis*. Sketch of a Motif in the 17th century Cistercian Reform at La Trappe.' This particular example is of course of a much more radical kind: in the late 17th century Armand-Jean de Rancé introduced his idea of reform in a monastery in La Trappe with manual labour playing a crucial role. Bruun illustrates how Rancé founded his ideas in a long monastic tradition, with the Rule of Benedict as an important inspiration, in order to authenticate his attempt. However, through this shines the personal ideals of the reformer: that manual labour was not only a matter of cultivation of land but a devotional practice of penitence and humility which he regarded should be the focal monastic deeds. Bruuns article is a demonstration of how change or revitalization is inseparably intertwined with continuity.

Rob Faesen's contribution 'The Great Silence of Saint Joseph: Devotion to Saint Joseph and the 17th Century Crisis of Mysticism in the Jesuit Order' is dedicated to the historiography of the devotion of St. Joseph. In the mid 17th century the Superior General of the Society of Jesus, Muzio Viteleschi, attempted to prohibit devotion to St. Joseph in what he regarded as a 'new and unusual manner'. By investigating the writings of a young Jesuit, Jean-Joseph Surin, a contemporary of Viteleschi's, Faesen shows that devotion to St. Joseph can be affiliated with a mystical tradition deeply rooted in the Middle Ages, which spoke of the 'indwelling of Christ' as a complete mutual love between man and God. However, Christian thought of the 17th century, as represented by the Superior General of the Jesuit Order, was heavily influenced by nominalism and the idea of the individual. 'Indwelling' was incomprehensible within this regime of thinking and regarded as mere imagination. Viteleschi regarded the contemplative dimension of the devotion to the father of Jesus as a threat to the identity of the Jesuit Order. Faesen's article contributes with a demonstration of how devotional practice and theological thought sometimes collide and challenge the established identity of a religious society.

The last contribution in this section is Fred van Lieburg on 'The Medical Market Compared with the Pastoral Market: A Perspective from Early Modern Dutch History.' Lieburg argues that there are several affinities between the medical hierarchical division of labour and the pastoral in the 17th century. The pastoral sector had its doctores and quacks too, which were to some extent controlled by market mechanisms. Different clientele sought different kinds of healers, be it medical or pastoral. In spite of the Old Testament words: 'O, everyone that thirsteth, come to the waters, and he that hath no money, come, buy and eat, yes, come buy wine and milk without money and without price' (Isiah 55.1) there seems to have been a subtle mechanism of service and reward. Lieburg thus touches on a very central theme in the history of religion and religiosity: the difference between practice and theory.

What binds the above mentioned articles together, in spite of their obvious differences in both theme and approach, is the idea that change and continuity of religion and religiosity is shaped by ideals, theological thought and doctrine as well as practices. There is no necessary contradiction between the two, but at times they collide and create an atmosphere of need for renewal, reform, and re-definition of religious and devotional identity. The contributions in the first section all illustrate such balances and tensions within the history of religious thought and practice.

Historical perspective is by no means absent in the second section, which deals more specifically with certain instruments of devotion, just as specific instruments are not absent from the contributions in the first section. The articles in the second section deals with the instruments themselves as the primary point of focus, and the contributors all attempt to shed light on the devotional qualities of specific instruments and the specific practices related to them. The materiality of the objects is the focal point. Perhaps it would clarify their devotional status to call them 'subjects', because after all, all 6 contributions in this section demonstrate how the meeting between instrument and devotee can be characterized as communication. The instrument is not just a silent object articulated by the one approaching it; it speaks and influences the devotional situation. The articles in this section illustrate the importance of instruments as well as their individual specificities as contributors to the devotional experience.

In his article 'Weapons of Redemption: Piety, Poetry and the Instruments of the Passion in Late Medieval Ireland' Salvador Ryan investigates a very common type of passion iconography which spread over the most of Europe in the late Middle Ages: the *Arma Christi*. Examples of such images, which often featured a variety of 'props' of the Passion story such as the cross, the lance, the nails, a hammer, the crown of thorns, the sponge, the flagellation column just to mention a few, and especially their meaning in an Irish context, are investigated by way of bardic poetry. Hence the article also introduces a little known poetic genre to a larger audience. Bardic poetry describes the Passion of Christ as a war against evil and shows Christ as a victorious militant hero, something which must have appealed to the medieval warrior society. This might help explain why images of the instruments of the Passion became so popular in late medieval Irish tomb-sculpture: the commissioners placed their trust in the saving power of Christ's Passion and death before they arrived before God on Judgement day, as Ryan concludes. As if the victorious Christ went to war for man with all his artillery.

The only contribution to deal with the relation between the Eastern and the Western Church is that of Peter De Mey. In his article 'Looking at the Mystery of the Incarnated God. Eastern and Western Iconography as a Source of Theological Reflection', the iconography and theological message of the Eastern Anastasis or Resurrection icon is compared with the Isenheimer Altar by Matthias Grünewald. De Mey argues that the visual traditions of both the Eastern and the Western Church have emphasized the catechetical value of images as tools for moving the hearts of the beholders. The two images in question here, both contain the message of Salvation: what they have in common is their communication of hope. De Mey concludes with a rhetorical question: 'Could God's love not ultimately touch the heart of every Adam and Eve of the Resurrection Icon, and even that of the most arrogant fallen angel of the Isenheimer Altar?' Thus he attempts to bridge modern theology of the Eastern and the Western Church by showing their affinities with outset in their visual expressions and instruments of devotion.

Nils Holger Petersen's article '*Sepolcro*: Musical Devotion of the Passion in 17th-18th Century Austria' deals with a specific musical genre associated with the devotional activities at the Viennese court under Leopold I (1658-1705). A sepolchro was a staging of a narrative related to the Passion of Christ performed in a church in front of an Easter sepulchre. By analyzing one particular sepolchro, *La vita nella morte* (Life in Death) by Antonio Draghi (music) and Niccolò Minalti (poetry), Petersen sheds light on some characteristics of imperial devotional practice at the time. *La vita nella morte* creates a space for theological instruction and devotional identification by combining theological discourse and representational technology which brings the beholder of the *sepolchro* directly to the Crucifixion by letting the Good Thief on the cross give an 'eye witness' report of the events. Music and drama can thus be understood as instruments of devotion. This type of religious drama in some respects resembles the medieval liturgical plays and Petersen argues that it might have influenced the music of the young Mozart.

In the 19th century a much more portable devotional edifice became widely popular. Eli Heldaas Selands article '19th Century Devotional Medals: A Presentation' introduces her ongoing research on devotional medals with some thoughts about how to define and analyze these often small objects. Most of them are mass produced and made of cheap materials and it makes little or no sense to speak of them as 'valuable' in a traditional sense. Numismatic research tends to systematize them under categories such as 'miscellaneous'. Anyhow, these medals or medalets have been connected with other kinds of values: many of them were blessed or had indulgences attached to them. As with most of the other instruments investigated in this anthology, medals were, and still are, associated with certain powers, reflected in the devotional practices related to them.

The article by Henning Laugerud, 'Visuality and Devotion in the Middle Ages' investigates late medieval conceptions of sight and vision in order to shed light on medieval reception of images. According to theological thinking of prominent figures such as St. Augustine and St. Thomas Aquinas, to 'see' was to 'know' and vision was regarded as the most important of senses. Seeing was not just an act of sensing which, in conjunction with images, could be used in the act of pious devotion: seeing had an almost sacramental character and an aspect of identification. Seeing could transfer grace because of its ability to give knowledge about God. The medieval visual culture, Laugerud argues, was far more complex than ours: medieval men and women 'saw' much more in images than the modern understanding of the verb 'to see' indicates today.

Along the same line as Laugerud, Laura Katrine Skinnebach's article '"the solace of his image": Images and Presence in Late Medieval Devotional Practice' investigates images as mediators of divine presence. Using a variety of visual and textual sources Skinnebach argues that images could produce a devotional experience which eliminated the barrier between Heaven and Earth and made the divine beings present to the devotee. Devotional practices related to images were largely directed by this 'longing for divine presence'. Much was acquired by the actual practice, however. Only if approached in an appropriate and devout manner could the images open the way for an experience of divine presence.

The purpose of this anthology is, as stated earlier, to present a variety of studies on devotion and its instruments and to give a presentation of the work of ENID and its individual members. The aim of our work is to shed light on what we believe to be central aspects of Christianity and its influence on and in European culture(s), and it is our hope that this anthology can present some new insights into the histories and cultures of Europe.

1st section

Piety, Practise and Process

Henrik von Achen

> Que vostre coeur, ô mon Jesus possede entierement le mien: Que le mien,
> ô mon Jesus! Soit entierement fondu dans le vostre. Que vostre Coeur et le
> mien ne soient plus deux coeurs; mais un seulement mon Jesus!
>
> *Pratiqve de l'amour de Dieu pour toutes sortes des personnes*, Paris 1672[13]

Particularly since the Late Middle Ages, the human heart has been a very popular
and obvious symbol to represent the innermost and most sincere quality of man,
his soul, his spiritual centre, or, indeed, human love, sacred or profane. Hence
it remains a very useful metaphor when heartfelt emotions, religious life and
the entire 'inner man' needs being described or visualized. The religious use of
the human heart as symbol and metaphor is at least as old as the Scriptures, yet
from the 14th century it was intensified, adding an increasing amount of pictorial
renderings to the already existing literary imagery. Having left the controversial
theology of the Reformation era behind, it became clear to Christians of most
denominations that salvation did not depend on simply holding the right beliefs,
but in loving God, in a 'change of heart', a constant conversion as one leaves oneself and the world behind in pursuit of God. Around 1600, on both sides of the
denominational border piety became a most important phenomenon, the heart
symbol therefore rising to prominence. Did not St. François de Sales define true
piety as nothing but the grace of true love for God?[14]

---

13   *Pratiqve de l'amour de Dieu pour toutes sortes des personnes*. Paris 1672, p. 15, by an anonymous author.
     In typical Baroque style, the quote testifies to the configuration of the devout to Christ as a perfect
     union according to St Paul in Gal 2.20: 'May your heart, oh my Jesus, totally own mine, so that my
     (heart) is totally dissolved in yours. May your heart and mine no longer be two hearts, but just one,
     my Jesus!'

14   François de Sales: *Introduction à la vie devote*. Lyon 1608, I,1: 'La vraie et vivante dévotion [...] pré-
     suppose l'amour de Dieu, ains elle n'est autre chose qu'un vrai amour de Dieu [...] la charité étant
     un feu spirituel, quand elle est fort enflammée elle s'appelle dévotion'. In this, one recalls engraving
     no. 8 of the series *Cor Iesv amanti sacrvm*, by Anton Wierix 1585-86.

Connected to a major work in progress on early modern religious heart symbolism, its preliminary title being 'Iconographia Pietatis', the present article presents a few reflections on practice and process based on the process of conversion as described in some of the early 17th century illustrated devotional literature, and as anticipated by the Late 14th century devotional treatise *The Scale of Perfection* by the English Augustinian canon Walter Hilton.[15]

Piety

The phenomenon of piety does not disappear in the shadows of the individual soul, but expresses itself as devotional practices and their instruments: books, pictures, music, devotional objects, liturgical and quasi-liturgical practices, structures, fraternities etc. Such instruments have played their part in the cultural construction of society and may be studied to understand the beliefs, attitudes and practices they manifest. Therefore, piety can actually be studied precisely through its devotional instruments; a study which by necessity is intrinsically and irreducibly interdisciplinary since the object studied expresses itself as a multifaceted phenomenon.[16] The history these objects or practices reveal has gained a particular importance today, as modern, secular Europe to a certain extent has become a world whose only Christian references are of a cultural nature.[17]

Christian piety may be defined as a personal, emotional and existential acceptance of the message of Christianity, in such a way that the individual not only believes certain things to be true, but holds a faith which interweaves his or her entire life, determining views, attitudes, actions and relations. Piety is always personal. The pious faithful experiences faith as an existential and emotional relation to God, faith being deeply and irretrievably integrated in the very fabric of his or her being. At the end of a century which had seen the apparent victory of Enlightenment, in 1793, the young Hegel thus stated an important truth: that the concept of religion concerns not only the science of God as a mere historical

---

15 See for instance von Achen, Henrik: 'Human heart and Sacred Heart: reining in religious individualism. The heart figure in 17th century devotional piety and the emergence of the cult of the Sacred Heart'. *Categories of Sacredness in Europe, 1500-1800*. Arne B. Amundsen and Henning Laugerud (eds.). Oslo 2003, pp. 131-158, and 'The Sinner's Contemplation'. *Images of Cult and Devotion. Function and Reception of Christian Images in Medieval and Post-Medieval Europe*. Søren Kaspersen (ed.). Copenhagen 2004, pp. 283-304. *The Scale of Perfection* was written in English in the years 1380-96. Originally written for nuns, it was also used by lay people. The text, appearing in print in 1494, was translated into Latin around 1500. See Hilton, Walter: *The Scale of Perfection*, book I-II, 1380-96. Thomas H. Bestul (ed.). Michigan 2000.

16 Schneiders, Sandra M.: 'The Study of Christian Spirituality. Contours and Dynamics of a Discipline'. *Studies of Spirituality* 8/1998, pp. 38-57, here p. 42.

17 As realized also by the Pontifical Council for Culture: *Towards a Pastoral Approach to Culture*. Vatican 1999, p. 3.

Fig. 1: The soul resting in the embrace of the Trinity in the 'house of the heart', representing the old man renewed by Grace according to Ephes. 4,22 and Col 3,9. Both texts define the 'new man' as a human being created according to the image of God. The stairs to the door is 'fear of God', the door of the heart itself, however, closed, to signify the pious heart as a hortus conclusus (Song of songs 4.12), in line with the late medieval tendency to interpret the Song of songs as an allegory of the relationship between Christ and a devout soul. Late 15th century manuscript coloured pen drawing in Mystisches Betrachtungsbuch, by a nun in the abbey of St. Walburg, Eichstätt, Bayern, C. 1470. Photo: Handschriftenabteilung, Staatsbibliothek zu Berlin – Preußischer Kulturbesitz / Hdschr. 417 bpk.

or rational knowledge, but as an interest of the heart.[18] As an existential involvement with Christ, piety as the experience of a mutual love belongs to the core of the Christian religion, and might be said, then, to be exactly that part of religion which is of interest to the heart (Fig. 1).

Christian theology is preceded by Christian experience, an experience of Christians which has, then, been reflected upon, articulated, to some extent systematized and eventually developed into a theology. From this stems a characteristic feature of piety, namely that it tends to concentrate on the relationship with God, being less occupied with dogmatic teachings. While this by no means indicates that denominational aspects play no role, the experiential basis of faith seems to emphasize the interdenominational aspects of piety, creating a common ground as it were, a sort of convergence towards the relationship between Christ and the individual. If such a relationship emerges as the only important or significant aspect of Christianity, separated from any outward manifestations, belief systems, articulated by a certain church or theology, do indeed become secondary, as do *a fortiori* all practices. This line of thought, where everything depended on an 'interior Christianity', might eventually develop into an irenic or spiritualist position. Hence, it was only natural that *Lebendige Hertzenstheologie* of 1691 by the mystical spiritualist Christian Hoburg was actually illustrated by the engravings of the *Cor Iesv amanti sacrvm*, of which we shall speak more below.

Even if elements of both Catholic and Protestant spirituality seemed to converge in the human heart as an almost un-denominational phenomenon, the main feature of this piety was its interdenominational character, a related piety using common means and often articulating itself in the same way. This seemed reflected in the relationship between the Lutheran devotional piety of Johann Arndt and Catholic Counter Reformation spirituality. While the devotional instruments of the opponent were not explicitly, let alone officially, recognized they were tolerated, sometimes, however, with some denominational adjustments. Still, Christians of various denominations met on a devotional level below school theology; here pictures and texts were used simply because they were devotionally attractive and expedient, of interest to the hearts, whether Catholic or Protestant. Basically, all imagery, musical, textual or visual, served but one goal: conversion; describing how the *imago Dei* was formed in man, Christ being born in the hearts of those who by the *unio mystica* are being con-formed to him, a theme developed by Meister Eckhart from its patristic roots. The process com-

---

18 'Es liegt in dem Begriff der Religion, dass sie nicht blosse Wissenschaft von Gott. […] nicht eine blosse historische oder räsonierte Kenntnis ist, sondern dass sie das Herz interessiert', in Hegel, Georg F. W.: *Theologische Jugendschriften*. Herman Nohl (ed.). Tübingen 1907, p. 5., and Hegel continues: 'dass sie (religion) Einfluss auf unsere Empfindungen und auf die Bestimmung unseres Willens hat'.

pleted, God literally dwells in the human heart, filling it; indeed, being 'deeper in me than I am in me', as St. Augustine said.[19] There is an analogy here: Like a sculptor does not add anything to the block, but removes material uncovering the sculpture hidden in the block, so the spiritual process sheds the *homo exterior*, uncovering the spiritual man, the *homo interior*, that inner man who practice and picture, then, provide with expression and form.[20]

Christian ceremonies, rituals and practices of a liturgical or collective nature cannot survive religiously, if they do not engage the hearts of the faithful. Indeed, as Durandus explained towards the end of the 13th century, the altar itself should be regarded by each member of the congregation as his or her heart on which one must sincerely sacrifice good deeds as offerings burned by love.[21] Therefore, in a Christian context, all ritual practices must to some extent become devotional practices if they were to survive as meaningful religious phenomena. This integration of form and contents was not universally recognized. Thus, the Puritan Richard Kilby in 1614 recommended the less serious devout to become Catholics, 'for that will so furnish you with outward works and ceremonies, that you shall not dreame of meddling with your heart'; even if the need for 'inwendighe aendachticheyt' was stressed often enough in the early modern Catholic books on Holy Mass.[22] The liturgy of the Church has always been a unity of individual and collective faith; hence, liturgical and quasi- or semi-liturgical practices are important in the history of devotion.

19   St. Augustine, *Confessiones* III,6: 'interior intimo meo'.

20   Meister Eckhart: Tractat *Von dem edlen Menschen*, Sermon on the noble man. The entire passage: 'Ouch hân ich etwenne ein offenbâr glîchnisse.gesprochen: sô ein meister bilde machet von einem holze oder von einem steine, er entreget daz bilde in daz holz niht, mêr er snîdet abe die spæne, din daz bilde verborgen und bedecket hâten; er engibet dem holze niht, sunder er benimet im und grebet ûz die decke und nimet abe den rost, und denne sô glenzet, daz dar under verborgen lac. Diz ist der schaz, der verborgen lac in dem acker, als unser herre sprichet in dem êwangeliô', see Quint, Josef (ed.): *Meister Eckharts Buch der göttlichen Tröstung und von dem edlen Menschen (Liber Benedictus)*. Berlin 1952, p. 73. The text was probably written in Strassburg c. 1320 as a homily for religious women. Earlier he had described the same parallel, the inner image coming about by 'expurgando, excicendo et educendo', see Quint 1952 p. 132.

21   Guillelmus Durandus: *Rationale divinorum officiorum* I-IV, I,ii,6 CCCM 140. Turnhout 1995, p. 30: 'Altare est cor nostrum in quo debemus offerre, unde in Exodo precepit Dominus: In altari offerres holocausta, quia de corde debent procedure opera igne caritatis accensa'. Durandus refers to Exodus 20.24.

22   In his *Hallelu-iah: Praise Yee the Lord, for the Unburthening of a loaden Conscience*, quoted from Hindmarsh, D. Bruce: *The Evangelical Conversion Narrative*. Oxford 2005, p. 39. On Catholics, see Luca Pinelli's SJ (ca. 1546-1609) explanation of the mass, translated into Dutch and published in Antwerp 1620: *De chracht ende misterie de h. Misse met verklaringhe der selve*. Particularly chapter XX on how to listen to the holy mass, pp. 174-179. The term 'inwendighe aendachticheyt' is used on p. 179. Further he defines three species of devotion, pp. 180-182. Or another Italian Jesuit, Andriotti, Fulvio: *Onderwys oft practycke om dickwils het H. Sacrament des avtaers*. Published in Dutch in Antwerp 1618.

Practice

Integral to any *praxis pietatis* is a certain order, a structure of this particular devotion, its process and apparatus not a mere question of form, but of substance. Most such practices have a clear instrumental (material) component, be it a book, a pattern of prayers, a structuring of the day, the use of devotional objects, pictures or songs etc. It belongs to the nature of practical piety that it is not just a question of pious thoughts, but also of something done in a certain way to evoke and structure such thoughts. A living religion "of interest to the heart" must express itself in devotional practices: fundamental in such practices are order and instrumentality, which create a significant relationship with the more generic concept of collective 'ritual'.

Like human love needs actions to establish relations and express itself, it belongs to the nature of faith that it seeks to express itself, since ultimately faith is not a question of knowledge or of certain teachings held to be true, but a communion with God expressed through certain actions, or practices. Such practices are called devotions, expressing a certain piety or spirituality. However, the piety expressed is not something which is merely articulated through any suitable devotional practice - the piety itself is intrinsically shaped and formed by its practice. A dialectical relation exists between the two, and it is not easy to determine where the exact border lies between piety and its practice, between mental and physical devotion. Form <u>and</u> substance often blend as a complete integration. Already in the 12th century William of St. Thierry was among those who reflected on the role of 'form' as a significant part of piety, its appropriation 're-forming' the devout as it were, leading him or her on the way towards God.[23] So, form, and thus physical objects as well as other outward phenomena, matter and should not be seen as something secondary. They are, to borrow an expression from Catholic sacramental theology, signs which produce what they signify.

Therefore, the instrumental aspects of a devout Christian life are highly important. If a certain devotional practice uses appropriate instruments to express a certain piety adequately, at the same time producing what it expresses, then the practice itself as 'form' is inseparable from the 'substance' of a given devotion. Thus, devotional life and its practice is a complex matter where it is not possible satisfactorily to isolate one component from the others. Of course the 'instrument' helps the devout to stay within the given structure, then, however, integrated in the devotion itself. A devout, slowly, painfully, climbing the Scala Sancta in Rome, will experience how the body and its gestures take part in a devo-

23 Cf. Waaijman, Kees: 'Transformation. A key word in Spirituality'. *Studies in spirituality* 8/1998, pp. 5-36, here pp. 13-19.

tional practice, his or her bodily experiences and sensations soon indistinguishable from the devotional 'substance' itself.

Approaching piety through its devotional practices and their instruments, by no means constitute an interest in secondary phenomena. Such instruments are not just rather inadequate manifestations of something which really is spiritual, but through them piety itself becomes accessible, describable and tangible, both as a historical and a religious phenomenon. Some instruments of devotion themselves actually articulated this access, visualizing the invisible and materializing the immaterial in a way which made it possible to render and describe spiritual processes which were otherwise inaccessible. In this the human heart played a leading role, conversion to a truly Christian life being nothing but an existential, all encompassing "change of heart".

The process of conversion

The most basic Christian spiritual process is conversion, *metanoia*, denoting that man has turned from various idols to the Lord, from darkness to light and from sin to virtue. Towards the end of the 14th century *The Scale of Perfection* calls this simply 'the reformynge of mannes soule'.[24] Conversion, however, is far more than the intellectual process of recognizing the Truth and then holding that belief, it is the state of mind, the way of life, of any devout Christian, the insight gained and the belief held influencing his or her entire life. Of course, apart from some obvious biblical examples, the very prototype of a conversion was described in all its details, using quite a number of textual images containing the heart, in the *Confessiones* of St. Augustine.

Another process did play an important role in Christian life: the process of ascent, of spiritual progress. Once converted, the task is a deepening and maturing of one's spiritual life. This process was often described as a ladder by which one reaches God, ascending step by step to reach an ever higher degree of perfection. The classical expression of this process was to walk the *via purgativa*, proceed by the *via illuminativa* to finally reach the *via unitiva* by which one would obtain the *unio mystica* with God. Though such concepts were developed in monastic settings, they were increasingly open to and influencing the devotional life of lay people as well. One might even suggest a certain correspondence between the three contemplative ways and the classic order of salvation: Should not all devout Christians be purged through *contritio*, be illuminated by *fides* and become united

---

24 *Scale of Perfection*, II, 2, p. 137.

with Christ as it would be reflected in a *nova oboedientia* to him, resulting in a new way of life? Thus a converted life became a redeemed life.

To all Christians, cloistered or in the world, the starting point of every spiritual growth would be a conversion, a reformation as it were, whereby the divine image in man, distorted by original sin, became reformed. Such is for instance the approach of Walter Hilton in his late 14th century *The Scale of Perfection*. Like Bunyan 300 years later, he too uses the metaphor of a pilgrim, overcoming a number of obstacles to reach the celestial city of Jerusalem. The reformed soul may now behold Jesus with a spiritual eye; this vision, however, is quite unlike any image produced by human imagination. In this Hilton conforms to the mystical tradition, which stressed the importance of not suffering the limitations of human concepts. Nevertheless, to describe spiritual processes and experiences, to view Christ and his doings with a 'spiritual eye'[25] pictures were made and functioned as devotional instruments.[26] Already here, in *The Scale*, one encounters a number of the themes depicted in the early modern descriptions of spiritual processes: The divine image in man, would that not be Christ in the human heart? Was true insight in your own interior not the prerequisite for any spiritual growth, anticipating early modern introspection? Did enlightenment not come from him and from within? Such themes bread pictures, describing the pilgrimage of the heart, and placed before the eyes of the devout what was otherwise only accessible to the spiritual eye of an advanced mystic.

In the world, however, turning from oneself or the world to God was a constant call, to be repeated over and over since it was a fundamental Christian experience, shared with St. Paul, that even if one has turned to God, one does not do the good things which one will, but the evil which one hates (Rom 7.14f.). Therefore, purging the soul, which, according to St. François de Sales, is the beginning of a devout life, shall never cease as long as we live.[27] The history of most Christians is the story of relapse, of flesh conquering the spirit, the outward man capturing and dominating the inward man, the *homo interior*. Conversion is the reverse of that fall (Fig. 2).

---

25 *Scale of Perfection*, I, 35, p. 68: The grace of the Holy Ghost provides an 'openynge of the goostli iye', or I, 39, p. 73: 'openeth the sight of here soule'. The image of a heart with an eye, drawing on Ephesians 1.18, reflects this textual image and was used by Daniel Cramer in his *Emblemata Sacra* of 1624, see I,6 and II,12.

26 On this see Lentes, Thomas: 'Der mediale Status des Bildes. Bildlichkeit bei Heinrich Seuse – stat einer Einleitung'. *Kultbild. Ästhetik des Unsichtbaren. Bildtheorie und Bildgebrauch in der Vormoderne.* David Ganz and Thomas Lentes (eds.). Berlin 2004, pp. 7-73, eg. p. 49.

27 François de Sales 1608, I,5: 'L'exercice de la purgation de l'âme ne se peut ni doit finir qu'avec notre vie'.

Fig. 2: The flaming heart inscribed with the name of Jesus (above a memento mori) weights more than the orb, denoting how the human soul rejects the world. Below the text is a quote from Psalm 73. 25: There is nothing upon earth that I desire besides Thee. Engraved illustration by an unknown artist, in a Danish edition of Pseudo-Augustine's Soliloquia; Siælens eenlige Samtale med Gud, København 1681, p. 194, illustrating chapter 19: On the desire of love (for God). The text presents a heartfelt prayer that God will kindle the fire of love in the devout soul, that she may love nothing but Him. Photo: Det kgl. Bibliotek, København, kort- og billedafdelingen, 1-487 octav, foto-nr. 193673.

Basically, one might divide conversion into three phases, all depicted by 17th century pious imagery: Recognition of oneself, unavoidably resulting in contrition filling the heart with the spirit of repentance. Hilton had described the first phase of conversion as a period when the Christian face to face with his wickedness 'is filled with great remorse and plenty of tears' as one beholds the dark and painful image of the sinful interior. Then, in faith, he takes heart, trusts in God and in redemption by Christ on the Cross[28], and now tries to follow Christ, to do God's will and live accordingly. Lapsing, but beginning again, falling, yet by the grace of God lifted up again, the Christian perseveres until the soul eventually matures in

---

28   *Scale of Perfection*, I, 34, p. 67: 'with gret conpunccioun and with plenté teeris'. And in I, 52, p. 90: 'A merk ymage and a peinful of thyn owen soule'; I, 39. p. 73: 'In tribulacion, ne in temptacioun oure Lord forsaketh not a man.'; I,44, p. 79:' aske oonli savacioun bi the vertu of His precious passion … and withoute doute thou schalt have it.'

Christian virtues and reaches its goal: God. This process reflected the classic *ordo salutis*,[29] making the human heart an appropriate dwelling for Jesus, anticipating the eternity of the saved – at least for a while.

If the human soul was truly *semper reformanda*, the process of conversion was not a once in a lifetime event, but something which had to be carried through again and again. Turning from oneself or from the world to God, was, then, a constant part of devout life. Indeed, when it has been said that particularly Puritan culture incubated a 'conversionist piety' in the first half of the 17th century[30], one feels inclined to extend this to more or less all Christian denominations of this period, thus explaining the popularity of Catholic emblem books dealing with this matter. This is why that particular process, or more precisely: the re-enactment of it by reliving it, virtually as it were, may be called a practice, and the rendering of that process an instrument. Did not the preface of the devotional book *Amoris Divini et Hvmani Antipathia* of 1629 spell out that the intention was to rekindle the dying flames of Divine love in the reader's chest?[31] Such instruments articulated the process, explained and described its various phases, dangers and promises, so that the devout might embark once again on a road to salvation, accompanied by texts and pictures and, indeed, guided by them. The final goal, was for the early modern pious Christian what it had been to the devout nun of the 14th century: that a true change of heart would take place, forever uniting the *anima humana* with the *amor divinus*, as its reciprocative aspect of this union was expressed in a small 18th century devotional card depicting the Sacred Heart above a fervent prayer which ended thus: 'Give me your heart and take mine / That we may stay together in all eternity, And I always with my heart and mind / Will be consumed by your love. Amen.'[32]

29 *Contritio, fides, nova oboedientia* (or *bona opera*), cf. *Confessio Augustana* art. XII, its roots going back to St. Bernhard, where the process of conversion is started by the 'contritio cordis'. A general account of the development of penitential theology until and including the Reformation was given by Reinhard Schwarz in his *Vorgeschichte der reformatorischen Busstheologie*. Berlin 1968.

30 Hindmarsh 2005, p. 42.

31 *Amoris Divini et Hvmani Antipathia*. Snyders (ed.). Antwerp 1629, p. 5f.: 'auiuer en ta poictrine les flames mourantes de l'Amour Diuin […]'

32 'Geeft mÿ u hert neemt gÿ het mÿn / Om seamen eeuwigh een te sÿn / En ick altÿt met hert en sin / Verslonden blÿf in uwe min. Amen.'

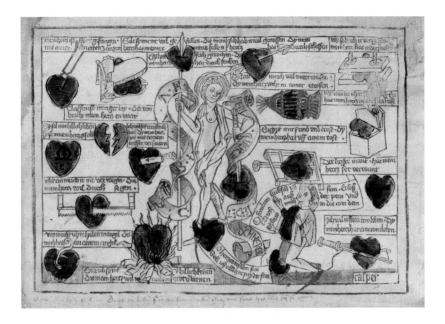

Fig. 3: Frau Venus und der Verliebte. The picture shows various ways in which the heart of the lover is treated by Venus, beauty, thereby offering a veritable compendium of visualized heart metaphors used in late medieval secular love poetry. Rendering metaphors in this way became a most popular feature in Baroque heart symbolism, and pictures of such painful treatments, usually administered by Christ or God to the heart of the devout as a kind of schooling and conversion, are legio in 17th century religious heart emblems. Handcoloured woodcut, single broadsheet, 25,7 x 36,5 cm, Meister Casper, Regensburg, c. 1485. Photo: Jörg P. Anders. Kupferstichkabinett, Staatliche Museen zu Berlin. /467-1908. bpk / Kupferstichkabinett, Staatliche Museen zu Berlin.

The human heart

The image of the Christ Child in the human heart, the main motif of the engraved series *Cor Iesv amanti sacrvm* from the end of the 16th century, was introduced by late medieval devotional literature and its illuminations, and the heart as an important symbol was soon to reappear after the Reformation[33] (Fig. 3).

---

33   Luther himself used the heart as part of his crest, and in 1550 Dirck Volchertsz Coornhert made an engraving after Marten van Heemskerck, showing the devil painting idle thoughts on a human heart, the heart placed like a canvas on an easel, henceforth a rather popular iconographical topos. In 1578 Hendrick Goltzius made some engravings using the human heart, one quite similar to the Coornhert-motif, and of course the 1584 altarpiece from Wittenberg, by Cranach the Younger, was itself shaped like a heart, the opened heart (corpus) showing the Crucifixion. A 15th century text anticipating the Cor Iesv-content was *Von Ihesus pettlein*, (*On the Little Bed of Jesus*), a manuscript from Nürnberg. A transcription is found in Hamburger, Jeffrey: *The Visual and the Visionary. Art and female Spirituality in Late Medieval Germany.* New York 1998, pp. 418-426.

When controversial theology of the Reformation era subsided, a new focus on the actually lived and felt faith emerged on both sides of the denominational border. As people in the later part of the 16th century settled in their religion, dogmatic questions seemed less important, the interest almost literally moving from the head to the heart. Thus the *homo interior*, the inner man, came into focus, and for almost a century particularly Protestant spirituality became marked by anxious introspection, to 'see' whether one was likely to be saved or not: 'First', the Puritan William Perkins wrote in 1590, 'take a narrow examination of thy selfe'; this, then, would necessarily lead to contrition.[34] Since the entire process was initiated by a contrite heart, a prior knowledge of one's sinfulness was presupposed. No wonder that the human heart, the focus of a number of views from science, poetry and religion forming a quite complex 'cultural unit', became of the utmost importance.[35] By using a representation of the human heart one might see the invisible and detect the status of that inner man on which everything depended. Through this instrument, the spiritual process of conversion could be seen, described and explained in great detail. Texts, emblems, symbols and metaphors, all placing the heart at the centre of interest, served exactly that introspective focus on the inner man.

Disregarding the rejection of pictures by the more radical and exclusive (monastic) mystical tradition of the Late Middle Ages and the general scepticism or rejection of imagery by the Reformation, early modern heart symbolism aimed at an edificatory effect addressing lay people, a group more and more involved in everyday devotion. Thus it was typical of the early 17th century that François de Sales with his introduction to devout life aimed explicitly at lay people.[36] To this end the veiled messages of the classical emblems of the 16th and 17th centuries, engaging theologians or learned intellectuals, were of little use. Therefore, the religious iconography of the heart consisted mainly of rather straightforward renderings of well known metaphors illustrating spiritual proceedings. Not only were many devotional texts illustrated, but the texts themselves contained a number of literary metaphors which, indeed, amounted to real 'word images', blurring the borders between literary and iconographic imagery. The illustrations including the human heart provided everybody with a 'spiritual eye', to behold what could not be seen by bodily eyes (Fig. 4).[37]

---

34 In his *Armilla Aurea, The Golden Chain*, published in 1590, quoted from Hindmarsh 2005, p. 35.

35 See Scholz, Bernhard: 'Het hart als "res significans" en als "res picta". Benedictus van Haeftens "Schola Cordis" (Antwerpen 1629)'. *Spiegel der letteren. Tijdschr. v. nederlandse literatuurgesch.* nr. 3, Leuven 1991, pp. 115-147, particularly pp. 122 and 131.

36 On the involvement of lay people, see eg. Chatellier, Louis: *The Europe of the Devout. The Catholic Reformation and the Formation of a New Society.* Cambridge 1991 (1987) and François de Sales 1608, the preface. On metaphors, see eg. Stambowsky, Phillip: *The Depictive Image. Metaphor and Literary Experience.* Amherst 1988.

37 The extremist position taken by Calvin rejected anything depicted which could not be seen with our (bodily) eyes, cf. Belting, Hans: *Das echte Bild. Bildfragen als Glaubensfragen.* München 2005, p. 171. On the position of Luther, see Belting 2005, pp. 163.

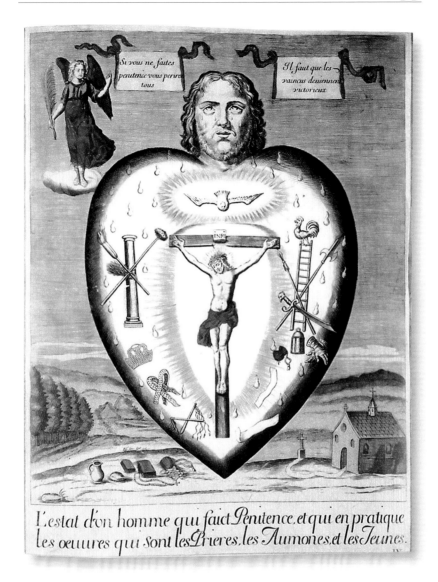

Fig. 4: 'L'estat d'un homme qui faict Penitence, et qui en pratique les oeuures qui sont les Prieres, les Aumones et les Jeunes', freely translated: The state of a penitent man, who is praying, giving alms and fasting. The heart presented as a symbol of the homo interior, showing what it contains, and hence the cause for penitence and the reason for the (exterior) face in tears.

Large, handcoloured, late 17th century engraving by Pierre Gallays. French catechetic motif, no. four of a series of Images morales, its function perhaps reflected in the size: 58,5 x 44 cm. Photo: Bibliothèque nationale, Paris.

In the last quarter of the 16th century, texts and pictures rendering the human heart thus became important instruments, well suited to visualize the otherwise invisible spiritual process of conversion – a change of heart, a true *cardiomorphosis* as it were. This insight was, then, provided by pictures 'in which your heart is shown to your heart', to quote Benedict van Haeften in *Schola Cordis*.[38]

In his book on muscles and glands, published in 1664, the Danish scientist, Niels Steensen, wrote: 'The heart has been seen as the very seat of inborn warmth, the throne of the soul, indeed, for the soul itself […] yet, if examined more closely, one will find nothing in it but a muscle'.[39] Since Harvey's earlier research on the heart and the blood, the human heart was slowly loosing its status as the physical core of the body. However, simultaneously the heart emerged as the religious organ par excellence, and thus suffered no loss of its importance as a symbol of faith, piety and devotion. Having converted to Catholicism and in 1677 ordained a bishop, Steensen himself chose as his crest a heart on which a cross was planted, signifying what Benedict van Haeften in his *Schola Cordis* had called the primary heart, *principalis cor*, the soul and central organ of the *homo interior*, different from the *cor carnalis* of medicine.[40]

Illuminating the story of conversion

To the early modern Christian, the introspect gaze on the condition of his or her soul revealed an entire world in which things happened as on a stage. The very centre of that microcosmos was the heart, as stated by the new stoicism of a Justus Lipsius.[41] On that stage the story of conversion was played, the characters and incidents by texts and pictures placed before the eyes of the spectator. Spiritual life was a journey, a pilgrimage, through many dangers and snares set out to prevent the Christian to reach his celestial home. The interest in this process of which everything depended, salvation or damnation, created a market for edificatory books describing it, combining the introspection with features of an autobiographical nature. Recently, this "conversion narrative" has been treated in 17th and 18th century evangelical context of spiritual autobiographies, testifying to the introspective piety which encouraged the focus on self-examination. Again,

---

38 Towards the end of the 13th century, Durandus had emphasized the ability of pictures to 'move the soul' better than texts in his *Rationale divinorum officiorum*. Van Haeften: 'In quo de corde tuo ad cor tuum loquitur', Benedict van Haeften OSB: *Schola Cordis*. Antwerp 1629, preface.

39 Stenonius, Nicolaus: *De musculis et glandulis observationum specimen*. Copenhagen-Amsterdam 1664.

40 Benedict van Haeften 1629 liber I, lectio IV: 'Mens igitur ac spiritus, principale cordis appellatur'. See in general book I, chapters III and IV. The bodily heart was regarded as neutral, see Benedict van Haeften, lecture VI.

41 Cf. Lipsius, Justus: *Physiologiae stoicorum*, 3rd book. Antwerp 1604.

this had been anticipated by Hilton, who stated that the soul seeking knowledge about spiritual matters, needed firstly to gain knowledge of itself.[42]

The original *metanoia* of the New Testament was never conceived as an isolated event, but as a comprehension of God and his will, the insight gained influencing one's entire life. Likewise, the early modern notion of the *ordo salutis* encompassed the results of conversion, named *nova oboedientia* or *bona opera*, new obedience or good works, the latter in a typical Protestant perspective by and large understood spiritually. Yet, since the sinfulness of natural man was a given, conversion was therefore always required. Indeed, it might be defined as the fundamental *praxis pietatis*. Conversion and its process was more a description of Christian life in general than focus on one single point in time. Indeed, to read a book on conversion of the heart and to contemplate its emblems was piously to meditate on the conditions of human life. Hence such an illustrated edificatory book was an instrument of devotion, a constant and constantly relevant companion through this life, the *picturae* of the emblems transforming its *minne-beelden* to *sinne-beelden*.[43]

Cor Iesv amanti sacrvm

In the work by Anton Wierix titled *Cor Iesv amanti sacrvm*, Antwerp 1585-86, (Fig. 5-6), a series of 18 unnumbered copper engravings, their original order must be provided by the general concept of the steps of conversion, or from the order provided by their insertion in a book. As various editions presented different orders of engravings, one might as well count the engravings of the original series according to the *catalogue raisonné*.[44]

The series depicts the Christ Child doing something to or in the heart, the heart itself being passive, as stated above, this might indicate a Protestant approach. Even if working in Antwerp, the Wierix brothers actually appeared in the

---

42 See Hindmarch 2005 and also Pettit, Norman: *The Heart Prepared: Grace and Conversion in Puritan Spiritual Life*. New Haven – London 1966. Cf. also the almost archetypal text of Bunyan, John: *The Pilgrim's Progress*, I-II. London 1678 and 1684 and its far less known illustrated Catholic forerunner, Boetius a Bolswert: *Duyskens ende Willemynkens pelegrimagi tot haren beminden binnen Ierusalem … Bescreuen ende met Sin-spelende Beelden wtghegheven*. Antwerp 1627, where two sisters, one pious and one stupid, are guided by Piety, an edificatory book for young women. On Hilton in *Scale of Perfection*, II, 30, p. 205: 'Hit needeth to a soule that wolde have knowynge of goostli thynges, for to have first knowynge of itself'.

43 To quote the title of Cats, Jacob: *Proteus Ofte Minne-Beelden Verandert In Sinne-Beelden*. Rotterdam 1627.

44 Mauquoy-Hendrickx, Marie: *Les estampes des Wierix. Catalogue raisonné*, vol. I, II, III.1-2. Bruxelles 1978-83, vol. I, no. 429-446. A simple comparison between editions from the 1620s documents the inconsistencies. The series was copied to illustrate *Lebendige Hertzenstheologie* by Christian Hoburg, published posthumously in Leipzig and Frankfurt a.M. 1691, but with a somewhat changed order, since the book was equipped with seven additional motifs of the same mould, leaving out some of the original motifs.

Sunt aufcultent qui Platoni, Tu ne verba vitæ fperne:
Aut facundo Ciceroni, Audi Patris æuiternæ
Aut Mundi ftultitiæ. Dicta Sapientiæ.

Antin .Wierx fecit et excud.

Fig. 5: Christ educating the human heart. Motif no. 11 from the series Cor Iesv amanti sacrvm, by Anton Wierix, copper engraving, Antwerpen 1585-86. There is no inscription apart from the text on the book: Erunt omnes docibiles Dei. (They (the devout Christians) shall all be easy for God to teach.) The subscription is Latin tercets, telling the reader that there are those who listen to Plato, Cicero or the foolishness of the world, but that he should listen to and not reject the words of life from the wisdom of the eternal Father. Photo: Statens museum for kunst, København. Kobberstiksamlingen.

lists of dissidents (Protestants) exactly in 1585 when the series presumably was made.[45] Protestant or not, they undoubtedly testified to 'the lasting appeal and utility of a metaphor first developed in medieval devotional texts'.[46]

The series begins with an engraving of a heart on which the title appears. A reasonable translation of the Latin title must be: The Sacred Heart of Jesus for him who loves. The meaning would be to show a conversion process in which the heart of a person who loves Jesus will be conformed to His Sacred Heart. On the title engraving, then, the Sacred Heart is depicted, adored by monastics as the very model or goal of that particular, spiritual change of heart which constitutes Christian conversion. Thus, *Cor Iesv* describes how the *homo interior* reaches a *conformitas Christi*. Even if Late Medieval passion iconography did occasionally represent the Sacred Heart as part of the passion iconography, this is actually a rather early direct use of it. Later, based on the visions of the nun Marguerite-Marie Alacoque (1647-1690) in the 1670s, the Sacred Heart should emerge as a major devotional cult, eagerly promoted by the Jesuits.

Initially, the human heart is shown captured by the world. Piety and devotion are the means to liberate the heart, all devotion being a *sursum corda*, which is shown by the winged, yet often chained heart in so many pious pictures. Prayer is an essential component, indeed, the core of any devotional practice, and prayer,

45 Mauquoy-Hendrickx, vol. III.2 p. 542, no. 38.
46 To quote Hamburger 1998, p. 403. He mentions the *Cor Iesv*-series as the closest pictorial analogue to the late medieval concept of the Child Christ in the devout heart.

Fig. 6: Jesus cordis perlustrator, Jesus cordis expiator, paintings copying motifs from the Cor Iesv amanti sacrvm series, on the parapet of the gallery in the cathedral of Stavanger c. 1660. Each section presents an emblem: Latin inscriptiones, Jesus, illuminator of the heart, and Jesus expiator of the heart, then the picture copied from Cor Iesv, and below subscriptions consisting of Danish two-liners, to the left: Huad skiult er i dit Hiertis huus / Det ser jeg i det klare Lius (What is hidden in the house of your heart, I see in the clear light), and to the right: Dit syndigt Hierte med mit blod / jeg rense vill om du giør bod (Your sinful heart I'll cleanse with my blood, if you do penance). Only parts of the parapet are still extant, now in Stavanger Museum. Photo: Terje Tveit, Stavanger museum, inv.no. ST-K.02977.

The *Scale of Perfection* had stated, is nothing but a strong desire for God while the mind is emptied of all earthly thoughts.[47] In the pedagogic illuminations of conversion, Baroque spirituality, with its love for dramatic contrast and opposing values, insisted on a strong dichotomy between heaven and earth. This world surely

---

47   *Scale of Perfection*, I, 25, p. 58.

tempts the *anima humana* who should loathe and despise the beauty of this world, as already Hilton had recommended in *The Scale*.[48] To help this lifting of the heart, liberating it, turning it away from the world, Jesus shoots his arrows to wound the heart, which means igniting a love for Him. The well known love metaphor of the heart wounded by love, going back to St. Augustine's 'written iconography' appears in *The Scale* too, when Jesus wounds the heart with the blissful sword of love.[49] Then he knocks at the door of the heart and is let in. Once inside, He starts out to conquer the darkness of the human heart by enlightening it with his light, and having created in man the necessary knowledge of himself, that is: of his sinfulness, Jesus then begins cleaning the heart. This cleansing from sins, says *The Scale*, encompasses removing fears and sorrows, bringing the light of Grace into it.[50]

After this initial phase of insight into one self, despairing when realizing the condition of one's heart, yet letting Christ in to bring comfort, trust and light, the cleansed heart now presents itself as a more worthy dwelling of Jesus, a house, lit by the fire of devout love, in which he now lives, sleeps, acts and reigns. Engraving no. 10 of the *Cor Iesv* series shows the Christ Child resting in the heart. In *The Scale* Wilton mentions that in a spiritual sense Jesus sleeps in the heart of the devout, drawing on the account of Jesus asleep in the boat on the lake of Galilee as related in Matthew 8.23f.[51] In no. 16 the Christ Child approaches the heart carrying passion symbols, which might be an illustration of what *The Scale* mentions as a spiritual vision of the passion of the Lord in the heart, the soul responding to such a vision with affectionate devotion.[52] As Lutheran reformers a few decades earlier had maintained that the true idols did not exist outside the body, but dwelt in human hearts, and hence the really dangerous images as well, it was only natural that Christ should take over as a new true "idol of the heart".

Not surprisingly, like *The Scale* the perhaps most popular devotional text of the Late Middle Ages, the early 15th century *De Imitatione Christi* treated a number of topics which anticipated Baroque imagery, not least a number of motifs in the

---

48 *Scale of Perfection*, I, 46, p. 83.

49 *Scale of Perfection*, I, 30, p. 62 where Jesus 'woundeth the soule with the blisful swerd of love'. Anticipating the exstacy of St. Theresa.

50 *Scale of Perfection*, I, 39, p. 73: 'putteth awei dredis and sorwes and merknesse oute of here hertes and bringeth into hire soules light of grace'.

51 *Scale of Perfection*, I, 49, p. 88: 'Jhesu slepeth in thyn herte gosteli …' Cf. Matthew 8.23f. To Wilton the point is like the apostles to wake up the Lord and ask him to save us.

52 *Scale of Perfection*, I, 35, p. 68: 'Thanne whanne the mynde of Cristis passioun … is thus maad in thi herte bi siche goostli sight, with devout affeccioun answerynge therto …' The Latin tercet of the *Cor Iesv*-engraving exhorts sweet Jesus to plant the cross deep in the little human heart, 'Bone Jesv, conde crucem … conde in imo corculo …'

Cor Iesv-series.[53] In the same way, the motifs of both late medieval texts and the *Cor Iesv amanti sacrvm* might be found, rendered in the dramatic way of an interaction between Divine love and the human soul in for instance *Amoris Divini et Hvmani Antipathia* of 1629. The last picture of the book shows the vision of love, face to face with the Christ child, admonishing the reader: if you love evil, you will be condemned, if you love the good, you will be crowned.[54] The final stage of conversion or devout life, when the world has been conquered and heaven is at hand, Divine love dwelling firmly in the human heart shows how the heart is glorified, given the crown of life (cf. Rev 2.10) and lead into union with Christ, whose image has now been reformed in it. Also to *The Scale* glorification of the soul is the final stage as it is now configurated to Christ.[55]

Christian heart symbolism came in two variants: one where the heart was used as a requisite (Fig. 3), something carried or something done something to, and one where the heart was opened to reveal the inside and thereby its spiritual condition (Fig. 1, 4-6). The first type is known from the Late Middle Ages. A later prominent example is the heart emblems of the Lutheran Daniel Cramer, published in his *Emblemata Sacra* from 1624.[56] The other type, the opened heart, is also known from the Late Middle Ages. As one of the early examples of this type, the *Cor IESV* series became widespread and popular as illustrations in a Jesuit booklet, *Le Cœur devot, throsne royal de Iesus Pacifique Salomon* [...] Douai 1627.[57] The first edition of Étienne Luzvics (1567-1640) *Le cœur devot* had appeared in Paris the previous year, but without illustrations. Actually, the Douai-edition of 1627 was a double edition with Luzvics text from 1626, and the text *Les saintes faveurs du petit Jésus au cœur qu'il aime et qui l'aime* by Étinne Binet (1569-1639), this too published in Paris in 1626, yet already translated into Flemish the same year.

Other edificatory books with a similar interest in the conversion process offered a series of pictures where the course of conversion was rendered as interactions between *amor divinus* and *anima humana*. As a devotional theme, this way of describing devout life was introduced by Otto van Veen in 1615 in his *Amor Divini*

---

53 Cleans and illuminates, *Cor Iesv* no. 5-8 corresponding with *De Imitatione* 2nd book 4,2 and 5,1, Teaches, *Cor Iesv* no. 11: 3rd book 1,1; Sings, *Cor Iesv* no. 12: 4th book 16,4; crowns, *Cor Iesv* no. 18: 3rd book 49,6 etc.

54 *Amoris Divini et Hvmani Antipathia*, p. 169, last paragraph.

55 *The Scale of Perfection*, II, 28, p. 201: 'glorifiynge, that is whanne the soule schal be fulli reformed in the blisse of hevene.'

56 On Cramer, see Mödersheim, Sabine: *Domini Doctrina Coronat: Die geistliche Emblematikk Daniel Cramers (1568-1637)*. Frankfurt a.M. 1994.

57 Cf. Höltgen, Karl J: *Faksimile. Henry Hawkins: The Devout Hart (1634)*. Ylkley 1975, introduction pp. 2-16, here pp. 9-10. Höltgen dates the Wierix-series to c. 1600. Cf. Praz, Mario: *Studies in Seventeenth-Century Imagery*. Rome 1964, p. 407 and Dimler, Richard: 'A Bibliographical Survey of Jesuit Emblem Authors in French Provinces (1618-1726)'. *Archivum Historicum societatis Iesu* 47. 1978, pp. 240-250.

Emblemata, published in Antwerp. The main players on the stage are the two personifications, the heart often appearing, yet reduced to a requisite. As examples of that line of representations one might mention the Jesuit Hermann Hugo's *Pia Desideria*, published in Antwerp 1624, the *Heliotropium seu conformatio humanae voluntatis cum divina*, by another Jesuit, Jeremias Drexel, first published in Munich 1627, using the sunflower as a symbol of the human soul. Another example is the *Amoris Divini et Hvmani Antipathia* by an unknown author, its earlier versions appeared in 1626 and 1628, the final edition published by Snyders in Antwerp 1629, the very same year in which Benedictine Benedict van Haeften published his *Schola Cordis*.[58]

Even if one in an early modern perspective might speak of a religious translation of the *amor-psyche* topos, the interactions between *amor divinus*, the Christ Child, and the human soul, *anima humana*, seem to have their roots just as much in the late medieval concept of the relationship between Christ and the loving soul, 'die minnende Seele' (cf. Fig. 1).[59] In addition the classic movement towards union between Christ and soul is described in a number of scenes, where the *amor divinus* purges, measures, invites, teaches, deepens the relationship, accompanies and finally is united with *anima humana*. The rendering of a human heart to which something is done might to some extent be said to articulate a Protestant approach, the human heart being a passive receptor. Describing the process as an interaction between God and man might, then, reveal a more Catholic approach, where the initiative and power belongs to God, man, however, collaborating with Grace according to the classic Catholic position. Likewise, the Reformed order of salvation, calling, justification, sanctification and glorification, seemed to emphasize the actions of God to a passive man, more than the classic *ordo salutis*. Thus, Protestants like Cramer and Wierix logically chose the passive role for the heart, while the Catholics, Hugo, Drexel and van Haeften, focused on the interaction, reflecting the traditional position of Thomas Aquinas, repeated by Wilton in *The Scale*: 'For He (God) does everything; forms and reforms. While He forms by himself alone, He reforms together with us; for this is all done by the Grace given, and by conforming our will to the Grace received'.[60]

---

58 *Sonnenwend, das ist, von Gleichförmigkeit deß Menschlichen Willens mit dem Willen Gottes: In fünff Buecher abgetheilt.* München: Leysser 1627. It came in a Flemish edition in Antwerp 1638: *De Zonne-Bloeme ofte Overeenkomminge van den menschelijcken wille met de godtlijckeke*. Only occasionally the *Amoris Divini* used the figure of the human heart in its emblems.

59 On the house of the heart and late medieval monastic mysticism, see the chapter 'The house of the heart' in Hamburger, Jeffrey: *Nuns as Artists. The Visual Culture of a Medieval Convent*. Berkeley – Los Angeles – London 1997, pp. 137-175, on late medieval and early modern heart symbolism.

60 *The Scale of Perfection*, II, 28, p. 199: 'For He dooth al; He formeth and He reformeth. He formeth oonli bi Hymsilf, but He reformeth with us; for grace goven, and appliynge of oure wille, werketh al this'.

In both cases, Protestant or Catholic as their point of departure may have been, the spiritual introspection regarding the inner man, the state of the heart, and the description of the spiritual process of conversion, was shown in a number of very popular, illustrated books, meant to edify the pious reader and make his or her own conversion easier and more lasting. Cramerian emblems could quite easily be used by Catholics, and motifs from at least three of these Catholic books were used as models for devout pictures in some Lutheran churches in Scandinavia, thus testifying to the interdenominational qualities of that particular pious imagery.[61]

The very reason for using heart emblems was to illustrate and convey spiritual matters in a way which made it easier to understand the message. The text interpreted the picture, the explained picture now more suited to educate the laity than mere words. Thus texts and pictures cooperated to instruct the devout reader-spectator. Even when no actual pictures were used, many pious texts painted veritable "word-paintings" for the reader, as we saw Walter Hilton do back in the late 14th century. Such textual pictures could quite easily be converted into actual paintings, or more precisely: applied emblems.

The emblem, as it emerged as a distinct genre during the 16th century, is a combination of texts and picture which aims at conveying a spiritual message in an indirect, artificial way. The classic emblem has three components: The title, the *inscriptio*, offers the overall theme, the image, *pictura*, renders this by analogies or metaphorically, the explanation, *subscriptio*, explains how this picture may illustrate the overall theme.[62] The emblems were originally meant to convey a spiritual truth to the learned, the pictures not immediately disclosing their spiritual content, but doing so indirectly, veiled, requiring learning and a sharp mind to penetrate the veil and reveal the meaning. Hence it was a mark of quality that such emblems were clever, and difficult to understand. Basically, however, the really popular emblems were quite simple and easy to understand, more like offering a didactic device than presenting an intellectual challenge.

---

61 Emblematic illustrations were widely used in both religious and secular buildings etc., concerning secular use see eg. Harms, W. and Freytag H. (eds.): *Ausserliterarische Wirkungen barocker Emblembücher*. München 1975, and on emblems in churches eg. Kemp, Cornelia: *Angewandte Emblematik in süddeutschen Barockkirchen*. Berlin – München 1981. As examples of Catholic emblems in Lutheran Churches one might mention the late 17th century copies from *Schola Cordis* on the parapet of a Danish church, now in the chapel at the manor of Overgaard, Eastern Jutland, and the paintings from c. 1675, copying *Cor Iesv*, in the chapel of the Swedish manor Venngarn, north of Stockholm.

62 There is a considerable body of publications on emblems. Here, we shall mention only a few of the more important ones: Heckscher, William, Wirth and Karl-August: 'Emblem/Emblembuch'. Reallexikon zur deutschen Kunstgeschichte vol. 5. Stuttgart 1959, col. 85-228; Henkel, A., Schöne, A.: *Emblemata. Handbuch zur Sinnbildkunst des XVI. und XVII. Jahrhunderts*. Stuttgart 1967; Höpel, Ingrid: *Emblem und Sinnbild. Vom Kunstbuch zum Erbauungsbuch*. Frankfurt a.M. 1987; Scholz, Bernhard F.: 'Emblem und Emblempoetik'. *Wuppertaler Schriften 3*. Berlin 2002; Warncke, Carsten-Peter: *Symbol, Emblem, Allegorie. Die zweite Sprache der Bilder*. Köln 2005.

Concluding remarks

Now, when one compares such a late medieval spiritual text to a series of engravings made a hundred years later, is becomes obvious that its themes, indeed, its textual visualizations, to a fairly high degree anticipated early modern devotional imagery, which, therefore, did not emerge without forerunners. Protestant devotional piety and Catholic Counterreformation spirituality converged on the human heart, advocating a sincere, heartfelt, emotional Christianity, expressing itself in a life of prayer following certain patterns and structures thought to be expedient in terms of sustaining the *nova oboedientia* of the order of salvation, to stay in Grace as long as possible or successfully to convert again. This practice became the 'house' in which God was worshipped, filling the 'house of the heart' with Jesus himself. Contemplating the process of conversion: each phase, each fall and each step forward, comparing with your own place in this, viewing this quite literally in pictures and succinct texts, became in itself a devotional practice rooted in late medieval piety, highlighted by the Baroque concept of dramatic tension between godly things and the world. Indeed, withdrawing into the heart might be interpreted as a reaction to the perception of the general development as an ever increasing secularization. Conversion itself consisted in rejecting the temptations and promises of this world. The devout left what seemed to be an ever more secularized macrocosm, withdrawing to his or her heart – a microcosm which Jesus could and should dominate.[63]

It may seem as if the Reformation for a generation or two simply interrupted the development of a pious, edificatory and devotional iconography, and when it was resumed, this new turn to some extent simply meant a rekindling of Late medieval spirituality. However, the Middle Ages had passed and piety as well as theology had to face new challenges, recognizing the new existential situation of man and therefore establishing new relations between God and man, world and man, and between men, now in a denominationally divided Europe bringing about a significant and profound change of mentality. Hence, even if early modern thoughts and imagery seem to testify to a 'longue durée', they did not simply reintroduce late medieval piety. Yet they were still related, operating by a sort of 'analogue iconography' reflecting the new possibilities of printing and reproduction. Changed, but still related: 'St. Bernhard', Daniel Cramer exclaimed in 1623, 'is ours too'.[64]

---

63 Cf. von Achen, Henrik: 'Verdensbilde og billedverden. Menneskehjertet som religiøs figur og metafor: Et mottrekk mot sekulariseringsprosessen i nyere tid. En tentativ synsvinkel'. *Mellom Gud og Djævelen. Religiøse og magiske verdensbilleder i Norden 1500-1800.* Hanne Sanders (ed.). Copenhagen 2001, pp. 17-40.

64 Daniel Cramer in *Arbor Hæreticae Consanguinitatis.* Strassbourg 1623, making the point that devotion was not exclusively Catholic.

The Cultural Turn of Catholicism

Mario Perniola

The title of my essay could be *Catholicism on the boundaries of mere reason*. That is a paraphrase of the title of a very important work of Kant. But affinities stop here, because my perspective is very different and even opposite to the Kantian philosophy.

I would like to take my starting point from a very recent work edited by Susan L. Mizruchi, *Religion and Cultural Studies*.[65] In her Introduction, she states that 'Religion is now a "cutting edge" field of research': 'some of the most exciting academic work in disciplines such as literary criticism and history is now being done in specializations devoted to the subject of religion'. 'Like its companion term, the aesthetic, religion has until recently been considered the special province of cultural conservatives. All this has changed. The boundary line of religion and culture at the turn of the twenty-first century is a major site of intellectual action and interaction'. In fact, religion has been one of the most neglected subjects of Cultural Studies.

Mizruchi's methodological premise in the book seems to me also to be very interesting, namely that 'religion is understood as nonuniversal in theory and practice. Religion is a particular phenomenon only apprehended through language, which is in itself historically particular. Thus, the analytical terms we apply to the religious instances we study are themselves subject to historical scrutiny.'

This stance implicitly accepts the methodology proposed by one of the most important protestant theologians in the last twenty years, George A. Lindbeck,

---

65   See Mizruchi, Susan L. (ed.): *Religion and Cultural Studies*. Princeton – Oxford 2001.

who lent the greatest importance in the study of religion to cultural and linguistic aspects.[66] More specifically, Lindbeck refutes two other conceptions of religion that are widely acknowledged. The first position that Lindbeck refutes is the *cognitive-propositionalist* interpretation of religion. This confers a determining importance to doctrines understood as 'propositional claims about reality'. It treats doctrines as 'informative propositions or truth claims about objective realities'. The second theory rejected by Lindbeck is the *experiential-expressivist theory* that 'interprets doctrines as noninformative and nondiscursive symbols of inner feelings, attitudes or existential orientations'. According to this theory, religious experience is grounded in a pre-linguistic and unmediated form of experience where inner experience is primary. Religious doctrine, symbols, myths and rituals are secondary expressions of this fundamental inward state.

To these two theories of religion, Lindbeck opposes its own that he sums up as follows:

> A religion can be viewed as a kind of cultural and/or linguistic framework or medium that shapes the entirety of life and thought […] Like a culture or language, it is a communal phenomenon that shapes the subjectivities of individuals rather than being primarily a manifestation of those subjectivities. It comprises a vocabulary of discursive and nondiscursive symbols, together with a distinctive logic or grammar, in terms of which this vocabulary can be meaning-fully deployed.

A fundamental element of this theory is the concept of *intrasystemic consistency* that opens the way to the study of the identity of the single religious cultures taken in their specific aspects.

Cultural Identity of Catholicism

After this methodological premise I pass to the fundamental question of what is the cultural identity of Catholicism. On this issue two recent works have been published that are close and yet very far from one another, the *Catholic Imagination* by the American sociologist Andrew Greeley[67], and my own *On Catholic Feeling. The Cultural Form of a Universal Religion (Del sentire cattolico. La forma culturale di una religione universale).*[68]

---

66 Lindbeck, George A: *The Nature of Doctrine: Religion and Theology in a Postliberal Age.* Philadelphia 1984.

67 Greeley, Andrew: *The Catholic Imagination.* Berkeley – Los Angeles – London 2000.

68 Perniola, Mario: *Del sentire cattolico. La forma culturale di una religione universale.* Bologna 2001.

What brings together both books is, first of all, the strong emphasis on the aesthetic character of Catholicism and the putting aside of dogmatic and didactic aspects. For Greeley 'Catholics live in an enchanted world'. The rituals, the arts, music, architecture, prayers, the stories, create an aesthetic climate that is an essential part of Catholic imagination and confer a metaphoric character to it. 'The Catholic imagination loves metaphors; Catholicism is a verdant rainforest of metaphors'. This aesthetic character is unfortunately misunderstood by scholastic, moralistic and dogmatic Catholicism. But as the great philosopher Whitehead put it: 'Religions commit suicide when they find their inspiration in dogma'. The aesthetic dimension is what differentiates Catholicism from Protestantism which has always been very suspicious with respect to the metaphorical imagination. The protestant imagination distrusts metaphors; it tends to be a desert of metaphors. Catholicism stresses the like of any comparison (human passion is like divine passion), while Protestantism, when it is willing to use metaphors (and it must if it is to talk about God at all) stresses the unlike. Greeley's book is full of examples of this enthusiastic and vehement passion for the arts, not only taken from Catholic writers of the past (Bernini, Mozart, Joyce and Eliot) but also from today's film directors as Martin Scorsese. In this sense the Catholic imagination is something broader than a profession of faith. It has a cultural meaning that concerns very general forms of feeling and thought that have to do with people that are not even aware of them. Greeley defines them as 'cultural Catholics'.

My book too is characterized by putting aside moralistic and dogmatic aspects as these are not the essential characteristics of Catholicism. What I propose is precisely 'a Catholicism without orthodoxy' and 'a faith without dogma' that has its fulcrum not in a subjective profession of faith, but in a mentality that persists in its fundamentally equal lines even when it does not present itself in a confessional aspect. To account for a religion in its cultural aspect rather than in its fideistic aspect is something obvious for Protestantism. In fact, in its history it has had many cultural developments. Modern philosophy is in large part influenced by Protestantism (Kant, Hegel, Kiekegaard, hermeneutics, dialectical theology, and the problematic of difference). The same cannot be said of Catholicism that with the centuries has become hardened into an always more rigid dogmatic orthodoxy. The aesthetic aspect has been hidden by an intrusive and authoritarian clericalism. If Catholic feeling has been able to survive the ideological deluge that has drowned the Church ever since the Restoration we owe it especially to writers, to theatre and movie people, to musicians, in short to artists, those who have been able to manifest and pass on freely an experience focused on suspension and ritual without remaining trapped in orthodoxy and orthopraxis. Hence the paradox that Catholic feeling has developed in an extraneous and independent manner from the Catholic Church which, in order to react to the climate of cultural hostility created by Enlightenment and Positivism, has been forced to close itself in a dogmatic and ideological asphyxiating shell. Because of this ecclesiastical closure, writers and artists of Catholic feeling have almost never been aware of their relation with essence, least of all with the cultural heritage of Catholicism which, as a result, was removed and completely hidden as much by clerical arrogance as by artistic rebelliousness. Writers and artists of Catholic feeling have been in large part nonconfessional and nonorganic. After all, in an era characterized by the triumph of vitalism and subjectivism, an institutional feeling as the Catholic one, could have only been preserved by a total independence and autonomy with respect to the spiritualistic and communitarian ideologies embraced by the Church.

That is why, in my book, I give great importance to the Swiss theologian Hans Urs von Balthasar, author of a monumental work, *Herrlichkeit. Eine theologische Aesthetik*, in which the centre of Catholic feeling is placed within a vast and comprehensive aesthetic experience that integrates within itself all aspects of living, thinking and action[69]. The work of Balthasar constitutes a vigorous affirmation of the aesthetic character of Catholicism. The subtitle of his work is very important: *A theological Aesthetics* and not *An aesthetic Theology* since it makes explicit the idea that God reveals himself not simply as truth or goodness, but as beauty. Consequently, Christianity is not simply a collection of true dogmas or a way of life, but the response to a vision that inspires and deeply influences one's way of life.

The second aspect that Greeley's book and mine have in common is in considering the experience of the world as an essential aspect of Catholicism. Catholicism, for Greeley, tends

> to emphasize the presence of God in the world, while the classic works of Protestant theologians tend to emphasize the absence of God from the world. The Catholic writers stress the nearness of God to his creation, the Protestant writers the distance between God and his creation; the Protestants tend to emphasize the risk of superstition and idolatry, the Catholics the dangers of a creation in which God is only marginally present. Or, to put the matter in different terms, Catholics tend to accentuate the immanence of God, Protestants the transcendence of God.

Greeley maintains very effectively that in Catholic sensibility 'God lurks in aroused human love and reveals Himself to us through it'. He confers great im-

---

69 Von Balthasar, Hans Urs: *Herrlichkeit. Eine theologische Aesthetik, 3 bnd.* Einsiedeln 1961-67.

portance to the verb to lurk in the sense of to linger furtively. 'God leaves all kinds of hints of His presence'.

According to Greeley, this worldly character of Catholicism is manifested under many aspects and is connected with the sacramental character of Catholic theology. As you know, the churches that issue from 16th-century Reformation generally limit the term sacrament to the two principal Christian rites: baptism and the Lord's Supper (Eucharist). On the contrary, the Roman Catholic Church has recognized seven rites as sacraments in the full sense of the word. The fact that even marriage is considered a sacrament is very significant. On the basis of his sociological data, Greeley claims that 'Catholics have sex more often, they are more playful in their sexual encounters, and they enjoy sex more'. Many works of art, of which Bernini's St. Therese is the most explicit (Fig. 1), shows that sexual desire is viewed by Catholicism as a sacred desire. 'Erotic desire is a part of human life and an important part at that. Like all powerful human energies, it can turn demonic, but it is not evil in itself'.

Another aspect of the worldliness of Catholicism is for Greeley its social sense: 'Catholics tend to communalism in their ethical concerns, Protestants to individualism'. 'Catholics tend to picture society as supportive and not oppressive, while Protestants tend to picture society as oppressive and not supportive'. As a result, they tend to attribute great importance to organization: 'The Church is not a chaotic mass of independent individuals but an ordered community in which diversity pervades both leadership and membership'.

In my book too the notion of world plays an important role. Catholicism and, in particular, that of the 16th century is, in my view, the secularized religion par excellence because it placed at the centre of its concerns a reflection on the world and its dynamics. That is why I attribute to the historian and political man Francesco Guicciardini and to Ignatius of Loyola a very important role in the elaboration of Catholic feeling. Even though they are very different men, they both paid the greatest attention to an examination of the historical process and its human events. Secularization, however, does not imply a declining religion. In Guicciardini's and Ignatius of Loyola's mode of feeling it is precisely worldly events to excite wonder and astonishment. One could sum up this sensibility in a single phrase: 'Nothing disappoints me. The world has bewitched me'.

In other words the choice of world does not imply the adoption of a technical programming mentality. World is the place of difference that the Protestant mentality tends to attribute to God. Loyola's *Spiritual Exercises* and Guicciardini's *Ricordi* point to a method to find one's own way in the world. The fundamental condition is leaving aside one's subjective affections and knowing how to com-

Fig. 1: The Extacy of St. Theresa by Gianlorenzo Bernini. The Cornaro chapel, Santa Maria della Vittoria, Rome.

bine a realistic vision of life with a hope without superstition. Loyola was called a 'contemplative in action'. The expression points very well to the type of spirituality that he inaugurated. In it the accent is not placed so much on God as on God's will, on history and on the world.

Greeley's book and mine have in common these two points: Catholicism as aesthetic religion and as religion of the world. Now I would like to consider some questions that remain open. The first concerns the relation between Christianity and the religions of the world. This issue has become central to theology as a result of missionary activities. The Jesuits were the first to focus on the problem with seventy-three volumes of their *Relationes*, from 1610 to 1791. There is a discrepancy between Catholicism's universal pretensions and its roots in the West. The missionaries that refused to be agents of colonialism looked for common aspects between Christianity and the religions of the people they visited. The greatest effort in this direction was undertaken by Jesuits in China. In their attempt to adjust Christianity to the Chinese mentality they went so far as to conceal Christ's disgraceful death on the Cross. As we known, this process of adaptation to the Chinese mentality in the 18th century led to the controversial 'Chinese rituals' that became one of the reasons for the dissolution of the Society of Jesus in 1773.

In the last thirty years the problem has become topical again with both Protestants and Catholics. The former speak mostly of *contextualization*, the latter of *inculturation*. These different names, however, refer to the same problem which is the necessity of finding points in common between Christianity and local cultures.

Now, according to Greeley, Catholicism is more suitable than Protestantism to this dialogue with non-Western cultures. In fact,

> [Catholicism] has never been afraid (at least not in principle) of contaminating the purity of spirit with sensible and often sensual imagery […] All the other religions and quasi religions (like Platonism) have abhorred the practices and images of nature religions as defilement of spirit. Catholicism, in its better moments, feels instinctively that nature does not defile spirit, but reveals it. Hence Catholicism (again, in its better moments) has not hesitated to make its own the practices, customs, and devotions of nature religions wherever it has encountered them - never more systematically thoroughly, or creatively than in Ireland.

On the contrary Protestantism has always feared the danger of sorcery and paganism. 'In one sense, the Reformation was a protest of a segment of the clerical elite and the newly emerging middle class against the continuation of paganism at the time when the Dark Ages had been definitively left behind'.

Here we begin to detect the differences between Greeley's study and my own. His focus is centred above all on Irish Catholicism and its developments in the United States that is a particular Catholic culture, which is different, for example, from English, Spanish or Polish Catholicism. In other words, the Catholic imagination that he describes is already the result of a process of inculturation and, therefore, it is more an Irish than a Catholic imagination. One must not forget that the Latin adjective *catholicus* means universal. The problem, therefore, is whether it is possible to reconcile the universality of Catholicism with the individuation of specific characters.

Now, in my opinion, these specific characters cannot emphasize content rather than form, otherwise a relapse in a type of ethnocentrism is inevitable. This identity can only have a formal and methodological character. Let me explain with an example. The *Spiritual exercises* of Ignatius of Loyola constitute a method for finding one's own way in life, but do not point to the best absolute condition. The validity of the choice is always relative to the premises from which those doing the exercises begin. In effect, they can also be done by an agnostic or a pagan. The ecumenism of Catholic feeling is not a relativistic irenics that wants to get along with everyone but the indication of spiritual methods of reflection and concentration that can be beneficial to everyone, independently of one's beliefs.

A profound difference between Greeley's and my point of view is the so-called *enchantment* of Catholicism. For Greeley 'Catholics live in a world that is enchanted, despite the fact that church leaders and thinkers are incorrigibly prosaic and seem to have hardened their hearts against the poetry of religion'. But, in my view, the *enchantment* cannot be considered a specific trait of Catholicism because it also belongs to many other religions and constitutes, without doubt, an essential element of ancient Greek paganism.

In fact, at the basis of Catholic feeling there is a much more complex experience that one can describe with an oxymoron: an enchanted disenchantment, a non-partaking participation, an external feeling, etc. This experience found its greatest manifestation in Catholicism between the 16th and 17th centuries and is not without its ties to neo-Stoicism. All my work in the last twenty years refers to this experience presented under various aspects and especially in the volume *Enigmas. The Egyptian Moment in Society and Art* published in English by Verso in 1995. At present, however, it is important to insist on the religious aspect of this experience

An important key to understanding what is meant by the so-called nonpartaking participation is provided by Ignatius of Loyola when he declares *indifference* as the fundamental condition for achieving good results in the *Spiritual Exercises*. He claims that it is necessary to 'make oneself indifferent toward all things created in the world in such a way that we no longer desire health rather than sickness, wealth rather than poverty, honour rather than dishonour, a longer life rather than a short one'. The *Spiritual Exercises*, therefore, entail a moment of suspension that the Jesuitic tradition calls, *indifference*, which is never thought of as a point of arrival, but only as a temporary stage, a transitory stage necessary to free oneself of one's own identity, a zero degree in the will's change of orientation. Ignatius' indifference has nothing to do with quietism, fatalism or pantheism. It is not an abolition of one's identity in the identity of Being, God, the Cosmos, but the overcoming of any obstacle to access the difference of history. It is necessary to become nothing in order to be available to the best. Since the best is extraneous, other, different, its knowledge will be precluded to those who are prisoners of an identity.

Therefore, before the *enchantment*, of which Greeley speaks, there is a moment of radical disenchantment, 'In tristitia hilaris, in hilaritate tristis'. In sadness cheerfulness, in cheerfulness sadness, as the Baroque saying goes. The Austrian writer Robert Musil was the great interpreter of this sensibility. He defined it as a relation of 'active passivity' towards himself and to things. Ulrich, the protagonist of *A man without qualities* feels in an impersonal way as if he were not the one to feel: 'his behaviour is both passionate and unperturbed'. This implies a complete detachment to vitalism. To be sure he possesses some qualities but these do not belong to him intimately: 'when he is angry something in him laughs. When he is sad he embarks on some venture'.

In many other poets and writers of the period between the 16th century and the 20th century, we find this enigmatic convergence between the extreme coldness of apathy and the extreme heat of poetic transport. As a last example I would like to mention Walter Benjamin's analysis in *Ursprung der deutschen Trauerspiels* (1928) where he shows that the Baroque entails the total abandonment of the medieval path of indignation and apocalyptic prophesying, an earth-bound solution to all metaphysical questions and entrance into a perspective of troubling serenity, of dizzying calm.[70]

The second question on which my interpretation of Catholicism diverges from Greeley concerns the question of the sacred. As is well-known, the notion of the sacred is inherent in a syncretistic intention that aims at comparing Christi-

---

70 Benjamin, Walter: *Ursprung des deutschen Trauerspiels*. Berlin 1928.

anity to superstition. On the Protestant and Jewish sides there have been outcries against the notion of the sacred. Memorable is Levinas' phrase according to who the sacred is the twilight in which sorcery flourishes. Furthermore the same opposition between sacred and profane has been put into question in most recent studies. The inherent risk in Greeley's position is that of comparing Catholicism too much to forms of popular religiosity that verge on superstition.

My proposal moves into another direction, toward the ritual. It connects to a whole series of previous studies that are collected in the volume *Ritual Thinking. Sexuality, Death, World*. In this work the notion of a ritual thinking is outlined and is very different from mythic and functional thinking.

It is essential to Catholicism to attribute to the institution a determining importance. As it has been rightly observed,[71] the Catholic Church has never recognized as its own the movements of reform that in the name of freedom of the spirit or of faith have set themselves free from any relation to the institution. At the same time, however, to the essence of Catholicism is extraneous that close relation between institution and ideology that characterizes modernity. Catholicism has been obliged to move on ideological ground in order to react to Enlightenment. The Restoration of the first half of the 19th century is precisely this reaction within which Catholicism still finds itself today. It has transformed it in an apparatus whose strength seems to depend on the adherence to a doctrinal system and to meticulous moral precepts. In the world now exits a hiatus between catholic identity, on the one hand, and the actual knowledge of the dogmas and the deep-seated belief of the correctness of the norms, on the other.[72] This discrepancy is generally considered a sign of superficiality and opportunism, if not of bad faith and hypocrisy. It would seem that Catholics, even more than Protestants, have difficulty internalizing the moral and cognitive aspects of their religion. In other words, it seems that they are lacking the coherence and transparence as a result of a historically sedimented propensity for tendentiousness and simulation. This accusation hides a profound misunderstanding of Catholic feeling which is not subjective, and least of all ideological, but *ritualistic*. On the other hand, this misunderstanding has been somewhat helped along by Catholicism itself, which has been obliged to engage in a relation of mimetic rivalry with Protestantism and Enlightenment, instead of reflecting independently on the specificity of its own feeling. For this reason, it was said that Catholicism is amongst the least known of the great religions.[73]

---

71 Danielou, Jean, Honoré, Jean and Poupard, Paul (eds.): *Le catholicisme: Hier-demain*. Paris 1974, p. 131.

72 See Garelli, Franco: *Forza della religione e debolezza della fede*. Bologna 1996.

73 Casanova, José: *Public religions in the modern world*. Chicago and London 1994.

Ritual Feeling

What do we mean by *ritual feeling*? At first the expression appears to be an oxymoron, which is the coupling of two terms that appear opposite to each other. In fact, in today's thinking, feeling is thought to be something essentially subjective, spontaneous, immediate and anti-formalistic, while to ritual are attributed the character of formality, conventionality, stereotypy and inflexibility.[74] The point of view presented in *Ritual Thinking* subverts this common opinion inspired by an anti-ritual prejudice very much rooted in modernity that privileges the spiritual over the corporeal, the internal over the external, life over form and intention over work.[75] The 'anti-Rome complex' is based,[76] in large part, on this prejudice, on a critique of Catholicism devoid of truthfulness, honesty and authenticity.

The studies that have been conducted in many disciplines on the essential meaning of ritual have variously identified it with the realization of an original myth,[77] the preservation of social ties,[78] the exercise of political control,[79] the preservation of tradition,[80] the mastery of anxiety and fear,[81] the legitimacy of social distinctions,[82] the resolution of tensions and conflicts,[83] the production of symbolic forms,[84] the elaboration of paradigms of thought and action,[85] and many other functions and finalities.[86] Even though all these explanations of ritual attribute to it a positive role, they remain nonetheless caught in ideology precisely because they pretend to explain it by recourse to a meaning, an intention, or to a subjective experience. Thus, it escapes them that ritual is an act and not a

---

74 These are the traits attributed to ritual by Stanley J. Tambiah, in *Culture, thought and social action: an anthropological perspective*. Cambridge, Mass. 1985. Most of the vast literature on the subject does not depart from this definition, exception made for some recent contributions amongst which the most important are Bell, Catherine: *Ritual Theory, Ritual Practice*. New York and Oxford 1992 and Terrin, Aldo Natale: *Il rito. Antropologia e fenomenologia della ritualità*. Brescia 1999. My theory of ritual feeling is dealt with in the book *Ritual Thinking. Sexuality, Death, World*. New Yok 2001.

75 On the anti-ritualistic prejudice and its spreading within Catholicism see the important remarks of Terrin 1999, p. 51; p. 205; pp. 302-6; p. 374. The entire work is a courageous indictment of the ideologization of Catholicism and of the prevailing attitude within it of a parenetic and didactic attitude, devoid of effectiveness and connection with the experience of those that it addresses.

76 von Balthasar, Hans Urs: *Der antirömische Affeckt. Wie lässt sich das Papsttum in der Gesamtkirche integrieren*. Freiburg i.B. 1974.

77 Eliade, Mircea: *Das Heilige und das Profane*. Hamburg 1957.

78 Durkheim, Emile: *Les formes élémentaires de la vie religieuse*. Paris 1912.

79 Radcliffe-Brown, Alfred R.: *Structure and Function in Primitive Society*. London 1952.

80 Douglas, Mary: *Natural Symbols*. Harmondsworth 1970.

81 Malinowski, Bronislaw: 'Magic, Science and Religion'. *Science, Religion and Reality*. J.A. Needham (ed.). London 1925.

82 Firth, Raymond: *We, the Tycopia*. London 1936.

83 Gluckman, Max: *Essays on the Ritual of Social Relations*. Manchester 1962.

84 Langer, Susanne: *Philosophy in a New Key*. Cambridge, Mass. 1942.

85 Bourdieu, Pierre: *Esquisse d'une theorie de la pratique*. Genève 1974.

86 An excellent review of the various positive interpretation of ritual can be found in Terrin 1999.

mode of thinking! To be sure this act entails both a thinking and a feeling, but it is a question of a thinking and of a feeling that are extraneous to the logocentric and discursive formulations of modern subjectivism.

Actually these explanations cannot be considered erroneous from a strictly intellectual point of view. In some sense they are all correct, but they never grasp the essential point of ritual experience. This is comprehended much better by those who maintain that ritual has no meaning,[87] that ritual has no other function than that of producing ritualized people,[88] that ritual is a self-referential and autotelic experience.[89] One enters ritual experience only through a suspension of daily life, a truce with respect to the functional activities for the achievement of certain goals, a delay in corporeality. In fact, this *epoché* does not lead us to a mystical state of rapture, but on the contrary it makes us similar to a thing that feels, as if the impulse to action did not come from us. It has been said correctly that ritual is paying attention to and an affirmation of difference, an 'occupying space and making time', a 'staying close to things of the world without doing violence to them'.[90]

The access to ritual feeling implies above all a distancing to one's own subjectivity that constitutes an unavoidable condition of feeling from outside. To be able to see oneself with an external eye, to consider oneself as world and not as an I, to be present at what is born and at what becomes without caging it into a prepackaged interpretation, or into a logic of personal interests, these are all aspects that originate in classical antiquity and that have been handed down to Catholicism often under the cloak of humility, piety and devotion. What Guicciardini calls 'reputation' and Ignatius of Loyola 'indifference' is precisely a movement of estrangement that enables one to find a common world on which, even in an extreme variety of opinions and perspectives, private worlds can converge.[91] However, this does not mean forming a community, and not even to think of society as a great family. The convergence on a common world is neither ideological nor affective. Hannah Arendt's invitation to never confuse the sphere of visible action with the invisible one of morality and love must be fully heeded. With the Protestant Reformation human beings were not projected into the world but in themselves. An important consequence of Reformation was precisely the loss of a common world. The rise of Capitalism, which Max Weber connects precisely to the spirituality of Protestant sects, implies therefore not a loss or an alienation

---

87   Staal, Frits: *Rules without meaning.* New York, Bern, Frankfurt a.M. and Paris 1989.
88   Bell 1992, p. 211
89   Terrin 1999, p. 171
90   Terrin 1999, p. 252
91   Arendt, Hannah: *The Human Condition.* Chicago and London 1958.

of subjectivity (as Marx thought), but on the contrary a loss and an alienation from the world. The origins of industrial Capitalism are possible 'only at the cost of sacrificing the world and the worldliness of man'. According to Arendt, modern mass ideological movements, as well as national states, are founded on an a-worldly mentality that considers interiority as well as sociality as subjective modes of being. In other words modernity is founded on a feeling from within that misunderstands the world, as well as the true nature of the political which is constructed on what is visible and tangible. The classical political-worldly distinction between public and private is substituted by the modern politico-ideological distinction between social and intimate. Unfortunately, the actual crisis of ideologies and nationalisms is not accompanied by an inversion of tendencies. If universalization is thought as an extension of modernity's emotional and affective categories to humanity as a whole, founded on a feeling from within, we are only taking a further step toward the destruction of common worlds.[92] Love, writes Hannah Arendt, can be falsified and perverted only when it is used for political purposes such as the changing and salvation of the world. The ideas of fraternity and solidarity are not only inadequate but also dangerous to the construction of common worlds. In fact these are not in the conscience or in the life of people, but in forms of action, in rituals, in works that are very visible. Goodness 'is not only impossible in the public domain but it is also destructive'.

The importance assumed by the concept of life in Catholicism falls within the process of subjectivization and ideologization to which it was forced to submit especially after the Reformation. The idea that life itself, and not its immortality, that is the world, constitutes the highest good, revealed itself to be very destructive for ritual feeling. Vitalism, which starting from Restoration is a very important aspect of Catholic ideology favours a demographic overproduction that provokes the opposite effect to any effective valorization of the poor, that is, an inflation, devaluation and humiliation of human bodies. Contrary to what we commonly believe, this depreciation does not depend so much on the reification of the human body, which does not constitute a novelty. It depends on the fact that cultural and ritual devices that make possible its valorization have deteriorated. The appeal to a subjective inwardness in which the dignity of the person supposedly resides, and the aversion toward any object and ceremonial dimension perceived as degrading, bring about a result which is precisely contrary to their intentions.[93] By wanting to deny value to actions, behaviours and visible works, one ends up

---

92 The notion of common world that is at the basis of Hannah Arendt's political theory can also be found in Luc Boltanski-Laurent Thévenot's important study: *De la justification. Les économies de la grandeur*. Paris 1992.

93 I take the liberty to refer to my own essay 'La merce umana'. *Agalma* 1. June 2000.

by totally abandoning the corporeal world to the manipulations of the so-called technique without soul or to the senseless practices of superstition. The subjectivistic formulation of modern culture and the vitalistic spirit that pervades it make it impossible for the single to be self-evaluated according to parameters that are shared by others, to become part of a world in which relative and continuously changing standards and classifications are in force, but that nonetheless are always felt by a plurality, however small, of individuals. Self-evaluation requires the feeling from outside, the becoming thing, being able to see oneself with an eye that does not belong neither to me nor to you, the access to a neutral and external dimension, the estrangement from what is intimate and one's own. As long as the value that one attributes to oneself depends only on intentions and not on actions, one fluctuates between vanity and disheartenment, arrogance and abjection.

After estrangement, attention to the real is the second aspect of ritual feeling. Guicciardini calls it 'discretion' namely, discernment, the faculty of grasping differences. It is not only a question of knowing how to determine affinities between apparently distant things, and, vice versa, differences between things that are apparently similar. This attitude is based on a conception of the world as place of *difference*. As long as men are prisoners of their subjectivities, they are deprived of the possibility of confronting a common world that is never reducible to something identical and homogeneous. As Hannah Arendt remarks, dictatorships and mass societies pretend that the world is something identical: 'in it we see everyone behave suddenly as if they were members of one family, everyone multiplying and extending the perspective of his neighbour'.

However, the *difference* of the world must not be seen as something abstract and evanescent. It is strictly connected to its corporeity, namely to the fact that it contains a dimension irreducible to an idea, to a concept, to a thought, to a meaning. Ritual implies precisely this rooting in corporeity that is opaque, contingent, and inaccessible to any theorization. At this point one could speak of mystery, but this word implies something more, especially if it alludes to a transcendental, supernatural salvific plan. Ritual feeling implies, instead, a sort of 'stupor of reason' (*Erstaunen der Vernuft*) [94] with respect to the world and its actuality, without a reason. There is, therefore, a relation between ritual and those moments when the cultural and physical dimensions cross and are superimposed. Birth, sexuality, disease and death constitute moments of strong ritual intensity par excellence.

Arnold van Gennep was one of the first to study the relation amongst these moments and ritual and to determine in the transit from one state to another the

94 Pareyson, Luigi: *Ontologia della libertà. Il male e la sofferenza*. Torino 1995, 385ff.

very essence of ritual phenomenon.[95] In his view, ritual can be divided into three phases: an introductory one of separation from the previous state; a transitional phase of suspension of the social life that precedes it and follows it; and a post-transitional one of incorporation of the new condition. The importance that he assigns to the intermediary phase, which constitutes the key moment of this process, corresponds exactly to the importance that we attributed to the experience of the *epoché* in the determination of ritual feeling. The *difference* of the world, its irreducibility to an ideology, to an explanation, to a single meaning, is revealed mainly in the truce, in the delay, in this limbo of existence. Therefore, van Gennep also emphasizes the physical character of the phenomenon of ritual. Change has nothing purely spiritual about it, but is connected to a material, corporeal shift.[96]

Transition remains always a ritual condition anchored to the body and to the world. There is in ritual a reification of action that belongs essentially to it. The interpretation of those like Victor Turner who consider transition as an anti-structure, as an anti-institutional dimension par excellence, is tendentious. In fact it attributes to the ritual process traits that are precisely the contrary of ritual, namely immediacy, spontaneity, and vitalism.[97] According to Turner, transition makes possible the access to an egalitarian society, earmarked by transparent and non hierarchical relations that he calls *communitas* where individuals confront each other in free and creative exchanges, not conditioned by pre-existing roles. Turner himself is aware of the precarious character of *communitas* that has a very short duration and tends to be transformed into a new normative system or into a utopian ideology. Turner observes that Francis of Assisi's project to institute an order that would transform transition into a permanent choice encountered insurmountable difficulties, derived precisely by its inclusion in the ecclesiastical structure. However, this type of approach to transition gets caught in an ideological definition that identifies structure with formalistic conservatism, and anti-structure with spontaneous progressivism. Thus, one forgets that even informality has its rituals. Even rebellion has its models, its precedents, its paradigms. If rebellion wants to be realized in the world, it must free itself of the indistinct and undifferentiated sentiment of a *communitas* that is proud of itself. The essential aspect of ritual feeling is not feeling together, nor the dialectic between the you and the us, but the relation with an 'it', with a third term that is reducible neither to the subjectivity of a single nor to that of a community.

---

95   van Gennep, Arnold: *Les rites des passages*. Paris 1981 (1909)
96   van Gennep 1981, p. 275
97   Turner, Victor W.: *The Ritual Process. Structure and Anti-Structure*. Chicago 1969.

We are left with one last issue. Granted that Catholicism contains ritual aspects of the greatest importance; can one identify *Catholic feeling* with *ritual feeling*, tout court? There are other religions where the ritual dimension is more evident or even exclusive. For instance, Hinduism, Confucianism, as well as the religions of people that are the privileged object of anthropologists' observation, they do attribute a greater importance to ritual than Catholicism. We would be tempted at this point to accept the distinction between religions of the book that have a tendency to degenerate ideologically, and religions of costume, where ritual is the mode par excellence to transmit the past.[98] However, if I attribute special importance to ritual in determining Catholic feeling it is not only for obvious reasons of cultural belonging. Catholicism, in fact, has been compelled into a relation of mimetic rivalry with subjectivism ever since the Protestant Reformation. This situation, which is enormously increased starting from the moment when modernity recognized itself in subjectivism, compelled it to remove the worldly, the ritual immanent dimension that deeply belongs to it. Ritual feeling dwells today in the Catholic unconscious,[99] while orthodoxy appears to make its triumphal march arm in arm with contemporary ideologies and sensologies.

98 Ortigues, Edmund: *Religions du livre et religions de la culture.* Paris 1981.
99 Terrin 1999, p. 205

Manual Labour as *praxis pietatis:*

Sketch of a Motif in the 17th Century Cistercian Reform at La Trappe

Mette Birkedal Bruun

I. Background

Prologue

In 1683, the Cistercian abbot Armand-Jean de Rancé published his main work *De la sainteté et des devoirs de la vie monastique*. In this book Rancé, in what amounts to about 1000 pages, offers a presentation of the reform that he had introduced some fifteen years earlier in an attempt to purge his own monastery and, if possible, the Cistercian Order of laxity, decay, and opulence. In *De la sainteté* Rancé pursues two goals. On the one hand, he marks out the key themes of the reform thus positioning his endeavours in the religious landscape of his days. On the other, he addresses the obligation generally facing those who in a religious context launch reform rather than revolution; the obligation, that is, to stage renewal as a matter of return.

In both prongs of the double ambition behind Rancé's work, the question of manual labour plays a crucial role. It is a link to the monastic tradition and thus a vital argument in the reformer's claim for authenticity and legitimacy, and archetypically Rancé corroborates his views on manual labour by means of a monastic genealogy ranging from Jesus, via the apostles, the Egyptian desert fathers of the 4th century, and the Rule of Benedict to the golden age of Cistercianism and the Order's main figure Bernard of Clairvaux (1090-1153) and onwards to contemporary figureheads. Manual labour is also one of the issues which most characteristically represents the tenor of the reform. Cultivation of crops and manufacturing of tools secure independence from the surrounding society and thereby promote the monastic estrangement from the world so vital to the abbot. At the same time, manual labour fleshes out his central ideals of penitent and humble devotion thus assuming the character of *praxis pietatis*. The primary interest of this essay lies with representations of the role played by manual labour in the reform of Rancé. A sketchy point of departure is taken, however, in its alleged foundations: the Rule of Benedict and the Cistercian ethos of the 12th century.

The Rule of Benedict

Written towards the middle of the 6th century, the so-called Rule of Benedict (*Regula Benedicti*) was originally intended for Benedict of Nursia's monastery Monte Cassino. When Charlemagne however sought to unify Frankish monasticism in the decades around 800, he decreed that the Rule of Benedict should be the one adhered to. This privilege was largely owing to the *Vita* of Benedict of Nursia by Gregory the Great (d. 604), which in the king's eyes endowed the abbot and his statutes with papal imprimatur.[100] Benedict's Rule in turn became the constitutive basis also for the offspring of the Benedictine Order, first and foremost Cluniacs (910) and Cistercians (1098).

According to the Rule of Benedict, monastic life rests on three pillars; *Lectio divina*: the meditative reading of Bible and Church Fathers, *Opus Dei*: the monastic liturgy, centred on the canonical hours where the monks assemble for chanting of Old Testament Psalms and readings seven times during the day, and *Opus Manuum*: manual labour. It is with this last issue that we shall here dwell.

'Idleness is the enemy of the soul. Therefore, the brothers should have specified periods for manual labor as well as for prayerful reading.'[101] Thus begins the Rule's chapter on manual labour. Then follows a passage which divides up the time between the prayers of the Office in slots dedicated to work and reading respectively. Both in the course of the year and in the course of the day. Monastic time is thus completely structured and charted according to the Rule's three main pillars. The Rule then proceeds to the issue of manual labour; the monks 'must not become distressed if local conditions or their poverty should force them to do the harvesting themselves. When they live by the labor of their hands, as our

---

100 Lawrence, C.H.: *Medieval Monasticism: Forms of Religious Life in Western Europe in the Middle Ages.* Harlow 2001 (1984), pp. 69-78.

101 'Otiositas inimica est animae, et ideo certis temporibus occupari debent fratres in labore manuum, certis iterum horis in lectione divina.' *Regula Benedicti* XLVIII.1, p. 248. Fry's translation in *RB 1980: The Rule of St. Benedict.* Timothy Fry et al. (eds. and transls.). Collegeville, MN 1981, p. 249.

fathers and the apostles did, then they are really monks. Yet all things are to be done with moderation on account of the fainthearted.'[102]

Manual labour not only takes up a substantial daily amount of time; it is also presented as a constitutive monastic occupation. The Rule's precepts for manual labour are of a pragmatic nature; work will prevent the monks from spiritually dangerous boredom and earn them an honourable living. In later realizations of the Rule's prescriptions there is a tendency that material and spiritual concerns are somewhat separated. Monks are still required constantly to engage in useful occupation, but when it comes to the sustenance of the monastery, their work is often not enough.

Manual labour in the Cistercian Order

Benedict's Rule does not specify the nature of the labour, but agriculture would have formed part of it, involving – at harvest – the assistance of hired labourers.[103] As from Carolingian times onwards the monasteries grew, a more general strengthening of the monastic labour force through lay labourers became necessary. But a growth in the introduction of extra-mural serfs meant a breech in the monks' estrangement from the secular world and a potential threat against monastic isolation.

The Cistercian Order, which was founded in 1098, was to adress this problem specifically. According to the foundation narratives written by later generations of Cistercians, the Order was founded with the ambition of renewing Benedictine monasticism through, among other things, a stricter adherence to the Rule of Benedict. Initially the monks were bent on doing the manual work required to run the monastery themselves, but it soon became clear that additional help was needed; and the more agriculturally successful the monasteries, the more urgent the need for extra hands. In the words of the foundation narrative Exordium parvum:

> Having spurn this world's riches, behold! The new soldiers of Christ, poor with the poor Christ, began discussing by what planning, by what device, by what management they would be able to support themselves in this life, as well as the guests who came, both rich and poor, whom the Rule commands to welcome as Christ. It was then that they enacted a defini-

---

102 'Si autem necessitas loci aut paupertas exegerit ut ad fruges recolligendas per se occupentur, non contristentur, quia tunc vere monachi sunt si labore manuum suarum vivunt, sicut et patres nostri et apostoli. Omnia tamen mensurate fiant propter pusillanimes.' *Regula Benedicti* XLVIII.7-9, p. 248-250. Fry's translation in *RB 1980: The Rule of St. Benedict*, 1981, pp. 249-251.

103 Lekai, Louis: *Cistercians: Ideals and Reality*. Kent 1977, p. 334.

tion to receive, with their bishop's permission, bearded laybrothers, and to treat them as themselves in life and death – except that they may not become monks – and also hired hands; for without the assistance of these they did not understand how they could fully observe the precepts of the Rule day and night [...] And since they had set up farmsteads for agricultural development in a number of different places, they decreed that the aforesaid laybrothers, and not monks, should be in charge of those dwellings, because, according to the Rule, monks should reside in their own cloister.[104]

As the quotation indicates, there is a basic tension between the various prescriptions of the Rule of Benedict. The demand for manual labour, if exercised on a grand agricultural scale, clashes with the daily liturgical curriculum, and the administration of farmsteads, sometimes situated far from the monastery, counteracts the Benedictine request for *stabilitas loci* (steadfastness). In the laybrother institution, lay labourers were integrated into the monastic community but on terms which allowed them to dispensate from the reading and most of the liturgical obligations and wholly dedicate themselves to the work; thus disturbance of the cherished isolation from the world was avoided while the necessary amount of workers was secured. This structure was not entirely new, but with the Cistercians it acquired dimensions hitherto unseen.[105]

Despite the laybrothers manual labour remained significant for the Cistercian monks. Manual labour appears in medieval monastic texts as a topos of mortification on a par with silence, fasts, prayers, and vigils, and it is endowed with more spiritual nuances than in the Rule of Benedict. It is considered a remedy for the edification of the soul, and as a feature in its own right it is above all associated with the initiatory struggles to leave wordly carnality behind. For instance, William of Saint-Thierry (ca. 1075-1148) prescribes that for the novice '[...] heavy work in the fields brings great devastation to the body, leading to devastation and humility of the heart, and the tribulation of its fatigue often brings forth a feeling

---

104 'Ecce huius sæculi divitiis spretis, cœperunt novi milites christi, cum paupere Christo pauperes, inter se tractare quo ingenio, quove artificio, seu quo exercitio in hac vita se hospitesque divites et pauperes supervenientes, quos ut Christum suscipere præcipit Regula, sustentarent. Tuncque definierunt se conversos laicos barbatos licentia episcopi sui suscepturos, eosque in vita et morte, excepto monachatu, ut semetipsos tractaturos, et homines etiam mercenarios; quia sine adminiculo istorum non intelligebant se plenarie die sive nocte præcepta Regule posse seruare [...] Et cum alicubi curtes ad agriculturas exercendas instituissent, decreverunt ut prædicti conversi domos illas regerent, non monaschi; quia habitatio monachorum secundum Regulam debet esse in claustro ipsorum.' *Exordium parvum* XV, Waddell 1999, p. 435. Waddell's translation in Waddell, Chrysogonus (ed.): *Narrative and Legislative Texts from Early Cîteaux*. Cîteaux 1999, p. 435.

105 Lekai 1977, p. 336.

of a more vehement devotion'.[106] This does not mean that manual labour is for novices only, but it is often represented as a step along the road to beatitude, the fruits of which in time give way to those of prayer and contemplative reading.

In the reform to which we shall now turn, however, the profound benefits of manual labour apply equally to all monks, and the topos is given a quite particular attention. The Rule of Benedict's pragmatical implications resound, and William's ideas of humility – and humiliation – loom large in the function ascribed to manual labour by Armand-Jean de Rancé. But the predominance and scope with which it is proposed are worth noticing.

II. Manual labour in La Trappe

The reformer

Armand-Jean de Rancé (1626-1700) was Richelieu's godson and the chaplain of Louis XIV's brother. He led the typical life of a French courtier of his time. He was the abbot *in commendam* of five monasteries of different Orders. The commendatory system entailed that the abbot received an income from the monastery without necessarily harbouring any administrative or ascetic aspirations, and it is typical for this institution that during his 22 years as abbot *in commendam* Rancé never visited any of his monasteries. In 1657 a series of events, among other things the death of his mistress from scarlet fever, turned him away from worldly pleasures. Rancé decided to sell his abbot-titles and withdraw to one of his monasteries. It was during this liquidation, that he first came to his Cistercian monastery La Trappe in Normandy.

A later record depicts the state of the monastery when Rancé first arrived: The buildings were falling down, birds nested in the dormitory, men and women walked freely in and out of the monastery and played *boules* in the refectory when bad weather prevented them from playing outside. The garden was overgrown with weed and bushes, and the neighbouring forests were crammed with vagabonds and murderers.[107]

This record was written by the Cistercian visitator Dominique Georges who made a statement as to the genuine Cistercian character of La Trappe at the General Chapter of 1686. It forms part of a praise of Rancé's reform and thus abides by hagiographic patterns. Even if Georges may have overstated things a bit, the fact

---

106   '[…] graviore rurali labore operum fit magna contritio corporis, usque ad contritionem et humiliationem cordis, et fatigationis suae pressura exprimunt saepe vehementioris affectum devotionis […]' William of Saint-Thierry: *Epistola ad Fratres de Monte-Dei*. J. Déchanet (ed. and transl.). Paris 1975, 86, p. 210.

107   Georges, Dominique: 'Procès verbal'. *La vie du très-reverend père Armand Jean Le Bouthillier de Rancé.* Paris 1709, Book VI, pp. 251-274, here pp. 264-274.

remains that Rancé was terrified by La Trappe's state – spiritually as well as materially – and decided to stay and reform the monastery. Rancé's very first meeting
with Cistercianism was his one-year noviciate in a monastery nearby. Here the
hard asceticism made the former courtier collapse when he was halfway; in the
end, however, he returned to La Trappe as a fully-fledged monk and there took up
the position as its proper abbot (Fig. 1).[108]

Armand-Jean de Rancé: The conception of manual labour
Rancé's reform was first and foremost centred on penitence. It prescribed hard
manual labour, silence, a meagre diet, isolation from the world, and renuncia-
tion of studies. The reform eventually made a significant impact on the Cistercian
Order, the stricter branch of which is now commonly known as the Trappists;
but Cistercians still disagree whether Rancé represented the true Cistercian spirit
or merely blind rigidity. Already at its instigation in the 1660s, the reform met
with equal measures of admiration and appal. The monks of La Trappe died in
considerable number presumably, rumours went, because of the dire asceticism.
Fear was voiced at the General Chapter that the zealous and strong-headed abbot
jeopardized the uniformity of the Order, and Rancé's slight knowledge of Cistercianism prior to his monastic profession was brought to mind. These were some
of the challenges that incited the abbot to write his grand oeuvre, *De la sainteté
et des devoirs de la vie monastique*, launching among many themes his doctrine of
manual labour.

Loyal to his general intention of grounding the reform in monastic tradition,
Rancé begins his chapter on this issue on a grand scale:

> There is no exercise of penitence, my brothers, which has been more prac-
> tised and more recommended among monks than manual labour. […] it
> has its source, as we have said, in the laborious life of Jesus Christ; it has
> been authorized by the example of the apostles, the opinion of the doctors
> of the Church, and almost all of the Rules of the Saints.[109]

---

108 For scrutiny of Rancé's person and reform, see the works by Bell, David N.: *Understanding Rancé:
The Spirituality of the Abbot of La Trappe in Context*. Kalamazoo 2005 and Krailsheimer, Alban John:
Armand-Jean de Rancé: Abbot of La Trappe. His Influence in the Cloister and the World. Oxford 1974.

109 'Il n'y a point d'exercice de penitence, mes freres, qui ait esté ny plus pratiqué ny plus recommandé
parmy les Moines que le travail des mains; […] puisqu'elle a sa source, comme nous l'avons dit,
dans la vie laborieuse de JESUS-CHRIST; qu'elle est autorisée de l'exemple de ses Apostres, du sentiment des Docteurs de l'Eglise, & presque de toutes les Regles des Saints.' Rancé, Armand-Jean de:
De la sainteté et des devoirs de la vie monastique, 2 vols. Paris 1683, XIX.1, vol. 2, p. 257. No attempt
has been made to harmonize the spelling of the 17th cent. texts; but for typographical reasons all
s'es have been modernized.

The abbot proceeds with an elaboration of the work of the Jesus, partly as a carpenter working for his poor parents, partly as a preacher: does not Scripture constantly refer to his travelling, his talks, how he was overcome with fatigue? All in all, Rancé concludes pointing to that biblical passage which forms the centre of gravity in this context, Jesus 'put into practice the obligation that God has imposed on every man and carried out literally the irrevocable judgement that he had pronounced against them in the words: *By the sweat of your face you shall eat your bread* (Gen 3.19).'[110] In short, manual labour is a matter of *imitatio Christi*. But it is also a response to what is here apparently conceived of as God's demand, rather than curse, that man toil in the wake of the Fall.

La Trappe did not dismiss laybrothers completely; Georges states that when he visited the monastery in 1685, there were thirty monks, fourteen novices, and sixteen laybrothers.[111] But the reform put a new stress on the spiritual and theological implications of manual work and introduced a radical definition of the kinds of occupation which rightfully belonged under that heading. The reformer lists five reasons why the monks should thus employ themselves: First, constant occupation fends off vices and protects the soul from deviation. Second, the monk must earn his own bread, fulfilling the demand of Gen 3.19. This has always, Rancé stresses, been the strategy of monks; both the first ones in the Egyptian desert and those of the Cistercian Order. Third, through manual labour the monks may exercise charity towards their neighbour. Fourth, the monks are thus an example to the rest of the world. Fifth, manual labour is part of the imitation of the Apostles required of monks.[112]

Furthermore a sixth point, according to Rancé, in itself offers sufficient inspiration for the love of work (*l'amour du travail*). This is the fact that manual labour 'makes the monks forget the splendour and delights of their past lives, and they acquire humility of the heart through the humiliation and difficulty of work [...].'[113] The argumentation is further that the disposition of the heart reflects the different states and circumstances in which man finds himself: 'The feelings of a man who sits on a throne differ from those of a man lying in the dirt. [...] Thus through base actions and humiliating occupations one loses any desire and any

110 '[...] de mettre en pratique cette obligation que Dieu a imposée à tous les hommes, & d'executer à la lettre cet Arrest irrevocable qu'il a prononcé contre eux par ces paroles: *In sudore vultus tui vesceris pane.*' Rancé 1683, XIX.1, vol. 2, p. 259.

111 Georges 1709, p. 251.

112 Rancé 1683, XIX.2, vol. 2, pp. 279-288.

113 '[...] faut que les Solitaires oublient le faste & les delices de la vie passée, & qu'ils acquierent l'humilité du cœur par l'humiliation & la peine du travail [...]' Rancé 1683, XIX.2, vol. 2, p. 288.

idea of glory and grandeur.'[114] Through their lowly activities, the monks are thus in fact working on the redirection of their hearts towards God, daily fleshing out the conversion instigated by their monastic profession.

Rancé understands the concept of manual labour in its most literal sense. One of the issues of his reform which seriously upset his contemporaries was his rejection of scholarly studies as a proper monastic employment. This stance led him into a controversy with one of the most learned men of his days, the Maurist Jean Mabillon, whose text critical work with the texts of, among others, Bernard of Clairvaux made a lasting scholarly and theological impact. Rancé's main argument in his dispute with Mabillon is that scholarly studies are basically incompatible with the aim of the monastery. To him, it is certain: '[…] that the monks are not destined for studies but for penitence; that their condition is one of crying not one of teaching, and that the plan of God in giving rise to monks within his church is not to form doctors but penitents.'[115]

Félibien des Abaux: The praxis of manual labour
In what kind of manual labour, then, did the brothers of La Trappe engage? Vivid renderings of the life at La Trappe are found in *cartes de visite*. These are accounts authored by visitors to the monastery, who offer an account of their impressions of the place and the life led there. One such *carte de visite* was written by Louis XIV's art historiographer Félibien des Abaux shortly after his visit to La Trappe in 1670.[116] Des Abaux goes through the monastic day from the monks get up at two o'clock in the night to they go to bed at seven o'clock in the evening. Let us follow La Trappe's monks from the morning.

> At seven o'clock they are ready to go to their work. This means that everybody leave their habit under what they call a cowl. And rolling up the one underneath they go to work. Some work on the land, others thresh, some carry stones. Everyone receives his task without any choice and without a selection of things to be done. The abbot [Rancé] himself is the first one to go to work, and more often than anyone else he employs himself with that which is hardest and most vile. When the weather prevents them from

114 'Les sentimens d'un homme qui est assis sur le trône sont autres que ceux d'un homme qui est couché sur le fumier […] Ainsi on perd par des actions viles, & des occupations humiliantes, tout desir & toute idée de la gloire & de la grandeur.' Rancé 1683, XIX.2, vol. 2, p. 289.

115 '[…] que les Moines n'ont point esté destinez pour l'étude, mais pour la penitence; que leur condition est de pleurer & non pas d'instruire, & que le dessein de Dieu en suscitant des Solitaires dans son Eglise, n'a pas esté de former des Docteurs, mais des penitens […]' Rancé 1683, XIX.4, vol. 2, p. 292.

116 Waddell, Chrysogonus: 'The Cistercian Dimension of the Reform of La Trappe'. *Cistercians in the Late Middle Ages*. Rozanne Elder (ed.). Kalamazoo 1981, p. 127.

Le R.Pere Dom Armand Jean Bouthillier de Rancé
XXIV.ᵉ Abbé Régulier de Noſtre Dame de la Maison-Dieu de la Trappe
De l'Etroite Observance de Citeaux, âgé de 57. ans.
Spiritu magno vidit ultima . Eccles.48.27.
P. Van-ſchuppen faciebat c.pr.1683.   F. Muguet excudit

Fig 1: *Not manual labour but celestial focus characterizes Pieter van Schuppen's engraving of Armand-Jean de Rancé on the frontispiece of* De la sainteté et des devoirs de la vie monastique *(1683). The abbot has his own work before him, but his gaze is directed towards the last things, epitomized in the quotation from Sirach. Reproduced by permission of Bibliothèque Nationale.*

being outdoor, they clean the church, sweep the cloister, do the dishes, do the laundry, or peel vegetables. Sometimes two or three of them sit on the ground opposite each other raking up roots without ever talking to each other. There are also places which are suited for roofed work. Here several monks are occupied; some with copying the books of the Church, others with proofreading; some with works of joinery, others with turnery. And thus employed with different useful activities, there are hardly any of the things needed in the monastery that they do not themselves produce. But they never dedicate themselves to any curious work which might attract the spirit in a much too agreeable way. For one of the maxims of this worthy abbot is that he who has withdrawn into the desert in order to possess nothing but God may not turn away in order to attach his affections to vain things but must continually remain turned towards God unceasingly keeping himself in the love of this supreme beauty who must be the object of all his desires.[117]

Des Abaux follows the rhythm of the monks' readings and prayers and dedicates an extensive passage to their scarce fare. His account underlines the tightness of the monastic schedule which is organized right down to 30 minutes' intervals:

At about one o'clock, the bell calls for work and for either retaining what was left in the morning or beginning something else. Thus twice a day they fulfil that prescription of Scripture which does not allow any person to eat who does not earn his food through his work. While themselves working on the land in order that they may live from their work, the sweat from their faces is the first water with which they water it. After one and a half hour of work, or sometimes two, the bell calls for retreat, and eve-

117 'Sur les sept heures on va travailler. C'est à dire que chacun quittant son habit de dessus quils appellent une Coule, & retroussant celuy de dessous, ils se mettent les uns à labourer la terre, les autres à la cribler, d'autres à porter des pierres, chacun recevant sa tâche sans choix , ny élection de ce qu'il doit faire. Monsieur l'Abbé luy même se trouve le premier au travail, & s'employe plûtost qu'aucun autre à ce qu'il y a de plus vil, & de plus penible. Lors que le temps ne permet pas de sortir, ils nettoyent l'Eglise, balayent les Cloistres, écurent la vaisselle, font des lescives, épluchent des légumes, & quelques fois ils sont deux ou trois assis contre terre, les uns aupres des autres à ratisser des racines sans jamais parler ensemble. Il y a aussi des lieux destinez à travailler à couvert, ou plusieurs Religieux s'occupent, les uns à écrire des Livres d'Eglise, les autres à en relier; quelques-uns à des ouvrages da menuiserie, d'autres à tourner, & ainsi à differen travaux utiles: n'y ayant guere de choses necessaires à la Maison, & à leur usage qu'ils ne fassent eux-mêmes. Mais ils ne s'appliquent jamais à aucun ouvrage curieux, & qui puisse attacher trop agreablement l'esprit, parce qu'une des maxims de ce digne Abbé est que celuy qui s'est retiré dans la Solitude pour ne posseder plus que Dieu, ne s'en doit point détourner pour s'attacher d'affection à des choses vaines, mais demeurer continuellement uni à Dieu; s'entretenant sans cesse dans l'amour de cette suprême beauté qui doit estre l'objet de tous ses desirs.' des Abaux, Félibien: 'Description de l'Abbaye de La Trappe à Madame la Duchesse de Liancour'. *Reglemens de l'Abbaye de Nôtre-Dame de La Trappe*. Paris 1718, pp. 36-38.

rybody leave their clogs, put back the tools in their proper place, take off their cowl, and retire to their room to read or meditate until Vespers which is sung at four o'clock.[118]

Des Abaux stresses the significance of the right kind of manual labour as one device in securing that attention remains directed towards God so that the monk may become 'uni à Dieu' and stays in the love of this 'suprême beauté'. Manual labour thus not only purges the monk's mind of his previous life, it also helps putting God in its place.

Conclusion

The role played by manual labour in La Trappe has several facets. The monks' work associates the reform tightly with the Rule of Benedict thus sustaining the reformer's claim for monastic authenticity. It also fulfils what is considered the basic post-lapsarian demand that man must earn his bread in the sweat of his face while furthermore promoting the monastery's independence from secular society. Above all, however, it embodies Rancé's ideals of penitence and humility. Through their labour, the monks at La Trappe cultivate not only their land but also their inclinations.

---

118 'A une heure ou environ, l'on sonne pour aller au travail, reprendre celuy qu'ils on quitté le matin, ou en commancer un autre. Ainsi ils accomplissent deux fois le jour ce precepte de l'Ecriture, qui ne veut pas que celuy-là mange, qui ne gagne point sa nourriture par son travail: Et labourant eux mêmes la terre pour vivre de l'ouvrage de leurs mains, la sueur de leur visages est la premiere eau dont ils l'arrosent. Aprés une heure & demie, & quelquesfois deux heures de travail on sonne la retraite, & alors chacun quitte ses sabots, remet ses outils dans un lieu destiné à cela, reprend sa coule & se retire dans sa chambre à lire ou à mediter jusques à Vespres qu'on dit à quatre heures.' des Abaux 1718, pp. 47-48.

The Great Silence of Saint Joseph:

Devotion to Saint Joseph and the 17th Century Crisis of Mysticism in the Jesuit Order

Rob Faesen S.J. (transl. Brian Doyle)

In 1629, the then Superior General of the Society of Jesus, Muzio Viteleschi S.J., wrote a letter to the Provincial Superior of Paris, Father Jean Filleau S.J., in which he prohibited the further veneration of Saint Joseph by young Jesuits in formation in what he referred to as a 'new and unusual manner'.[119] This, at first sight, rather strange ordinance is symptomatic of a profound crisis that was confronting the Jesuit Order at the time in relation to the question of mysticism. Michel de Certeau has provided an important analysis of the historical context of the said crisis with particular reference to the French Jesuits. Upon closer inspection, however, a number of passages from the work of Jean-Joseph Surin S.J. (1600-1668), one of the protagonists in the crisis, reveal the possibility of going beyond de Certeau's analysis, especially with respect to the content and scope of the issue. As we shall see below, the question at hand has its roots in the 12th century and has far reaching consequences for the development of Christian culture.

Mysticism and devotion to Saint Joseph

It is important to bear in mind in the first instance, however, that the evolution of devotion to Saint Joseph took a strikingly unusual turn in the 16th century. In

---

119   Letter dated April 5th, 1629 (unpublished), cf. de Certeau, Michel: *Correspondance de Jean-Joseph Surin*. Texte établi, présenté et annoté par Michel de Certeau, Bibliothèque Européenne. Paris 1966, p. 40.

the preceding century, we already witness the publication of the first tractates devoted exclusively to Saint Joseph, such as *Dictamen de laudibus beati Joseph* by the Celestine Peter Pocquet († 1408) or the lengthy poem entitled *Josephina* written by Jean Gerson († 1429), chancellor of the University of Paris.[120] Theresa of Avila, however, introduced an important modification into this increasingly popular devotion. As a matter of fact, it quickly became clear that Theresa had a particular attachment to the saint. Her veneration is based on the claim that she was cured of a serious illness upon the intercession of Saint Joseph when she was twenty-six years of age and that he had given ear to all of her prayers. Indeed, she suggests that the saint be taken as a guide for those who can find no one to teach them in prayer:

> I took for my advocate and lord the glorious Saint Joseph and commended myself earnestly to him; and I found that this my father and lord delivered me both from this trouble and from other and greater troubles concerning my honour and the loss of my soul, and that he gave me greater blessings than I could ask of him. I do not remember even now that I have ever asked anything of him which he has failed to grant. I am astonished at the great favours which God has bestowed on me through this blessed saint, and at the perils from which he has freed me, both in body and in soul. To other saints the Lord seems to have given grace to succour us in some of our necessities but of this glorious saint my experience is that he succours us in them all and that the Lord wishes to teach us that He was himself subject to him on earth (for, being his guardian and being called his father, he could command Him) just so in heaven He still does all that he asks. This has also been the experience of other persons whom I have advised to commend themselves to him; and even today there are many who have great devotion to him through having experienced this truth.
> [...] I only beg, for the love of God, that anyone who does not believe me will put what I say to the test, and he will see by experience what great advantages come from his commending himself to this glorious patriarch and having devotion to him. Those who practise prayer should have a special affection for him always. I do not know how anyone can think of the Queen of the Angels, during the time that she suffered so much with the Child Jesus, without giving thanks to Saint Joseph for the way he helped them. If anyone cannot find a master to teach him how to pray, let him take this glorious saint as his master and he will not go astray.[121]

120 Cf. the survey by Gauthier, Roland in *Dictionnaire de Spiritualité* VIII. Paris 1974, pp. 1308-1316.

121 See *The Life of Teresa of Jesus*. Translated and edited, with an introduction by E. Allison Peers. New York 1960, pp. 93-94. See also *Libro de la vida, 6-8, Obras completas*. Revision textual, introducciones y notas Enrique Llamas, Teofanes Egido, D. De Pablo Maroto e.a., director Alberto Barrientos. Madrid 1976, pp. 39-40.

This, for Theresa, is clearly not a matter of secondary importance. Indeed, its significance is demonstrated by the fact that she placed the foundation of the first reformed Carmel in Avila on August 24th 1562 under the protection of Saint Joseph. Eleven other new foundations acquired the same patron saint. Saint Joseph was ultimately (in 1590) to become the patron of the entire Carmelite reformation in Spain. The French Carmelite renewal movement likewise adopted Joseph as its patron saint from 1604 onwards.

While Saint Joseph enjoys an important place in the writings of the major French authors of the period – including Pierre de Bérulle, Jean-Jacques Olier and François de Sales – it is clear, nevertheless, that Theresa of Avila in particular placed singular emphasis on the saint by recommending him in her writings as a teacher in prayer and especially by choosing him as patron saint of the Carmelite reform movement. As a matter of fact, a connection was thus established between Saint Joseph on the one hand and the contemplative, mystical dimension of the life of prayer on the other. This connection is lacking with respect to earlier mystical authors who nonetheless exercised significant influence on the Carmelite reform movement and the French school. Indeed, Saint Joseph is more or less absent in the work of Jan van Ruusbroec, for example, or the anonymous authoress of the *Evangelische Peerle*. It is striking that Theresa explicitly states that she is referring to something she had learned from experience. She would appear to be conscious of the fact that she is introducing something new, and the only argument she can offer in support of her recommendations is that of personal experience and the experience of others.

Jean-Joseph Surin S.J. and devotion to Saint Joseph

Theresa thus states that Joseph is an excellent guide in the life of prayer, particularly for those who do not have a teacher. This is an important element that resurfaces in the well-known letter written by the French Jesuit Jean-Joseph Surin on May 8th, 1630 (Fig. 1).[122]

At that moment, Surin had just completed his so-called 'Tertianship', i.e. the period whereby a Jesuit concludes his formation according to the Constitutions of the Society of Jesus and during which he returns to and interiorizes the most important aspects of the life of a Jesuit after having dedicated himself to lengthy intellectual formation. Surin completed his Tertianship in Rouen, together with seventeen confreres, under the guidance of Louis Lallemant S.J. When the year

---

122 The letter in question has frequently been copied, passed on, reworked and printed. See de Certeau, Michel: 'L'illettré éclairé dans l'histoire de la lettre sur le Jeune Homme du Coche (1630)'. *Revue d'Ascétique et de Mystique* 44. Toulouse 1968, pp. 369-412.

Fig. 1: *Portrait of Jean-Joseph Surin; from: Henri Bremond, Histoire littéraire du sentiment religieux en France, vol. 5: La conquête mystique (Paris: Bloud et Gay, 1933).*

had come to an end, he was asked to travel to Bordeaux where he was to take up residence as part of the Jesuit community. Having arrived in his new community, he composed and despatched a remarkable letter to the community at La Flèche, where he had lived before his Tertianship. The letter contains a detailed account of an unusual encounter he had had during the journey from Rouen to Bordeaux. En route he had met a young man, roughly eighteen years of age and the son of a baker from Le Havre, who was on his way to Paris to enter a religious community as a lay brother. Surin was deeply impressed by this exceptional young man who, although uneducated, was initiated nevertheless in the deepest secrets of God, enjoyed an ongoing and intimate relationship with God and exhibited extraordinary personal insight into the mystical life. Surin's letter describes the conversations he had with this youthful mystic:

> I asked him if he was devoted to Saint Joseph. He answered that the saint had already been his protector for the last six years and that the Lord himself had given him as protector without anyone advising it. He added that he had clearly seen that this saintly patriarch was the greatest of all the saints after the Virgin Mary; that he possessed the fullness of the Holy Spirit in a manner completely different to that of the apostles; that he governed over souls, the virtue of which must remain hidden in this world – as was the case with his own soul –; that so little was known of him; that God on the other hand had desired that only the most pure souls should receive enlightenment concerning his greatness. He went on to say that Saint Joseph was a man of great silence; that he spoke very little in the house of our Lord, that Our Lady spoke less and that our Lord spoke even less than them both; that his eyes taught him enough, without our Lord having to speak.[123]

It appears thus that the young man cherished a particular devotion to Saint Joseph. Although completely uneducated and lacking any form of spiritual instruction, he had adopted Saint Joseph as his spiritual guide (*il était dominateur sur les âmes dont la vertu doit être cache en ce monde, comme la sienne l'avait été*). It is striking that the young man understood Joseph as one who did not speak (*un homme de grand silence*), but rather observed and thereby learned from Christ (*que ses yeux lui apprenaient assez de choses sans que notre Seigneur parlât*). In this sense, Joseph was indeed an excellent guide for those engaged in the contemplative life – the *contemplatio* observes and sees more than can be said.

---

123 de Certeau: *Correspondance*, Letter 18, p. 142.

The fact that Jean-Joseph Surin had inquired of his conversation partner whether he was *dévot à saint Joseph*, should not come as a surprise. As a matter of fact, he himself had undergone a mystical experience in 1612 – when he was roughly twelve years old, the same age as the baker's son when God had granted him Saint Joseph as *protecteur de son âme* – in the church of the Carmelite nuns in Bordeaux, which was dedicated to Saint Joseph. Surin's biographer describes the experience as follows: 'a supernatural light which made him discover, in an ineffable way, the indescribable grandeur of the most adorable being of God.'[124] The event had a profound effect of Surin's life and he would surely have never forgotten that it had taken place in a Carmelite church dedicated to Saint Joseph. How could he possibly have forgotten? His sister entered the same community a few years later in 1619 and his mother likewise ended her years as a Carmelite in the same community.

The youthful mystic, baker's son was not the only person Surin had met who was devoted to Saint Joseph. Two years later, in a letter addressed to a Carmelite nun, he writes in detail concerning another mystical figure, in this instance a woman named Marie Baron, the wife of a merchant in Marennes.[125] In his account of the woman's spiritual life he notes:

> It would be wrong of me to fail to mention Saint Joseph, the patron of virtually all the great souls of our day. This saint warned her and assured her of his protection even before she had any special devotion to him. One day, on his feast, he manifested himself to her by surprise and granted her considerable enlightenment with respect to the future.[126]

It is striking that Surin makes use of the expression *il la prenait sous sa protection*. The baker's son had likewise stated that Saint Joseph was *son protecteur*. The expression *son patron*, however, would have been more neutral in reference to a patron saint. *Protection* and *protecteur*, by contrast, would appear to place the emphasis on the fact that the spiritual life of these mystical individuals explicitly required protection. As we shall see below, it is likely that this was indeed the case. In any event, in his letter of April 5th 1629, Muzio Viteleschi S.J. had, as we noted above, forbidden young Jesuits in formation from continuing to venerate Saint Joseph in a 'new and unusual manner' – which would appear to allude to

---

124 Cf. Bouix, M. (ed.): *Oeuvres spirituelles du Père Jean-Joseph Surin: Traité inédit de l'amour de Dieu, précédé de la vie de l'auteur.* Paris 1890, p 8; Surin, Jean-Joseph: *Triomphe de l'amour divin sur les puissances de l'Enfer et Science expérimentale des chose de l'autre vie.* Collection Atopia. Grenoble 1990, pp. 281-282.

125 de Certeau: *Correspondance*, Letter 27 (20th December 1632), p. 168ff.

126 de Certeau: *Correspondance*, p. 180.

the renewal of devotion to the saint in line with that maintained by Theresa of Avila. The two letters in which Surin refers to Saint Joseph as protector of the spiritual life of mystical individuals were written one year and three years after the prohibition respectively. While it goes without saying that the anonymous baker's son and Marie Bourdon were not subject to the authority of the Jesuit superior, it nevertheless says a great deal that Surin, who had just completed his Tertianship, did not appear to be much inspired by the ordinances of his Superior General. He clearly adopts a different position.

The Jesuits and the crisis of mysticism – described by Michel de Certeau

Are we not dealing here with an incidental and barely relevant detail? Is it not possible that Surin was not even aware of what Father Viteleschi had written to Father Fileau? The latter, after all, was provincial superior in Paris while Jean-Joseph Surin was situated hundreds of kilometres away in the Jesuit Province of Aquitaine. On the other hand, the possibility that Surin was indeed aware of the said correspondence is fairly significant. The letter written by Father Viteleschi was part of a controversy in which an entire generation of young French Jesuits was also involved, namely the generation of Jean-Joseph Surin.[127]

The history of the said controversy is described in detail by Michel de Certeau.[128] He distinguishes two related aspects thereof, which primarily had to do with two different generations. The first aspect is evident from an official report sent to Rome by the provincial of the Jesuit Province of Aquitaine in response to a general question addressed to the entire Society of Jesus in 1605 by Claudio Aquaviva, its Superior General at the time. Father Aquaviva, the fourth successor to Ignatius, was not sure if the Order was still on the right tracks after the spectacular growth it had enjoyed in the first decennia of its existence. He was considering introducing reform and to this end he established a general inquiry into the *detrimenta* of the Order. Each province was asked to submit a report on the matter. The report of the Province of Aquitaine states, among other things, that one of the points that were causing genuine damage to the Order was the lack of interior life among its members. While it was true that they were doing their best

---

127 It appears from a letter written by Muzio Viteleschi (21st March 1631, i.e. two years after the letter written to Fileau and dated 5th April 1629), and addressed to Father Jean Ricard that Surin had written to Viteleschi. The letter in question has been lost, however, and nothing is known of its content (cf. de Certeau: *Correspondance*, pp. 146-147).

128 de Certeau, Michel: 'Crise sociale et réformisme spirituel au début du XVIIe siècle'. *Revue d'Ascétique et de Mystique* 41. Toulouse 1965, pp. 339-386, summarised in de Certeau: *Correspondance*, pp. 34-42 and pp. 433-462.

to excel in academic and intellectual matters and were inundated with pastoral obligations, they had tended to fall behind in prayer and spiritual reading. The reason, according to the report, was an *effusio ad exteriora*: the fathers were loosing themselves so much in exterior matters – instead of being turned inwards – that they were simply no longer capable of prayer, not even during the moments set aside for the purpose.

The second aspect is the converse of the first, as it were. Indeed, it would appear that many young Jesuits in formation enjoyed an intense spiritual life, and were fervent readers of mystical authors such as Theresa of Avila, Johann Tauler, Louis de Blois (Blosius) and Jan van Ruusbroec. This generation of young Aquitanian Jesuits had the impression that their elder confreres were not providing them with spiritual leadership. It is hardly surprising, therefore, that they had acquired a particular devotion to Saint Joseph and had understandably sought spiritual advice from the great mystical authors of the Christian tradition. This generated a considerable amount of critique and lack of understanding among the older generation and complaints ultimately found their way to Rome in which the younger generation were accused of letting themselves be led by 'a spirit alien to the Society of Jesus.'

The complaints represent a possible reflection of the fear that the Order was facing an imminent loss of identity. Father Claudio Aquaviva had died in the meantime and had been succeeded by Father Muzio Viteleschi whose intervention in the matter was severe (Fig. 2).

It would appear from a letter dated 1628 that his interpretation of the question agreed with that of the complaints.[129] The letter states that he considered the core of the problem to be the fact that the young Jesuits had allowed themselves to be led by a spirit that was alien to the Order. The safest path, he maintained, was to follow the normal customs of the Order, and obedience to one's superior offered the best guarantee against deviations. Indeed, the tendency to follow one's own insights would only lead to the total shipwreck of religious life in the Society of Jesus. The letter requested further information concerning the young Jesuits in question and insisted that measures be taken where necessary. Surin was one of them. At least two dossiers with complaints concerning him were despatched to Rome.[130]

In short, the General Superior of the Jesuits took the matter very seriously and even associated it with the identity and continued existence of the Society. From his perspective, the younger generations of Aquitanian Jesuits were, in the first

129   Quoted by de Certeau: 'Crise sociale' 1965, pp. 372-373.
130   de Certeau: *Correspondance*, pp. 438-460.

Fig. 2 : Portrait of Muzio Vitelleschi (1553-1645), General Superior of the Society of Jesus from 1615 till 1645; from: Arnold van Westerhout, Imagines Praepositorum Generalium Societatis Jesu (Roma, sumptibus Venantii Monaldini … ex typographia Bernabo et Lazzarini,1751).

instance, following their own insights. In his opinion, this was being promoted by their reading of certain mystical authors who themselves, moreover, were not even Jesuit authors. Only one simple yet efficient remedy existed to counter the problem, namely obedience, and such was surely not alien to "the spirit of the Society". The letter from the same Father Viteleschi concerning devotion to Saint Joseph should thus be understood against the background of this concern. Interest in Saint Joseph was threatening the very existence of the Jesuit Order.

Jean-Joseph Surin's interpretation of the crisis

Is the perception of Father Viteleschi and his advisors correct? Was it simply a question of a rebellious younger generation that was refusing to obey and was thereby endangering the religious life of the Order? In the last year of his life, Jean-Joseph Surin shed a degree of illumination on the content of the question in his book *Questions importantes à la vie spirituelle: Sur l'amour de Dieu*,[131] returning to the objections of Father Viteleschi – albeit without mentioning him by name – in order to counter them.

The said objections are referred to when Surin describes a specific experience that a person can encounter when he or she takes to heart the first of the commandments. In Surin's opinion, the love of God with all one's heart is the foundation of the spiritual life. This love may be imperfect at the beginning on account of self-interest, but it can grow into a more profound orientation towards the divine Other, whereby one forgets oneself completely and every other form of affection is taken up in its entirety into that singular orientation towards God:

> He loves God with all his heart, who has so attuned all his affection to God and to the service of God that there is nothing in his capacity to love that is not oriented towards God. To such an extent that if he loves anything other than God – just as the law obliges people to love their neighbour, and of the latter, a few in a more particular manner, such as one's father and mother – he does so for God, out of respect for Him and because He desires it so. […] Behold what it actually is to be a spiritual person, that is to be a person of God and that is to love God with all one's heart. This is the spirit of the saints, the perfect law of love, the service of those who worship in spirit and truth. […] Saint Francis de Sales said that if he

---

131 Although written in 1665, this text was first published as such in 1879. A paraphrase thereof appeared in 1799 under the title *Le prédicateur de l'amour de Dieu*. I quote here from the most recent edition: Surin, Jean-Joseph: *Questions importantes à la vie spirituelle. Sur l'amour de Dieu*. Texte primitif révisé et annoté par Aloys Potter & Louis Mariès. Paris 1930.

were aware of anything in his heart, however small, that was not oriented towards God, he would rip it out whatever the cost. Saint Ignatius, founder of the Society of Jesus, frequently spoke the following words: *Majus Dei obsequium semper intuendo,*[132] etc. In his rule, he orders his sons to seek God and cast off their love of created things in order to grant all their affection to the Creator.[133]

Such individuals, Surin writes, can be confronted by a particular experience to which Paul refers when he says 'the Holy Spirit bears witness to our spirit that we are children of God' (Rom. 8.16):

> [These words] point to a clearly identifiable effect, which is experienced by the souls that put into practise what we explained in the previous chapter. Indeed, when a person follows this direction in the spiritual life, and when he, with munificence and generosity towards God, gives himself completely and keeps nothing for himself but rather dedicates himself completely to the pure love of God, then a grace makes itself felt in such a person. Such a person feels an interior sense of confidence and peace that is unique to God's good and faithful friends. The divine Spirit which, as the faith teaches, lives in us, brings about his own grace as an expression of his presence, *propter inhabitantem Spiritum ejus in nobis.*[134] This takes place in such a free and elevated manner that the faithful heart remains convinced of it, not only on account of the insight of faith in general, but also on account of an experience [*sentiment*] that is child-like [*filial*] and wonderful. The soul recognises and knows thereby that it belongs to God, without fear of being subject to an illusion, and is particularly certain thereof. [...] There are many good and pure souls to whom our Lord, after they have lived long in his love and have often made the effort to seek him in all things, grants such an experience of his presence. He gives them the effect of his grace to such an extent that this can be called the witness of the Holy Spirit, who assures them that they belong to the number of the children of God. And this can be associated with the words of Saint John in his letter: Those who believe in the Son have the testimony in their hearts.[135] This testimony is the interior word of God, which the book

---

132 'Always with a view to the greater glory of God'.

133 Surin: *Questions importantes,* 2, pp. 6-7; cf. *Const. S.J.* [288], 3 in Padberg, John W.: *The Constitutions of the Society of Jesus and Their Complementary Norms. A Complete English Translation of the Offical Latin Texts.* Jesuit Primary Sources in English Translation, 15. St. Louis MO 1996, p. 124.

134 'On account of the Spirit who lives in us', cf. Rom 8. 11.

135 1 John 5. 10.

of the *Imitation* calls the *verbum consolationis*.[136] In the darkness that sometimes accompanies the faith in this life, this testimony steadfastly assures
that the soul is of God and God of the soul. And on occasion this testimony is so strong that the heart cannot doubt it. While it is not so strong
that it takes away all sorts of doubt, it nevertheless does not cease to be the
word of the Holy Spirit, adapted to this life. This is precisely what gives
support to the saints in their works. Not all those who are in a state of
grace have this. And it is seldom given to any other than those who seek
God with all their heart, that is, souls that have resolved to belong to God,
without reserve, refusing Him nothing and – in the state of life in which
they find themselves and the activities associated therewith – desiring
nothing other than his divine will.[137]

The description Surin provides at this juncture, which refers implicitly to a crucial
experience in his own life,[138] coincides for him with a long mystical tradition. Jan
van Ruusbroec, for example, developed the same theme in considerable detail in
his *Sparkling Stone*. On this very point, however, Surin points out that objections
had arisen. The first two objections to which he refers would appear to be a repetition of those first raised by Father Viteleschi several years earlier:

> In the first instance that those who desire to make the testimony of the
> Holy Spirit, namely that we are children of God, into a point of support,
> desire to promote singularity (*vouloir établir l'esprit particulier*). [And] that
> one is intent thereby on making spirits headstrong (*opiniâtres*), attached
> to their own intuition (*instinct*), and inclining them to give preference to
> what is said to them within above what is said to them by their superiors
> – something that represents a source of illusion.[139]

Surin insists, however, that this objection is totally without foundation:

> To this I would answer that the testimony granted by the Spirit of God to
> pure souls is always in conformity with the light of faith, and that it per-
> suades them and orders them in fact to subject themselves to obedience,
> and that this light is never so abundant as when the soul that receives it,
> follows the guidance of another. This testimony is nothing other than the

---

136 *Imit.* III, 1, 1, see Thomas a Kempis: *De Imitatione Christi*. Michael J. Pohl (ed.). Opera Omnia 2.
      Freiburg 1904, p. 143.
137 Surin: *Questions importantes*, pp. 8-11.
138 Namely his healing in 1656, cf. de Certeau: *Correspondance*, pp. 517-532.
139 Surin: *Questions importantes*, p. 20.

comfort of the Holy Spirit commonly given, not to everyone, but to those who embrace the way of mortification with genuine humility and complete self-renunciation. For God is especially generous to those who exhibit great generosity towards Him. He shares exceedingly great spiritual goods with them, rather via the way of humility than via the way of reason.[140]

This brings Surin to the third objection:

It happens with considerable frequency that many, even the most highly educated, given that they are used to acquiring the truth via the efforts of the intellect rather than via the way of love, cherish suspicion with respect to the inspirations (*instincts*) of grace and the touch of the Holy Spirit, and consider them to be the work of the imagination. They therefore despise them and think that it is safer to follow the light of the intellect. But they ought to consider that the Holy Spirit guides the human heart, not so much by way of reason but rather through a simple light and inspiration (*instinct*).[141]

Surin goes on to make a remark that proves he was in dispute with his fellow Jesuits, given the fact that he makes reference to the Constitutions of the Society:

The saintly Fathers and spiritual authors placed considerable emphasis on attentiveness and docility, which the soul owes to the stirrings of God. Many scholars reject this, however, placing such stirrings at the level of the imagination and preferring nothing other than their own argumentations. I would ask them, however, to explain what Ignatius, founder of the Society of Jesus, wrote at the beginning of his Constitutions, namely that 'the interior law of love that the Holy Spirit inscribes and engraves in our hearts must help the Society more than any other constitution.'[142] I ask them: what is this interior law of love and what does it consist of? Is it not to be found in the inner movements of grace and in the touch of the Holy Spirit, to which all the saints gave ear after having studied them fittingly? Those who follow the way of the senses are often ignorant hereof. Only those who live within, who are liberated and detached, and who are accustomed to seek God in all things, hear this law, value it and allow themselves to be

---

140 Surin: *Questions importantes*, pp. 20-21.

141 Surin: *Questions importantes*, p. 21

142 *Const. S.J.* [134], Preamble 1, 3 in Padberg: *The Constitutions of the Society of Jesus and Their Complementary Norms.* p. 56.

led by it without thereby rejecting obedience. As a matter of fact, this way of God is not as the scholars imagine it, those who present whatever objections they can against the mystics. And this way is likewise unlike that of those deceived into singularity (*l'esprit particulier*) by the devil. For it is a light that is exceedingly sweet, extremely general (*fort général*), very respectful, that cannot be better explained than by the 'interior law' to which Ignatius refers. This light is an extraordinary benefaction of the Holy Spirit, of whom we have spoken often, the one who prescribes this law. I ask, therefore, of all those who oppose that which falls outside the everyday course of affairs of imperfect Christians, that they tell me what this interior law of love is, written in the heart, if it is not that which the Holy Spirit addresses to everyone in order to bring them to perfection.[143]

We can now offer a summary of the issue as Surin himself presented it. The problem is related to a particular experience with which people who have completely and genuinely abandoned themselves in the love of God can be confronted. The experience in question of 'belonging to the number of the children of God'. In other words, in the human person's active practice of loving God, a person can experience being completely loved in the passive sense, a deeper love than one's own activities have the capacity to bring about. It is an experience of complete and mutual belonging between God and the human person ('This testimony ensures [...] that the soul is of God and God of the soul'). Surin refers to this experience as 'a touch of the Spirit'.

The experience in question is rejected by some as dangerous to the religious life because it would appear to undermine the vow of obedience to one's superiors. Surin immediately rejects this argument, arguing that an increase in obedience on the part of the human person constitutes part of the inner logic of the said experience.[144] Should the experience lead nevertheless to disobedience, then it represents a deviation ('as with those deceived by the devil') of something that in itself does not embrace such a tendency.[145]

---

143 Surin: *Questions importantes*, pp. 22-23.

144 It should be noted in passing that Claudio Aquaviva, Muzio Viteleschi's predecessor, had raised precisely the same objection: 'Neque tamen ea re veritati reluctandum est, aut testatissimae Sanctorum Patrum refragandum, et habenda despicatui contemplatio, vel ab ea nostri prohibendi, cum illud plurimorum Patrum sententia suffragioque perspectum sit et exploratum veram perfectamque contemplationem potentius et efficatius altera quaelibet piarum meditationum methodo, superbiantes hominum animos frangere, atque contundere, pigrantes ad abeunda Superiorum madata vehementius incitare, et languentes ad salutem animorum procurandam ardentius inflammare.' Aquaviva, Claudio: 'De oratione et paenitentia'. *Epistolae Praepositorum Generalium ad Patres et Fratres Societatis Jesu*. Rome 1615, pp. 228-229.

145 It is possible that Surin is thinking here, for example, of his ex-confrere Jean-Charles de Labadie. Cf. the comments he makes about the latter in his *Science expérimentale*, quoted by de Certeau: *Correspondance*, pp. 436-438.

Others reject this experience as the work of the imagination. The reason, according to Surin, is because they have become accustomed to 'acquiring the truth via the efforts of the intellect'. We should take care not to misunderstand Surin at this juncture. He is definitely not an anti-intellectualist. What he means is that some have acquired such an interior attitude of *active* love towards God that they no longer consider it possible to be loved by God in the *passive* sense, in a deeper and more fundamental manner than their own active orientation has the capacity to generate. Their own activities and efforts have ultimately become a stumbling block, obstructing God from making his stirrings felt.

Surin then alludes to the manner with which Ignatius of Loyola refers to this experience in the Constitutions of the Jesuit Order, namely as the 'interior law of love'. This is more than a simple *argumentum ad autoritatem*. Surin uses it to call to mind the mystical origins of the Society of Jesus. He is thus also convinced that the entire issue is a sign that the Society is losing its identity. While he does not state it explicitly, there can be little doubt that he is referring at this juncture to the well-known vision granted to Ignatius in the chapel of La Storta; the content thereof is precisely that to which Surin is alluding. The vision in question represents a turning-point in the life of Ignatius and is recognized by his companions as a crucial ingredient in the foundation of the Order. Ignatius describes the vision as follows:

> And being one day in a church some miles before arrival in Rome, and making prayer, he [= Ignatius] sensed such a change in his soul, and he saw so clearly that God the Father was putting him with Christ, his Son, that he would not have the wilfulness to have any doubt about this: it could only be that God the Father was putting him with his Son.[146]

Translations frequently tend to leave this statement vague, such that it is not clear what Ignatius means when he says that 'the Father was putting him with the Son'. It has to do with the experience of being loved by the Father as Christ was loved. Ignatius no longer experiences a distance between himself and the eternal Son.

146 'Cum vero quadam die, aliquot ante passuum millibus quam Romam intraret, templum quoddam ingressus oraret, ita animum suum moveri mutarique sensit, tamquam manifeste vidit quod eum Deus pater cum Christo filio suo poneret, ut de eo dubitare non auderet, quin eum Deus pater cum filio suo poneret.' In: 'Acta patris Ignatii scripta a P. Lud. Gonzalez de Camera'. *Fontes narrativi de S. Ignatio de Loyola*, vol. 1, MHSI 66. Rome 1943, pp. 497-99, transl. in: Saint Ignatius of Loyola: *Personal Writings*. Joseph A. Munitiz & Philip Endean (transl., introd. and notes). London 1996, p. 60. Several different descriptions of this experience have been passed down to us. In his detailed and thorough analysis thereof, Hugo Rahner has shown that the description quoted above is the most reliable, 'Die Vision des heiligen Ignatius in der Kapelle von La Storta', *Zeitschrift für Askese und Mystik* 10. 1935, pp. 17-35; pp. 124-139; pp. 202-220; pp. 265-282.

He experiences being *filius in Filio*.[147] This is precisely the experience Surin had described, which he had thus referred to as a 'touch of the Spirit'. Indeed, the Holy Spirit is the mutual love between the Father and the Son. 'To be touched by the Spirit' is to experience this bond of love.

The core of the question: the indwelling of Christ in the human person

This brings us to the core of the question at hand. A lengthy mystical tradition exists that offers reflection on a specific (contemplative) experience which consists in the realisation that in Christ one shares in the life of the Trinity. Jan van Ruusbroec, whom Surin considered one of the grand masters of Christian mystical literature,[148] offers a thorough analysis of this experience in various places in his writings. In his *Sparkling Stone* he writes:

> If we transcend ourselves and become so onefold in our ascent to God
> that bare love may embrace us in that height where it is engaged with it-
> self only, beyond all practice of virtues, that is in our origin from which we
> are born spiritually, we shall come to nought there and die in God to our-
> selves and all our self-consciousness. And in this dying we become hidden
> sons of God and we find a new life in ourselves, which is life eternal. And
> about these sons St. Paul says: You are dead and your life is hidden with
> Christ in God (Col 3.3).[149]

A theological question naturally arises at this juncture: does this mean that the contemplative man or woman has the experience that he or she is Christ? Do countless sons and daughters of God exist of which Christ is but one among the many? Jan van Ruusbroec is unequivocal in his response to this question: the created can never become the Creator, and the human person cannot thus become identical to the second person of the Trinity.[150] It is actually a question

---

147 Cf. the remark made by Ribadeneira: 'Moreover, during the years in which he wrote the Constitutions, Ignatius recorded the lights he received in prayer and his spiritual feelings daily in a notebook in which I read the following: "Today I experienced something similar as when the eternal Father united me with his Son."' ('Porro in commentariolo quoddam et in diario (in quod dum Constitutiones scriberet, affectus in oratione suos et spirituales quasi gustus Ignatius manu sua quotidie referebat) scriptum reperi: "hodie affectum sensi, qualem cum aeternus Pater me Filio suo commendavit". Ribadeneira, Pedro de: *Vita Ignatii Loyolae*. MHSI 93. Rome 1965, pp. 272-274.

148 Cf. Surin: *Guide spirituel pour la perfection*. Christus 12. Paris 1963, p. 178.

149 Jan van Ruusbroec: *Opera Omnia* 10. CCCM 110. Turnhout 1991, p. 144.

150 Cf., for example, Jan van Ruusbroec: *Opera Omnia* 1. CCCM 101. Turnhout 1989, pp. 128-132 and more extensively, Jan van Ruusbroec: *Opera Omnia* 7A. CCCM 107A. Turnhout 2000, pp. 96-113.

of the presence of Christ *in* the human person. Christ always remains other, but he is nevertheless actively present, transforming the interior person more and more into the likeness of Him, whereby likeness is related to one's experience of the love of the Father. The goal of Ruusbroec's magnum opus, his *Spiritual Tabernacle* – an extraordinary monument in the history of Christian literature – is to describe how Christ (and thus the entire Trinity) can be actively present *in* the deepest core of the human person, without the human person thereby becoming God.[151] As Ruusbroec states in several places in his writings, the contemplative life is precisely the awareness of this indwelling of Christ in the human person, and thus the awareness that the ultimate foundation of the human person is not the 'I' but rather the unfathomable relationship between Christ and the Father.

This is precisely the core of the problem. From the moment nominalist anthropology begins to consider the human person as an individual completely coincidental with him/herself, it naturally becomes intellectually impossible to understand what such an indwelling might mean. While this position reached its peak in the thought of Ruusbroec's contemporary, William of Ockham, it is, of course, much older than the 14th century. The 12th century debate between Peter Abaelard and William of Saint-Thierry deals, among other things, with the said topic. In contrast to Abaelard, William opted for a radically relational image of the human person.[152] While mystical authors were to follow him in this for centuries, their position became more and more marginal in relation to the intellectual life. The nominalist perspective gradually gained the upper hand, whereby the human person ultimately came to be understood in the final instance as an individual, an 'I'. When Jean-Joseph Surin's confreres refer to the experience he described as 'imagination', this is a clear indication that the intellectual framework within which they functioned was unfamiliar with the notion of 'indwelling' and even found it incomprehensible. As such, the experience could only be understood as the work of the imagination.

This suggests, therefore, that the problem with which Jean-Joseph Surin was confronted had two different aspects. The first is related to an element unique to the spiritual life, namely that the *active* devotion of the human person in his or her relationship with God becomes so dominant that it ultimately comes to form a shield between the said human person and God. The second belongs to the history of Christian thought, namely that a nominalist understanding of the human person as individual (rather than as person) had gained such prominence that the notion of the indwelling of Christ had become incomprehensible. The

---

151   Jan van Ruusbroec: *Opera Omnia* 5-6. CCCM 105 and 106. Turnhout 2006.

152   Cf. Tomasic, Thomas Michael: 'William of Saint-Thierry against Peter Abaelard: A Dispute on the Meaning of Being a Person'. *Analecta Cisterciensia* 28. Rome 1972, pp. 3-76.

experience of indwelling is ultimately refused because it is not understood and vice versa.[153]

It is at this juncture that Saint Joseph manifests himself as patron saint. At a time in which the indwelling of Christ in the human person and a living relationship with Christ was being rejected as 'imagination' – precisely because the intellectual framework of the day was no longer able to understand it – people who were nevertheless granted such an experience could expect nothing from their spiritual leaders. Indeed, Surin himself was personally confronted with such rejection during the most difficult years of his life.[154] Given the fact that Saint Joseph had concerned himself with the growth of the young Jesus during his earthly existence, it was logical therefore that one should turn to the same Saint Joseph in search of protection for the indwelling of Christ in the human person here and now. It is indeed the case that the contemplative life in which the human person becomes aware of the indwelling of Christ is vulnerable and clearly requires protection when spiritual leaders reject it as imagination. This explains the 'new' devotion to Saint Joseph – the great patriarch who was more a man of silence than of words – and it is precisely this devotion that Muzio Viteleschi desired to prohibit.

Viteleschi's prohibition represents one particular tendency within the Jesuit order but not, however, the only one. Some were well aware of the fact that the Society of Jesus exhibited a strong orientation towards the contemplative life in its early years. The reference made by Surin to the Constitutions of the Order is revealing. Indeed, he was not alone in maintaining this perspective. In 1640, the Dutch Jesuit Maximilianus Sandaeus wrote a short tractate on the occasion of the Order's centenary in which he endeavoured to illustrate the essentially contemplative character of the original Society of Jesus. The book was published with the full permission of his superiors.[155] Its title embodies its content: *Centenary Jubilee of the Society of Jesus, Owing to the Mystical Theology Practiced and Explained by Ignatius of Loyola and His Companions in the First Century After its Foundation.* Sandaeus presents a long series of Jesuit authors who had experienced or described mystical theology, or had reflected upon it in their writings. The resulting list was further supplemented in the 1922 edition of Sandaeus' volume. It would indeed appear

---

153 Cf. the polemic concerning Gal 2. 20 (*Vivo ego, jam non ego, vivit vero in me Christus*), Costa, Eugenio: 'La tromperie, ou le problème de la communication chez Surin. Notes sur quelques textes de la "Science expérimentale". *Revue d'Ascetique et de Mystique* 44. Toulouse 1968, pp. 413-424 (esp. 419). Cf. the intellectual difficulties encountered by Theresa of Avila in this matter, *Libro de la Vida*, ch. 18.

154 Cf. de Certeau: *Correspondance*, pp. 517-523.

155 *Jubilum Societatis Jesu seculare ob theologiam mysticam a fundatore suo Ignatio ejusque Sociis primo conditae Societatis seculo excultam et illustratam.* Cologne 1640. Reprinted in: Collection de la Bibliothèque des Exercises de Saint Ignace 77-78. Engien, Paris 1922.

to be the case that the Order originally enjoyed an unequivocally mystical orientation, at a time in which such was certainly far from evident. Significant in this regard, for example, is the fact that the Carthusians of Cologne dedicated their second edition of Herp's *Theologia mystica* (1550) to Ignatius and the Society of Jesus – a matter that clearly pleased Ignatius, [156] although he was also aware that Herp was open to misunderstanding.[157] The said mystical orientation gradually began to change around the beginning of the 17th century. Indeed, the fact that Sandaeus found it necessary to write his book represents evidence of this change as does the extraordinary devotion to Saint Joseph.

Conclusion

It is clear that the renewal in devotion to Saint Joseph among the younger generation of Jesuits during the first decades of the 17th century has an important symbolic significance. Joseph was the silent protector of the contemplative, mystical life, a life that was perceived to be under threat. The Christological dimension is evident: Saint Joseph had borne responsibility for Jesus' childhood and the early years of his earthly existence, it was thus appropriate to turn to the same Saint Joseph for protection of the indwelling Christ in the here and now. Indeed, the contemplative life is precisely the awareness of Christ in the here and now, alive in the deepest core of the human person. This awareness was rejected by some as the work of the imagination on the basis of an anthropology that understood the human person in the final instance as an individual. The General of the Jesuit Order considered it necessary to intervene firmly in the matter, fearing that it might lead to serious difficulties. Given the fact that he understood this extraordinary devotion to Saint Joseph – understand: the contemplative dimension – to represent 'a spirit alien to the Society of Jesus', he forbade it. For Viteleschi, the very identity

---

156 'De Mistica theologia Henrici Herp gaudemus in Domino quod sit excusa'. Letter of December 18th 1556 to Lenaert Kessel S.J.: *S. Ignatii de Loyola epistolae et instructiones*. t. 10, MHSI. Rome 1968, p. 349. The book was to be forbidden shortly thereafter (in 1559) by the Spanish Grand Inquisitor Fernando de Valdés, and placed on the Index in 1585. A 'corrected' edition was approved in 1598.

157 'Alguno dellos como Henrico Herp, tiene, sin duda, necessidad de ser glosado en algunos lugares, para que se sufra lo que dize'. *S. Ignatii de Loyola epistolae et instructiones*. t. 12, MHSI. Rome 1968, p. 650. Cf. Albert Deblaere on Herp: 'Herp unit la spiritualité affective de la méditation bonaventurienne à la doctrine mystique de Ruusbroec. Mais surtout, il s'efforce de fondre à nouveau le language de la théologie scolastique et celui de la mystique, séparés depuis des siècles, quoiqu'employant les mêmes termes, mais dans un système référentiel fort différent. Or, l'unité dans laquelle Herp fond ces deux languages a été une source d'ambiguïtés et de problèmes pour les lecteurs qui l'étudient dans le cadre de l'histoire de la pensée ; d'autre part, et c'est un fait remarquable, les mystiques des générations suivantes, presque tous lecteurs assidus de Herp, ont toujours trouvés dans ses ouvrages l'enseignement dont ils avaient besoin et qui les aidait à mieux se comprendre, tandis que ces mêmes ouvrages paraissent avoir peu aidé les théologiens à comprendre les mystiques.' *Essays on Mystical Literature*. BETL 177. Leuven 2004, p. 313.

of the Order was at stake. Jean-Joseph Surin, who never exercised a function of responsibility within the Order and was even held in the infirmary for several years considered unfit for any form of apostolate, suggests at the end of his life that the Order was losing its spiritual identity and had departed fundamentally from what Ignatius had understood to be its essential characteristic (Fig. 3).

A problem confronting the Jesuit Order of the 17th century thus serves to illustrate a phenomenon that had in fact confronted European culture as a whole: humanism in its original form with its theocentric understanding of the human person was gradually being abandoned. The fact that the contemplative dimension survived in spite of everything – albeit in the margins of the intellectual life – is perhaps due to the protection of Saint Joseph, who silently bore responsibility for the beloved Son of the Father.

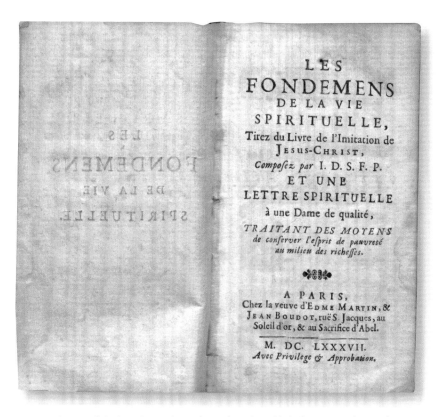

Fig. 3: *Title page of the first edition of one of Surin's works, published anonymously – as the superiors of Surin did not allow him to publish anything – Les fondements de la vie spirituelle, tirez du livre de l'Imitation de Jesus-Christ, composez par I.D.S.F.P. (Paris, chez la veuve d'Edme Martin & Jean Boudot, 1687). The book contains excerpts from his Dialogues Spirituels.*

The Medical Market Compared with the Pastoral Market:

A Perspective from Early Modern Dutch History

Fred van Lieburg

Introduction

In 1690 the Reformed consistory in the Holland city of Rotterdam censured a critical woman member of the congregation. She had said to some lady friends that she doubted 'whether a dear Christian is allowed to listen to the Reverend Velingius, for I do not know if he has one drop of grace, and he stands on the pulpit like a quack'.[158] This statement is interesting because of the ambiguous comparison of a clergyman to an irregular healer. Given her disqualification of his religious inner self, she must have seen him as a bad healer of spiritual disease. In her eyes a good theologian should be a good physician, certainly when he is preaching. But she was also referring to his outward appearance or, to put it in another way, his corporal eloquence. His appearance may have been so exuberant that the churchgoers possibly imagined themselves to be in the theatre or on the marketplace.

Be that as it may, the comparison between religion and medicine is as old as Jewish-Christian tradition. In the Old Testament God is called a Healer and in the New Testament we read how Jesus combined his preaching with healing trough wonders. The *Christus-medicus*-motif as well as the sin-sickness-symbol appears throughout the whole of church history. In the Middle Ages and also during the Reformation and the Renaissance a strong unity of soul and body was assumed.

---

158 *City Archives at Rotterdam, archives of the Reformed consistory of Rotterdam*, vol. 7, acta 4 October and 22 November, 1690. When the church council discussed this case, pastor Wilhelmus Velingius had already died on 24 June, 1690.

Clergymen often also acted as medical men. Until well into the 17th century, even Calvinist ministers connected pastorate with medicine, and even magic. Suffice it to mention at this point that academic studies in theology and medicine were sometimes combined.[159]

Let me make a further comparison of both realms. There is a historical similarity between the structures of the medical and the theological fields. I am concerned here with the Dutch situation during the early modern period, that is to say, with the period from the 16th to the 19th century.[160] During that time, the medical sector was divided, roughly speaking, into three groups. At the top were the *doctores medicinae*, who were received an academic education and graduated in medical science. Through their knowledge of the classical languages, they had access to scholarly traditions from Hippocrate to Vesalius. Since they were physicians, doctors were mainly concerned with theoretical matters, making diagnoses, giving advice, and writing prescriptions. Handwork was usually left to practitioners lower in the medical hierarchy.

This second group of healers consisted mainly of surgeons, sometimes also known as barbers. They were skilled in blood-letting, tooth-drawing and curing injuries or infirmities. These skills were usually acquired through a master-pupil-relation. In contrast to the *doctores*, who had a free profession, surgeons were organized as craftsmen in guilds, at least in towns. Also in contrast to the doctors, many surgeons were found in the country-side. To this second group also belonged 'specialists' such as herniotomists, lithotomists, oculists and bonesetters. Their work was complementary to that of the surgeons, as far as they had more knowledge and skill.

I now come to the third group engaged in medical practice, the quacks or bunglers. These are men who claimed to possess the means to cure people from their diseases – glib persons who, travelling through local markets, tried to sell all sorts of salves and drinks as the best remedies to the gullible people. We must, incidentally, consider that the notion of quackery was rather subjective. It concerned more the results obtained by healers, whatever name or qualification they might have had. Quacks could do much damage, but they could also obtain success and distinction. Moreover, many were permitted by local governors or guilds to do their work as legally as doctors and surgeons did.

In order to compare the medical with the theological professions, I shall focus on the situation in the Dutch Reformed Church during the 17th and 18th cen-

159 See in general Gijswijt-Hofstra, Marijke, Marland, Hilary and de Waardt, Hans (eds.): *Belief, trust and healing in Europe, sixteenth to twentieth centuries*. London and New York 1997.

160 See in general Marland, Hilary and Pelling, Margaret (eds.): *The task of healing. Medicine, religion and gender in England and the Netherlands 1450-1800*. Rotterdam 1996.

turies.[161] This was the 'public church', as Calvinism was the politically privileged religion of the United Provinces. At the top of the Dutch Reformed Church were the ministers who, like the *medicinae doctores*, had received a university education. Directly after the Reformation gifted lay men were ordained as preachers too. Theological candidates were never obliged to graduate, since a double examination by the church itself sufficed to obtain the pulpit. From the early 17th century, only academically trained theologians were admitted as *proponenten* and ministers. They were versed in the biblical languages and could also read the Latin writings of church fathers, scholastics and protestant reformers. Theologians and medical doctors shared the exclusivity of being learned.[162]

However, the social positions were different. Physicians worked only in the towns and therefore ranked almost as high as the town ministers. Graduated doctors ranked even higher. Sometimes ministers were sons of surgeons and ministers' children studied medicine or married with physicians to move upwards socially. Furthermore, clergymen were occupied not only with theory, but even more with the practical side of their profession. Besides preaching every week, they had to administer their flocks daily. On the other hand, ministers in the towns were aided by special helpers who visited the sick. This was caused by the size of congregation, but perhaps also by the same reservations which drove the *medicinae doctores* to leave their patients to the care of surgeons.[163]

The second category of pastoral occupations which I mentioned just now included above all the comforters of the sick and the male and female catechizers. Besides these there were functionaries like lecturers and singers in church services, organists and carillon players, sextons and people who put the chairs in place. These church jobs were additional to a normal primary source of income. A primary function was often that of schoolmaster, since it was closely affiliated to the ministry. However, I will not digress on the social range of public education – with its professors, preceptors and schoolmasters - nor on the strictly ecclesiastical offices of elders and deacons.

Of greater importance to the issue I am discussing may be the third group of people concerned with pastoral activity. I am thinking here of persons who with-

161   See in general Hsia, R. Po-Chia and van Nierop, H.F.K. (eds.): *Calvinism and religious toleration in the Dutch Golden Age.* Cambridge 2001; van Eijnatten, Joris: *Liberty and concord in the United Provinces. Religious toleration and the public in the eighteenth-century Netherlands.* Leiden 2003.

162   See also van Lieburg, Fred: 'Preachers between inspiration and instruction: Dutch Reformed ministers without academic education (sixteenth-eighteenth centuries)'. *Dutch Review of Church History* 83. (2003); Clemens, Theo and Janse, Wim (eds.). *The Pastor Bonus. Papers read at the British-Dutch Colloquium at Utrecht, 18-21 September 2002.* Leiden and Boston 2004, pp. 166-190.

163   de Niet, Johan: 'Comforting the sick: confessional cure of souls and pietist comfort in the Dutch Republic'. *Confessionalism and Pietism. Religious reform in early modern Europe and North America.* Fred van Lieburg (ed.). Mainz 2006, pp. 197-212.

Fig. 1: *Scenes from before and after a death-bed. The Title-page from Jacob Sceperus' Schat-Boeck Der Onderwysingen voor Kranck-Besoeckers. A handbook for comforters of the sick. Published in Amsterdam in 1671.*

out specific education and often also without formal permission or admission were engaged in preaching the Word of God or provided spiritual consultation. The bulk of this group was formed by the so-called *oefenaars*, literally: exercisers or practitioners, but better simply translated as 'lay preachers'. They were men and sometimes women who acted as uneducated and unqualified speakers in private meetings of pious people. The Dutch Reformed Church of the 17th, 18th and 19th centuries had many of such lay preachers, and the same can be said for strict Calvinist groups until the present day.[164]

Lay preaching and quackery

To understand the position of lay preachers in Dutch Reformed church life, we have to go back to the age of Reformation. Protestant theologians, opposing Roman Catholicism, tried to restore the 'priesthood of all believers'. Every Christian is allowed to read and interpret the Bible, although the correct exegesis is the prerogative of the church community. While the clergy may have more knowledge of the Scriptures than the laity, the Holy Spirit can also reveal the meaning of God's Word to common church members. An important legitimisation for this conviction was found in Paul's letter to the Corinthians. The apostle dealt with the spiritual gifts to the faithful, including the gifts of healing and prophecy, the latter refers speaking in the congregation through divine inspiration (1 Cor. 12.9 and 10; on prophecy: 1 Cor. 14).

One problem involved was the question whether these capacities were given by immediate revelation or by an education enabling professional acting. The great Reformers opted for the latter way. Just as the gift of healing applied to the *medicinae doctores*, the art of preaching presupposed academic theological training. However, this did not alter the fact that leaders in several protestant centres of 16th-century Europe experimented with lay activity. Zwingli in Zürich, Bucer in Strasburg and A Lasco in London organized so-called 'prophesyings'. In such meetings church people could put forward questions about the Bible or personal faith experience, to which ordained, ministers theological students or admitted laymen provided answers.[165]

Nevertheless, neither in Lutheranism nor in Calvinism was a formal position created for free preaching by the uneducated during public meetings. Besides

---

164 Cf. van Lieburg, Fred: 'Pasteurs calvinistes et prédicateurs laïcs piétistes. De l'anticléricalisme dans l'Église Réformée néerlandaise, 1550-1750'. *L'anticléricalisme intra-protestant en Europe continentale (XVIIe-XVIIIe siècles)*. Yves Krumenacker (ed.). Lyon 2003, pp. 103-125.

165 See Kaufman, Peter Iver: 'Prophesying again'. *Church History. Studies in Christianity and Culture* 68:2. New Haven and Tallahassee 1999, pp. 337-358.

anxiety concerning the theological and pastoral qualities of lay sermons, there were fears regarding deviation from orthodoxy and the social consequences of religious excess. In particular, 16th -century Anabaptism, which rejected all theological education and church order and stressed the 'inner Word' and visionary revelations, traumatized religious sensibilities in this regard. Meanwhile, popular prophets could appear everywhere and at all times. In the Lutheran areas around the Baltic Sea, for example, there were hundreds of unlettered preachers claiming to have received angelic messages and healing the sick by means of prayer.[166]

In the Dutch Republic, Roman Catholics and protestant dissenters were tolerated beside the Calvinists. In most churches there was no place for lay preachers. Only among the Mennonites, the peaceful heirs of the Anabaptists, church members served as 'admonishers' or 'preachers by love'. They combined this role with common occupations in society. It is remarkable that a well-known preacher who was also a *medicinae doctor*, Galenus Abrahamsz. de Haan, at the end of the 17th century strove for a theological school for Mennonite pastors. Although the Mennonite fraternity has never abolished lay preachers, since the 18th century its intellectual elite had been able to compete with the clergies of other churches.

As I mentioned at the beginning of my essay, academic education was a practical requirement in the Reformed Church. Only the offices of elder and deacon and the functions of catechizer and comforter of the sick were open to common (though exclusively male) church members. Praying and interpreting the Bible was bound to liturgical forms and books on the catechism that were approved by the clergy. Those who wanted more and liked to hold edifying speeches, had to be content with a private role in the family, their circle of friends, or meetings of believers, usually called 'conventicles'. The possibilities for lay preaching were therefore limited, but of course everyone could try to extend it and to exceed the limits of public performance.

In actual fact, in the Dutch Reformed Church there have been hundreds of men (and a small number of women) who during varying lengths of time were more or less active as 'preachers'. Their work field was constituted by the conventicles that serious church members held on Sunday evenings or during the week. These were edifying house meetings where people came together to discuss the church sermon, to read a book, to talk about personal faith or to listen to someone's account of the 'way of conversion'. In addition, specific catechisations were held at different places, where a minister or another person with formal permission taught the catechism, and the members of the congregation were allowed to ask and answer questions.

---

166   Beyer, Jürgen: *Lutheran lay prophets, c.1550-c.1700*. Leiden 2007.

As a matter of course, men came forward in these conventicles and catechisations who attracted attention through their personal image, their eloquence, their knowledge of the Bible and Reformed tradition, their assured faith and their pastoral abilities. If such people had gained a certain spiritual self-confidence and charismatic authority, they could begin to act as lay preachers. Most of them originated from the lower middle class and had received only a primary education. In respect of theology they were self-taught men, as a result of ardent reading and visits to services, catechisations and conventicles. Several lay preachers were schoolmasters or filled offices as catechizers or comforters of the sick. In these cases, lay preaching was an authorized but limited form of speaking and teaching.

Certain groups of lay preachers did not only appear in their own places of residence or region, but travelled across the country. These include travelling merchants, skippers and booksellers as well as people who were on the move all the time since they continually got into trouble with the church. Furthermore, many young and single men roamed the Dutch country side. In contrast to the local lay preachers, tended to be loyal to the church, the wanderers were often suspect, especially when their elusive assemblies appealed to sectarianism and heterodoxy.

The lay preachers' power and the reason for their success was indubitably a result of their rhetoric abilities. Having a ready tongue, they spoke popular language and also mastered pious idiom. Apart from their theological knowledge, they relied heavily on experiential insights into religion, both their own and those they gathered from the spiritual autobiographies of pious people. As self-made preachers they alluded to their own personal association with the Lord and their vocation to edify their fellow believers. They did not provide philological interpretations, but practical applications of Scriptures in their sermons. With a special voice modulation and body performance they were able to evoke emotions among their listeners.

Reformed lay preachers usually belonged to the right wing of their church, being pietistic rather than orthodox. The true doctrine, they believed, should be experienced and practised. Pietism flourished from the last decades of the 17th century, as rationalism and enlightenment conquered the church establishment. Lay preachers played a significant role in the religious revivals in the middle of the 18th century, a phenomenon characterized by deep faith and strong body language. In general, they were trusted by the pietistic section of the clergy. Middle orthodoxy, however, detested their appearance, condemning their theological amateurism, their pastoral ignorance and the disturbance and dissension they caused in society and the church.

The governors of the Republic agreed with the church's critical attitude. The pious subculture within the public church was seen as a potential danger for the religious and social order. Meanwhile, ad hoc legal developments provided for a measure of recognition. Many regulations concerning the conventicles and lay preachers were laid down by local and regional authorities as well as church councils and synods. Often resulting from incidental conflicts, they tended to lose their force and were not maintained for long. Legal measures always had the intention of making the gatherings of the pious conform to rules of church order and catechisation. They never entailed the formal appointment of lay preachers, recognition extended no further than registration, examination or permission.

The regulated position of lay preachers in church and society resembles the non-legalized but tolerated position of quacks in the field of health care. It should now be clear that the profile of lay preachers similarly corresponds to that of the irregular healers. These similarities include the following: the way they legitimised their activities by claiming to have a divine mission or simply through popular belief in their effectiveness; their personal charisma and self-taught knowledge, together with the verbal and non-verbal instruments used to reach their customers; their high geographical mobility, which could be connected with local and regional competition; and the way in which they tried to cater to the special needs of the common people.[167]

I am not the first to compare lay preachers with quacks. In 1743, in a controversy about the legitimization of conventicles, a Dutch Reformed minister referred to 'self-styled preachers' who only aimed to further their own interest and profit, expecting for example a free meal. They 'went out and sold God's Word all over the country as spiritual quacks'.[168] Above we encountered the minister as a quack; here the lay preacher is seen as a quack as well as a merchant. Apart from their negative connotation, it is clear that these comparisons connect the theological and the medical to an economic dimension of culture. Before discussing this issue further, I will first go into the development of medical and pastoral professions during the transition from the early modern to the modern period.

Once more the two professions

I began my essay by distinguishing three groups of medical and theological professions. I mentioned a top layer of academic experts, a group of recognized and specialized workers, and a group of unattached and self-appointed pedlars. In

---

167 See also de Waardt, Hans: 'Breaking the boundaries: irregular healers in eighteenth-century Holland'. *Illness and healing alternatives in Western Europe*. Marijke Gijswijt-Hofstra, Hilary Marland and Hans de Waardt (eds.). London and New York 1997, pp. 141-160.

168 van Gennep, Arnoldus: '*Onpartijdig en onzijdig opstel (…) over de zamenkomsten en oeffeningen der particuliere ledematen (…)*'. Dordrecht 1743, pp. 68-69.

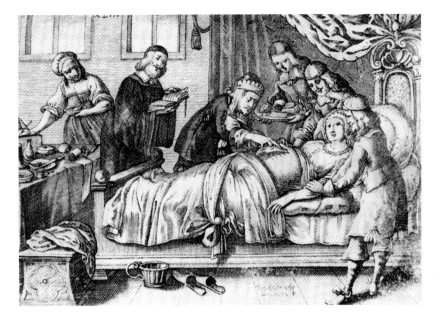

Fig 2: A Caesarean section in presence of a minister. Illustration from Johannes Scultetus' Auctarium ad armamentarium chirurgicum, published posthumously in Leyden in 1653.

the medical domain these were the *medicinae doctores*, the surgeons and many specialists, and the quacks. I have left apothecaries, who were often better trained than surgeons, as well as midwives, who did not have any medical qualifications at all. In the ecclesiastical I have distinguished between the ministers, the catechizers and comforters of the sick, and the lay preachers.

In fact, we should speak only of two professional ranges. In both domains distinctions were made between theory and practice, science and art, reflection and action, scholarship and skill. Medicine and theology were theoretical sciences for professors and doctors. Several professions were concerned with the practical care for the body or the soul. It is well-known that ministers combined theory and practice, theology and spiritual care. Doctors also practised medicine, but most of the people were dependant on the help of surgeons and other healers. The view that early modern doctors only dealt with book learning and did not do practical work at all is a misconstruction (Fig. 2).

The main problem was the relationship between theory and practice, the question whether medical or spiritual care, regardless by whom it was given, was in accordance with official medical or theological knowledge. In this respect, the formal bipartite between theory and practice was a cultural tripartite in reality. Among the non-academics there were practitioners who conformed to generally accepted knowledge, besides people who offered a more or less unorthodox medicine or pastorate. From this point of view, those who concerned with theory and those concerned with practice – that is, doctors and surgeons, respectively ministers and their assistants – with at a distance, dubious alternatives such as popular quacks and preachers.

Church and government as public institutions aimed at, and mostly succeeded in, bringing together the theories and practices of faith and health care. They were able to do this by simply controlling the competition between the various kinds of 'specialists'. In medicine civic ordinances and the rules of medical colleges and surgeons' guilds regulated the activities of quacks. They were allowed, on payment of fees, to offer medical remedies and services at a certain location and during a limited time, for example at fairs or markets. Established doctors and surgeons delivered the aftercare that was frequently needed, and maintained the more permanent local and regional customs.

The Dutch Reformed church was concerned with the spiritual care for congregation members and people in public orphanages, prisons and hospitals. Church councils, just like the guilds supported by the government, controlled the examination and admission of theological candidates, ministers, catechizers and comforters of the sick. The latter pastoral workers lacked academic training, but conformed to the clergy's confessional and ethical norms and values. The same applied to the majority of lay preachers. Combining this role with a church office, or being acknowledged in the congregation, they subscribed to the Reformed doctrines and rules. In fact, only dissenters and sectarians appear to have acted medical quacks.

The negative image of non-intellectual practitioners of medicine and theology, and the way they were identified with incompetent colleagues, was mainly the result of the process of professionalization at the turn of early modern to modern times. In this development, the top layer of both sectors began to control or even annexed the middle group, while the lower echelons were marginalized or even eliminated. The aim was adaptation to and monopolizing of a new professional model. Medicine was now dominated by the empirical sciences, and theology could not escape the influence of Rationalism and Enlightenment.

These developments in Dutch society were mirrored in literary works. Writers often ridiculed preachers and healers who were not satisfied with the prevailing standards of scholarship. It is not accidental that around 1820 Jacob Vosmaer, in his medical satire on the life of a surgeon, satirized a simple shoemaker and spiritual admonisher.[169] Multatuli mocked a preaching interloper, who according to

---

169   Jacob Vosmaer: *Het leven en de wandelingen van Meester Maarten Vroeg.* J. Wagelaar (ed.). Culemborg 1978.

him belonged to 'the class of catechizers and comforters of the sick, corresponding to a real minister as a quack to a doctor'.[170] This is a fine quote supporting my argument, but at the same time it is a ridiculization of pastoral workers who were theologically accepted in the past.

In the 19th century there was a far-reaching transformation of all kinds of professions and competences. During the Republic, it had already been attempted to improve the education of surgeons, chemists and other occupations in accordance with scientific developments in medicine. After abolishing the guilds, the national state (which followed the Republic) made new laws to ameliorate and maintain the level of health care. In addition, academically trained *doctores* of a 'second medical rank' were introduced, consisting of town-doctors and rural-doctors, man-midwives, midwives and pharmacists. The introduction in 1865 of the doctors' certificate, a strict academic declaration of competence regarding all medical activities, completed the process of professionalization.[171]

In theology, too, there was a growing emphasis on academic standards since the 18th century. The University Act of 1815 and the General Regulation of the Dutch Reformed Church eliminated the possibility becoming a minister without full university training. By means of ecclesiastical examinations, the established clergy promoted the admission of well-educated candidates and tried to inhibit the entry of young men from the lower social classes. However, the relationship between the Church and the universities remained a much debated issue. The faculties taught academic theology free from confessional ties, but at the same time students had to be prepared for the ministry. In an attempt to resolve this contradiction, the *duplex ordo*, a separation between a 'state curriculum' and a 'church curriculum', was introduced in theological education in 1878.[172]

The development of the *clerus minor* is of interest because of the similarities with the 'second medical rank'. From 1816 catechizers had to be trained by a minister and were examined by the Church before being allowed to teach the youth. Furthermore, comforters of the sick were now selected from the best catechizers. In this way the traditional combination of the two functions was fixed and their activities came under preventive control of the 'first pastoral rank'. By the end of the 19th century, the comforting of sick and dying people was left to the ministers, analogous to the manifold tasks of physicians.

---

170 Multatuli [pseudonym for Eduard Douwes Dekker]: *De geschiedenis van Woutertje Pieterse*. N.A. Donkersloot (ed.). Amsterdam 1938. p. 43 and 70.

171 Cf. Marland, H. and van Lieburg, M.J.: 'Midwife regulation, education and practice in the Netherlands during the nineteenth century'. *Medical History* 33. London 1989, pp. 296-317.

172 van Rooden, Peter: 'History, the Nation, and Religion: The Transformations of the Dutch Religious Past'. *Nation and Religion: Perspectives on Europe and Asia*. Peter van der Veer and Hartmut Lehmann (eds.). Princeton 1999, pp. 96-111.

The continuing and successful professionalization of medicine and theology implied the control or elimination of private enterprise. As to irregular healing, traditional quacks lost more and more ground by the rising monopoly of official medical practitioners. But they never quite disappeared. Instead, they returned in a socially more accepted way in the circles of homoeopathy and alternative medicine. It is not accidental that around the turn of the century, after the field of medicine had been fully professionalized, physicians founded the Association for the Fight against Quackery.

In a sense there was a similar development in the domain of religion. After the Secession of 1834, the first exodus of orthodox and pietistic members out of the Dutch Reformed Church, lay preachers were found in the small free groups, who wanted to continue along the lines of the old public church. It is true that there was a measure of professionalization in these communities. In fact, the tradition of free prophecy has been maintained only by the less organized and semi-official congregations, such as those of the evangelical movement, which are comparable to esoteric currents from a sociological point of view.

The medical and pastoral markets

The comparison between medical and pastoral activities in the early modern period and the respective developments in professionalization can be extended to historiography. Only during the last three decades research into the different levels of professional practices has been done. This has been a consequence of developments in medicine as well as in theology. In health care, the 'professional dominance' of doctors began to be criticized during the sixties. People defended the rights of irregular healers and the legitimacy of alternative cures. In church, participation of lay members increased at the same time and tended to be consumptive. The self-evident authority of theologians, preachers and pastors decreased.

These contemporary developments were reflected in the view of the past and in historical research. In the past, medical historiography was heavy oriented towards the development of and progression in academic medical science. The work of healers on the secondary level was neglected and the perceptions of patients were not taken into consideration at all. Because research was done by doctors about doctors, historiography was in effect a legitimization of their traditional scientific monopoly. This state of affairs has now largely changed. Medical as well as non-specialized historians are doing 'medical history from below', taking into consideration also the perspective of patients and other people.[173]

173 Huisman, Frank: 'Shaping the Medical Market. On the Construction of Quackery and Folk Medicine in Dutch Historiography'. *Medical History* 43. London 1999, pp. 359-375.

Church history has been broadened in a similar way. It would perhaps be an exaggeration to claim that traditionally church history was written by ministers about ministers. But traditional interest was concerned mainly with regular church life and academic theology. Everything else was mostly described as a deviation from orthodoxy and church order. Dutch church history was marked by a rational, scholarly and professional view of faith experience and religious practice, and phenomena such as Mysticism, Pietism or Revivalism were criticized. Since some decades, however, 'profane historians' in particular have begun to pay more attention to popular religion, piety in everyday life, or to put it in another way, on 'church history from below'.

Modern medical historians have been using the concept of the 'medical market' for more than a decade. This concept implies the application of the economic model of supply and demand to the interactive relations between patients and healers. The model takes into consideration the fact that different kinds of people seek health and healing. They consult themselves, their relatives and others, buy mixtures and ointments, read books and periodicals, and apply self-medication. They may consult medically qualified professionals at the same time or at a later moment. Treatments are tried out and sometimes rejected. All sorts of healers compete to gain the patients' favour and money, using different theories, diagnoses, therapeutics and prescriptions, whether they are recognized by science or not. They can profile themselves by referring to previous successes in their practice or by focusing on certain social and cultural groups.

Can this market-model be transferred to religious history? At first glance, the applicability of an economic dimension seems unlikely. Faith is no more negotiable by supply and demand than health, according to the well-known text in the Old Testament: 'O, everyone that thirsteth, come to the waters, and he that hath no money, come, buy and eat, yes, come, buy wine and milk without money and without price' (Isaiah 55.1). Pious Reformed people, in their own 'language of Canaan', like to speak about the 'market of sovereign grace'. Neither money nor property is essential to the preaching of the Gospel.

To return from theology to history, it should be noted that on the medical market money had a real function. Patients could spend their fees for advice only once. *Doctores* found customers among the rich classes, unless they were employed by the government to serve the poor. Most people were dependant on the cheaper help of secondary healers. In religious care there was no such financial dependence, at least not in the public church. Reformed ministers received a fixed salary from the state, sometimes consisting of, or supplemented by, local church funds. The believers themselves could contribute to church collections or bestow gifts.

Lay preachers acted out of their own free will and were religiously motivated: they did not work for payment. Nevertheless, there was a subtle mechanism of service and reward. In conventicles sometimes collections were held for the expenses of the host or for a gift to the preacher. According to the passage quoted above, they could expect a free meal or free accommodation. I know of lay preachers who took the place of ministers during burials, and who were, of course, paid by the relatives. A number of lay preachers were out of work, dependant on charity and seeking for other means to obtain an income. Some of them travelled as peddlars to sell spiritual literature personally to pious men and women.

The book market itself shows a clear parallel between the worlds of faith and health in the early modern period. Theological knowledge was not the exclusive possession of a lettered elite able to read Latin. A large part of Christian tradition was accessible, directly or indirectly, in the vernacular. In addition to oral education by preaching and teaching, Christian faith was popularized for the common believers. This resulted in a large theological lay culture, represented in particular by skilled church members. Analogous to the appearance of numerous popular-scientific books on diseases, religious literature could supply remedies to faith problems. Authors, translators and publishers were sometimes called 'spiritual apothecaries'.

It is also possible to compare the patient to the believer in respect of the latter's pursuit of help and support in his experience of, and the forming of his relation with God. He consulted himself in prayer and meditation, read the Bible and edifying literature, in the company of his family or his friends, in worship, conventicles or catechisation. He would receive many answers, and be guided by the advice most suited to his individual problems. For professional pastoral care he would be dependant primarily on ministers, but also on catechizers or comforters of the sick. But seekers of assurance of faith are not always satisfied by the diverging or contradictory answers to his questions.

In Biblical terms, all people are sick because they are sinful, but not all are aware of this and seek healing by believing in Christ. 'It is not the healthy who need a doctor, but the sick', said Jesus himself (Mark 2.17). Only serious, active, pious Christians were the appreciative consumers of the work of pastoral mediators. And only among them, freelance preachers did seek and find an audience. In spite of regular ministers and their official helpers, lay pastors had the specific means to supply to the needs of pietist patients. They had the gift of speaking not only to the mind but also to the hearts of people. Their 'spiritual knowledge', originating from an experiential conversation with the Lord, contrasted sharply with the 'literary knowledge' of learned theologians.

The 18th-century pietistic clergyman Wilhelmus Schortinghuis, who underwent conversion when he was already a minister, denoted simple true believers as 'little professors', educated in the 'heavenly academy'. This qualification applies even more to lay preachers. They were able to comfort and admonish people excellently, without being ordained as ministers. They led seekers of salvation effectively, pointing out their spiritual patients the way to the great Healer by means of the 'heavenly apothecary'. Hence in pietistic circles lay preachers were seen predominantly as true pastors, and many professional theologians as blind guides. The woman in Rotterdam at the start of my article, who pictured her minister as a quack, in more than one way is a case in point.

Conclusion

The relationship between early modern religion and medicine was not restricted to the Christian vision of man and thought about soul and body. It extended to the social and cultural contexts of professional activity. *Medicinae doctores* are comparable to *ministri divini verbum*, and surgeons and medical specialists to catechizers and comforters of the sick. Where healers conformed to medical science and to regular practices, lay preachers were more or less loyal to orthodox theology and church order. These corresponding factors legitimate my introduction of the 'pastoral market' as an analogy of the 'medical market'.

Of course, it is not my aim to propose only the term or the model, or even the metaphor or the comparison as such. Projecting a modern economical concept on early-modern culture and society cannot be done without frictions. Yet virtual market-thinking can help to understand relations between individuals, groups and institutions in the complex fields of faith and health and to clarify their historical development. Moreover, it helps to understand the context in which religious belief is connected with religious ritual both in public and private devotions. In that respect, the pastoral market reveals certain dynamics of the interplay between piety and its practices and instruments.

2nd section

Weapons of Redemption:

Piety, Poetry and the Instruments of the Passion in Late Medieval Ireland

Salvador Ryan

Perhaps at no other time in history has the theme of Christ's passion and death more confidently occupied the devotional stage than during the later Middle Ages in Europe, when it became the 'great preoccupation of souls'.[174] The increased emphasis which new religious orders such as the Franciscans put on the practice of affective devotion (mental and emotional involvement with the person of Christ in the various situations in which he found himself, sympathy with his pain, hardship, suffering etc.) necessitated the production of suitable material on which and by which the devotee could meditate. Works such as Johannes de Caulibus's *Meditationes Vitae Christi*, St. Bridget of Sweden's *Revelationes* and, most famously perhaps, St. Thomas à Kempis's *Imitatio Christi* responded to this trend. With the arrival of print in the 15th century, works such as these could be more widely distributed. Similarly, the development of passion iconography, which depicted in increasingly graphic detail the extent of Christ's sufferings, became more accessible by means of the use of woodcuts, whereby small, cheap images and engravings could be produced for the mass market and sold cheaply at locations such as popular pilgrimage sites, often carrying with them the promise of pardon from sin for those who gazed at them with love and with sorrow.[175] Images which were once

---

174 Mâle, Émile: *L'art religieux de la fin du moyen âge en France*. 7th ed. Paris 1995, p. 87.

175 Lewis, Flora: 'Rewarding devotion: indulgences and the promotion of images'. *The Church and the Arts*. Diana Wood (ed.). Oxford 1992, pp. 179-94.

the preserve of the wealthy who were able to afford to commission lavish Books of Hours also became more widely accessible (albeit in inferior reproductions) in the late 15th and early 16th centuries when these devotional objects moved downmarket.[176] By the close of the Middle Ages, therefore, depictions of elements relating to the passion of Christ, which were once the preserve of church architecture and furnishings, lavish tombs and expensive Books of Hours had become the popular currency of devotion. The development and elaboration of passion piety across Europe throughout the later medieval period was reflected with surprising clarity at the very peripheries of the continent, as in the case of Ireland.[177]

One of the most instantly recognizable features to be found on images relating to the passion from this period is the range of what have become known as the 'instruments of the passion' or the *Arma Christi*.[178] These 'instruments' might be understood as the 'props' of the passion story, i.e. the various symbols connected with the story of Christ's condemnation, torture and crucifixion. Variously, they consisted of the cross, the spear or lance which pierced Christ's side, the scourges, pincers, nails, hammer, ladder, crown of thorns, dice, robe and the sponge held on a hyssop stick. The flagellation column is also found widely along with ropes, the titulus board (INRI) which was affixed to the cross, the faces of those who spat at Christ, the thirty pieces of silver (or purse) belonging to Judas, the basin in which Pilate washed his hands and the sword and ear of Malchus, the high priest's servant. The choice of symbols did not rely solely on accounts found in the canonical gospels: apocryphal accretions to the passion story such as the handkerchief of Veronica and the cock and pot from the Gospel of Nicodemus also featured frequently.

Devotion to the instruments of Christ's passion can be traced to the 12th-century crusades and the Sack of Constantinople after which the West became flooded with relics of the passion hitherto unknown.[179] Among the 'new' relics which were discovered by the West were the tools with which the cross of Christ was erected (the ladder, the pincers and hammer) and the dice by which soldiers cast lots for Christ's clothes, which feature prominently among the 'instruments' in late medieval iconography as described above. Irish fascination with the acquisition of new passion relics can be seen in an entry in a native Irish chronicle for 1492:

176 See especially Duffy, Eamon: 'Elite and popular religion: the books of hours and lay piety in the later Middle Ages'. *Elite and popular religion: Studies in Church History 42*. Kate Cooper and Jeremy Gregory (eds.).

177 For a detailed discussion of continental influences on Irish devotion see Ryan, Salvador: *Popular religion in Gaelic Ireland, 1445-1645*. PhD thesis, National University of Ireland Maynooth 2002, 2 vols., volume 1, chapter 1.

178 For Irish examples see Roe, Helen M.: 'Instruments of the Passion: notes towards a survey of their illustration and distribution in Ireland'. *Old Kilkenny Review* 2:5. Kilkenny 1988, pp. 527-34.

179 Schiller, Gertrud: *Iconography of Christian art*. trans. J. Seligman, 2 vols. London 1972, ii, p. 190.

A portion of the wood of the Holy Cross was found in Rome, buried in the ground i.e. the board that was over the head of the Cross on which was written Jesus Nazarenus Rex Judaeorum and it was found written in the same place that it was St Helena that buried it. The head of the lance with which Longinus wounded the body of Christ was sent to Rome in this year by the sovereign of the Turks.[180]

The rediscovery of such relics and the knowledge of their existence undoubtedly made meditation on the passion a more rewarding experience for many. An Irish translation of the *Meditationes Vitae Christi* text, made in the mid-15th century by a choral canon in Killala, County Mayo, encouraged its audience to:

raise the eyes of your mind now and you will see a band of them thrusting the cross into the ground, and another group preparing a sign and another gang readying a hammer and another crew preparing a ladder and other instruments […][181]

We know that this invitation was taken seriously by many of Ireland's most prominent families. The 16th-century O'Shaughnessy tower house at Ardamullivan, County Galway, for example, devoted a large chamber on its second floor to wall paintings depicting the passion cycle, which have lately been the subject of conservation and research.[182] By helping to bring elaborate images such as these out of the vicinity of the church and into one's home, families such as O'Shaughnessy of Ardamullivan were responding to the preaching of orders such as the mendicant friars which encouraged greater interiority of devotion. Increased interest in passion relics ensured that when important Gaelic Irish families commissioned the compilation of devotional collections in the late 15th and early 16th centuries, the traditional story of the finding of the true cross by St. Helena was a favourite.[183] It was important that these items could be proved to exist and the retelling of the story of the discovery of the cross was used as evidence of its veracity. The rulers of Ulster, Hugh O'Neill and 'Red' Hugh O'Donnell, reputedly visited the famous

---

180   Hennessy, William M. (ed.): *The annals of Loch Cé.* 2 vols. London 1871, reprint Dublin, 1939, p. 1492. For a good introduction to the native Irish annals see Cunningham, Bernadette and Gillespie, Raymond: *Stories from Gaelic Ireland: microhistories from the sixteenth-century Irish annals.* Dublin 2003, pp 13-28.

181   Ó Maonaigh, Cainneach (ed.): *Smaointe beatha Chríost: innsint Ghaeilge a chuir Tomás Gruamdha Ó Bruacháin (fl.1450) ar an Meditationes Vitae Christi.* Dublin 1944, p. 146.

182   Morton, Karena: 'A spectacular revelation: medieval wall paintings at Ardamullivan'. *Irish Arts Review* 18. Dublin 2002, pp. 105-12.

183   For the content of late medieval Irish devotional manuscripts see Ryan, Salvador: 'Windows on late medieval devotional practice: Máire Ni Mháille's "Book of piety" (1513) and the world behind the texts'. *Art and devotion in late medieval Ireland.* Rachel Moss, Colman Ó Clabaigh and Salvador Ryan (eds.). Dublin 2006.

Fig. 1: FitzEustace, Baron of Portlester's tomb, c. 1496. Kildare, New Abbey, Kilcullen. Photo: Edwin Rae, TRIARC, Irish Art Research Centre.

site of Holycross Abbey in County Tipperary in the 1590s to pray at the shrine of the relic of the true cross and to invoke its blessings. When the northern earls fled Ireland for the continent in 1607, it is reported that the head of the lance used by Longinus to pierce Christ's side was shown to O'Neill and his cohort at Rome along with the handkerchief of Veronica.[184] Clearly, avid interest in the tangible elements of the passion story had not waned by the early 17th century.

Representations of the instruments of the passion became increasingly common in Ireland from the 15th century onwards, appearing on wayside crosses, tomb sculpture, as in the FitzEustace, Baron of Portlester's tomb at Kilcullen, *c.* 1496 (Fig. 1), in church decoration and even on vestments and chalices, indicating their wide appeal across ecclesiastical and lay boundaries.

The only Irish wall painting specifically depicting the instruments can be found at the Franciscan friary at Askeaton, County Limerick, where it is located in the friars' dormitory.[185] Its location in the dormitory may hint at a *memento mori* theme for it is around the subject of death that the instruments played their

---

184 Ryan 2002, 'Popular religion', p. 90; Tadgh Ó Cianáin, *The flight of the earls* (1607), ed. Paul Walsh. Dublin 1916, pp 177-79.

185 See O'Farrell, Fergus: 'Passion symbols in Irish church carvings'. *Old Kilkenny Review* 2:5. Kilkenny 1988, pp. 535-41; also Morton, Karena: 'Aspects of image and meaning in Irish medieval wall paintings'. *Art and devotion in late medieval Ireland.* Rachel Moss, Colman Ó Clabaigh and Salvador Ryan (eds.). Dublin 2006.

Fig. 2: Tomb of Piers Butler and Margaret Fitz-gerald. West end of south side. Kilkenny, St. Canice's cathedral. Photo: Edwin Rae, TRI-ARC, Irish Art Research Centre.

most prominent role, appearing frequently on 16th-century Irish monumental tomb sculpture. The tomb of Piers Butler, 8th Earl of Ormond and his wife, Margaret Fitzgerald c.1539, which is to be found in St. Canice's cathedral, Kilkenny, is a good example. The south side panel has a crucifixion scene at the centre. On the left hand side is the indented Butler coat of arms, with Ormond inscribed above it. On the right is a depiction of Christ bound to the column, with a shield bearing the instruments of the passion (in effect, Christ's 'coat of arms'). The instruments include the spear, crown of thorns, robe, hammer, pincers, scourges, nails and dice (Fig. 2).[186]

A later tomb chest, that of Richard Butler, Viscount Mountgarrett (1571), also in St. Canice's cathedral, carries a shield with the indented coat of Butler arms between the letters R and B. On the right hand side of the slab the instruments of the passion are featured, including the scourging pillar, robe, scourges, ladder, cup on pole, hammer, pincers, heart surrounded by the crown of thorns through which two daggers run.[187] Other depictions of the instruments are simpler in style, as in the case of the tomb of unknown Butler knights dating from the first half of the 16th century (Fig. 3). The instruments here appear on two shields, the first showing the cross, ladder, column and scourges and the second the robe and dice. Perhaps the sum of the numbers that appear on the three dice is significant: six, four and five make fifteen, a number which was traditionally associated with the pains or sorrows of Christ's passion.[188]

186 See Hunt, John: *Irish medieval figure sculpture 1200-1600: a study of Irish tombs with notes on costumes and armour.* 2 vols. Dublin 1974, i, p. 188; ii, pl. 285.

187 Hunt 1974, pl. 299.

188 Ryan 2002, pp. 95-100.

Fig. 3: Tomb of unknown Butler knights. First half of the 16ᵗʰ century. Kilkenny, Gowran. Photo: Edwin Rae, TRIARC, Irish Art Research Centre.

Although the parallel drawn between the coat of arms of Butler and that of Christ can be quite readily understood, tomb sculpture, by its very nature, can only partially reveal the significance that the instruments were believed to have at the hour of death. For a greater insight into how these images were interpreted, we must examine another kind of source: bardic religious poetry.

From the 13ᵗʰ to the 17ᵗʰ centuries, families of professional Gaelic Irish poets were hired by Ireland's ruling elite to compose secular praise poetry in their honour and, on occasion, religious verse. Bardic poetry was designed to be recited aloud in public or semi-public settings and the themes that it dealt with needed to be intelligible to both the patron and the larger audience.[189] The religious sentiments expressed in the almost four hundred devotional poems that survive reflect not merely insular religious concerns but, more often and more widely, broad European themes. There was a sense in which the patron may have wished to demonstrate that he was *au fait* with the very latest continental devotional fashions. Among the many subjects dealt with in bardic religious verse, the instruments of the passion or the *Arma Christi* loom large, particularly in later 15ᵗʰ and 16ᵗʰ century compositions. It is here that the meaning behind many of the tomb sculptures bearing the instruments can be grasped.

189 For a more comprehensive introduction to bardic religious poetry see Ryan, Salvador: 'A slighted source: rehabilitating Irish bardic religious poetry in historical discourse'. *Cambrian Medieval Celtic Studies* 48, Winter. Wales 2004, pp. 75-99.

Accounts of Christ's passion and death in late medieval bardic poetry borrow heavily from a variety of Christian apocryphal, patristic and literary traditions, creating an impressive, but often quite complex montage. Christ's journey towards his passion and death is variously described as a war against the devil and against humanity which has entered into a pact with him. The idea of Christ going to war against the devil to reclaim territory that was once his own (the world and its people), which appears in many bardic poems, has its roots in the second half of the first millennium when the crucified Christ was frequently depicted as a victorious warrior who easily defeated his enemy and scooped souls out of Hell to safety. Iconography of the crucifixion scene up to the 11th century thus depicted a self-confident kingly figure rather than an emaciated and tortured one. The 6th-century mosaic of *Christus Miles* in the archiepiscopal chapel at Ravenna attests to the influence of the warrior-Christ image as do the hymns of Venantius Fortunatus (*d.*609) which refer to Christ ruling from the tree (of crucifixion). The famous Anglo-Saxon *Dream of the Rood* text (dating from perhaps as early as the 8th century) depicts Christ as stripping himself for battle and embracing the cross in preparation for combat.[190] The 16th-century Irish bardic poet, Diarmuid Ó Cobhthaigh, borrows from this tradition when he speaks of Christ as 'a young prince set on asserting his right to his inheritance', riding a steed (the cross) and 'paying no heed to death'. Carrying a 'shield of love' in his hands, Christ charges his foes and storms the enemy fort.[191] While the image of the warrior remains, the emphasis is somewhat different, however. From the 12th century onwards, with its increased emphasis on courtly love and chivalry, the image of warrior-Christ gradually evolved into that of lover-knight. The battle scenes remained but the motivation for battle changed. Christ was now depicted as motivated by an intense love for his people.[192] This shift in emphasis accompanied the evolution in styles of passion iconography and meditative treatises, which now began to focus on the horrific physical sufferings of Christ. Muirchertach Ó Cobhthaigh, a kinsman of Diarmuid, captures the image of Christ as princely saviour, suffering victim and ardent lover in the following verses:

> In saving us from our foes' designs he showed a princely valour well worthy of him who was called thy Son; he freed us from our sore chains. When his body's veins tortured him and broke open the door of his heart for his folk they had almost lost the game (of salvation) and no other man came to save them.[193]

---

190 See Woolf, Rosemary: 'Doctrinal influences on the Dream of the Rood'. *Medium Aevum* 27. Oxford 1958, pp. 137-53.

191 McKenna, Lambert (ed.): *Aithdioghluim Dána*, 2 vols. Dublin 1939-40, poem 65, stanza 26; also poem 64, stanzas 15-21.

192 See Woolf, Rosemary: 'The theme of Christ the lover-knight in medieval English literature'. *Review of English Studies* 13. Oxford 1962.

193 McKenna, Lambert (ed.): 'Christ our saviour'. *Studies,* 1949, p. 188, stanza 32.

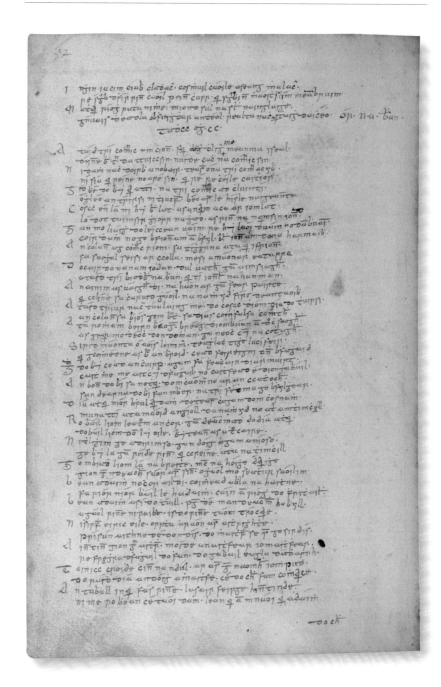

Fig. 4: Bardic poem from the Book of O'Gara' (1655-59), p. 59. Royal Irish Academy Ms 23 F 16. I wish to thank Dr. Rachel Moss of TRIARC and the staff at the Royal Irish Academy for their assistance in providing me with the images to this article.

When referring to Christ 'opening his heart', Ó Cobhthaigh draws attention to the heart wound of Christ, which was considered to be the most efficacious of the Five Wounds, which were widely invoked by late medieval Christians as symbols of God's love and mercy.[194] Another 16th-century poet, Maolmhuire, son of Cairbre Ó hUiginn, further emphasizes the heroic nature of Christ's foray by stating that he continued fighting despite suffering the most horrific wounds:

> The cross was his steed when he was wounded; there would be nothing strange in a wounded man riding a steed were it not that he was wounded in the heart […]

> No man wounded in the heart could have recovered as Christ did; scarce anyone survives a heart-wound; it was always dreaded.[195]

Here, once again, Christ is depicted as a fearless warrior but the heart-wound refers not just to the physical wound inflicted by the lance of Longinus, according to one popular account of Christ's passion, but also the wound of love inflicted by the human race which has rejected God. Although the secular eulogies composed by the bardic order often described their subjects as braving chest wounds in battle, the reference to Christ's wound was designed to appeal to the sensibilities of audiences who, when assured of Christ's love, would be reduced to copious tears.[196]

The image of Christ as victorious military hero, which had appealed to early medieval warrior societies, encountered some difficulty in the later Middle Ages with its increasing emphasis on a tortured and bloody Christ on the cross. How could one stress Christ's victory in the face of such stark iconography? The answer lay, partly, in the arming of the warrior. In 14th-century Latin allegory, Christ is well equipped when he goes into battle: he has a spear, a shield, a helmet (the crown of thorns), gloves and spurs (the nails in his hands and feet) and rides a horse (the cross).[197] The twist in the allegory is, of course, that far from protecting him (as it might have been expected to do in the early medieval period), the armour is turned against Christ himself. The 16th-century poet, Tadhg Óg Ó Dálaigh, remarks in one poem that nothing but the wounding of God could have

---

194 For devotion to the five wounds in Ireland see Ryan, Salvador: 'Reign of blood: devotion to the wounds of Christ in late medieval Gaelic Ireland'. *Irish history: a research yearbook.* Joost Augusteijn and Mary Ann Lyons (eds.). Dublin 2002, pp. 137-49.

195 *Aithdioghluim Dána* poem 65, stanza 36.

196 For a good example of the use of the heart-wound in secular poetry see McKenna Lambert (ed.): *The book of Magauran.* Dublin 1947, poem 11, stanza 18.

197 Woolf, Rosemary: *The English religious lyric in the Middle Ages.* Oxford 1968, p. 54.

made good the losses to humanity's ranks.[198] The weapons of Christ are depicted in the same poem as leading humanity back to Christ's heart: 'God wished not us to be kept out of his heart; the spear in his breast points the way for us [...]'.[199]

The weapons or arms at his disposal in the battle for victory over sin now become emblazoned upon his standard as the *Arma Christi* and invite those who behold them to literally return to Christ's heart in repentance.

The image of the 'Man of Sorrows' or *Imago Pietatis*, depicting Christ displaying his five wounds to the viewer and surrounded by the instruments of his passion, which appeared frequently in woodcuts that spread from Italy to France and then to England in the 14th century, quickly became popular in Ireland also. Its popularity was linked to the enormous indulgences attached to it for those who recited five paters, five aves and five gloria patris before it.[200] A fine example of this image is located in the Franciscan friary in Ennis, County Clare, dating from the late 15th or 16th century.[201] With the increasing availability of portable images of the 'Man of Sorrows' in the form of small printed sheets, many could respond to the invitation to 'pyteously behoild these Armys Christi', as found in English examples.[202] An English allegory of the 14th and 15th centuries, which was adopted also in Ireland, detailed how Christ brought an end to his war against humanity by the drawing up of a charter of peace.[203] Here the instruments of the passion also had a central role. The parchment on which the charter was written was Christ's skin, the lance or nails functioned as the pen with which it was written, Christ's blood formed the ink, his wounds the letters and his breast or heart-wound was the seal by which it was authorized. A poet visiting the famous medieval Irish pilgrimage site of St. Patrick's Purgatory in the late 16th century reflected on 'the generous testament of love thou didst leave to thy race', proceeding to recall 'the pens that wrote it [...] were the hook-bearing thongs'.[204]

Those who were moved to repentance by images of the wounded Christ surrounded by instruments of his passion sometimes asked to participate in his sufferings as an act of reparation. One poet makes reference to many of the passion instruments when requesting that they be turned against him in order that he might be saved:

198 *Aithdioghluim Dána* poem 71, stanza 17.

199 *Ibid.*, poem 71, stanza 35.

200 See especially Ryan 2002, 'Reign of Blood'.

201 See O'Farrell, Fergus: 'Our Lord's pity in Ennis friary'. *North Munster Antiquarian Journal* 22. 1980.

202 Lewis 1992, pp. 179-94.

203 For a more detailed discussion of the Charter see Ryan 2002, 'Popular religion', i, pp 92-5.

204 Leslie, Shane: *St Patrick's Purgatory: a record from history and literature*. London 1932, pp 167-72, stanzas 18-19.

May the scourges drawing thy blood in full streams over thee draw my blood too, living and streaming.

May I be an anvil struck by the hammers that struck thee; may they crush my body's vigour when I am cast out into misery owing to thy misery.

May also the pincers that seized thy flesh bite me and tear the tender part of each of my limbs, so that my sin's pardon may be assured.

May the points of the pricking thorn-spikes be (as) hooks tearing my skull and gnawing it, O Christ, so that at this thy fierce anger may relent.

The points piercing his head, the spike in his feet, the spear in his breast, the nail in his hands – may these wound me, O God, though my wound is small payment for thy blood.

May I bear my cross with thee; may I drink of thy draught of gall; may I join in that banquet with thee, though its drinking be bitter to me.[205]

This approach is reminiscent of that found in Jacopone da Todi's famous 13th-century hymn *Stabat Mater dolorosa*, which requests that the devotee be pierced through and that every wound of Christ be renewed in his heart.[206] This hymn became widely popular in the 14th and 15th centuries. Such sentiments arose perhaps from a fear that if contrition and penance were not willingly embraced in this life the instruments of the passion would be turned against the sinner in a far more ominous manner after death. Irish bardic poets certainly feared the vengeance of Christ on judgment day towards those who did not avail of his mercy. While both the five wounds of Christ and the instruments of his torture could be profitably invoked by sinners on this earth, these very symbols of redemption could become heralds of perdition later on. The late 16th-century Clare poet, Domhnall, son of Dáire Mac Bruaideadha, appears anxious when he remarks 'We should fear too the flashing reddened spear, tempered in the Lord's blood, and the rope that dragged out his bright arms so that neither of them was left unwounded'.[207] The 15th-century poet, Cormac Ruadh Ó hUiginn, likewise feared retribution on account of humanity's part in the crucifixion in the words

---

205 *Aithdioghluim Dána*, poem 92, stanzas 12-17.
206 Blume, Clemens and Dreves, Guido Maria (eds.): *Analecta hymnica medii aevi*. Leipzig, 1886-1922, 54, p. 312.
207 *Aithdioghluim Dána*, 58, v. 21.

'My share in the spear through his heart I have not requited; may Mary pray to her nursling for me, saving me from that spear'.[208] Laoiseach Mac an Bhaird, who composed in the 16th -century also noted that on the Day of Judgment 'his cross will make his crowded folk anxious; he will display it to the world'.[209] Others were not as pessimistic in their outlook. Maolmhuire, son of Cairbre Ó hUiginn listed the ways in which some of the instruments of the passion would help him to attain Heaven:

> I was even helped by the spear, which the Blind Man [Longinus] drove
> into Christ's breast; Christ thought the side wound necessary and he was
> not a man to shirk doing all that kin-love required.

> He built Heaven's holy house – eye has not seen its like; with three nails
> Heaven's Lord fortified for us a castle large enough for us all.[210]

Elsewhere, in two separate poems, Diarmuid Ó Cobhthaigh likens the spear that pierced Christ's side to a plough preparing the soil for new seeds of life and also an oar by which humanity is rowed to safety out of dangerous waters.[211] The 16th -century poet, Muirchertach Ó Cionga, also asserts that 'the lance, a shaft from vine stock, was able to avert stern justice'.[212]

Clearly, the distinction between the instruments of the passion as symbols of redemption and tools of condemnation was in the eye (or rather, heart) of the beholder in much the same way as is found in the five wounds devotion where the blood of Christ could alternatively provide a refuge for the repentant and a deluge for the obstinate.[213] Bardic poetry provides a valuable insight into how these instruments were perceived by various individual poets and/or their patrons. It also explains why the instruments of Christ's passion appear so frequently on tomb sculpture. Those who commissioned such works clearly wished to place their trust in the saving power of Christ's passion and death before they arrived before the judgment of God. Many had already done so during life while gazing at images of the 'Man of Sorrows' in their churches or, privately, at home in cheap woodcut reproductions or in Books of Hours. Believing in the promises attached, many who could afford to do so, wished to provide for a permanent testament of

---

208 McKenna, Lambert (ed.): *Dán Dé*. Dublin 1922, poem 22, stanza 38.
209 *Aithdioghluim Dána* poem 55, stanza 9.
210 *Ibid.*, poem 77, stanzas 9 and 15.
211 *Ibid.*, poem 65, stanza 30; poem 63, stanza 35.
212 *Ibid.*, poem 60, stanza 13.
213 See especially Ryan 2002, 'Reign of blood', pp. 144-6.

that belief in stone on their tombs, identifying themselves as having had recourse to these instruments of salvation during life, hopeful that this would provide for their safe delivery through death.[214]

214 For more on stone sculpture in late medieval Ireland see Moss, Rachel: 'Permanent expressions of piety: the secular and the sacred in later medieval stone sculpture'. *Art and devotion in late medieval Ireland*. Rachel Moss, Ó Colman Clabaigh and Salvador Ryan (eds.). Dublin 2006.

Looking at the Mystery of the Incarnated God:

Eastern and Western Iconography as a Source of Theological Reflection

Peter De Mey

The Resurrection Icon Lends Itself to Contemplation of God's Universal Will for Salvation

I shall begin by considering an icon that symbolises the descent into hell, although the Latin designation *descensus ad infernos* speaks of Christ's sojourn in the underworld, the realm of the dead, in a more neutral sense. I 'see' in this icon a confirmation of the universal saving will of God. The question is whether the same connection is made in aesthetical studies of this icon and what contemporary theology teaches on this subject.

For Christians from the West it is perhaps peculiar that an icon known as the *Anastasis* or Resurrection Icon should depict the descent into Hell. According to one tradition, which is not preserved in the Gospels but in the Creed, Jesus descended to the realm of the dead after his death on the cross. There he conquered the power of death and freed its captives. This is however not a complete liberation, because the souls of the departed remain in the realm of the dead until the Resurrection of the Dead on the Last Day. Certainly, the icon also seeks to convey that the unity of Christ's human soul and his divine nature was intact, even though his body was lying in a tomb. Nevertheless, it is not the Christological but rather the soteriological theme that is central – the salfivic meaning of Christ's Resurrection for the whole of humanity.

The *Anastasis* is thus certainly not an illustration of a second-rate theologoumenon, the descent to hell, but rather expresses the message of the Resurrection itself in the double significance of the Resurrection of Christ and the Resurrection of the Dead. That is why, in the icon of the Twelve Great Feasts, this icon is depicted in the centre with the other feasts around it: The four feasts in honour of the Mother of God (the birth of the *theotokos,* the presentation of the *theotokos* in the temple, the Annunciation and the Assumption) and the eight feasts of Christ (the Nativity of the Saviour, the presentation of Christ in the temple, the baptism of Christ, the Transfiguration, Palm Sunday, the Ascension, Pentecost and the Exaltation of the Cross).

Sources of Inspiration for the Iconographer
Previously, the apocryphal Gospel of Nicodemus was one-sidedly referred to as the source of inspiration for the Resurrection Icon. Today the prevailing opinion is that the tradition forming the basis for this icon is much richer. Besides, there are too many differences between the protagonists in the Gospel of Nicodemus and those depicted in the icon to accept that this text is the only source of inspiration. Isaiah and Seth, who occupy a prominent place in the text, are, for example, never depicted in the icon, while King Solomon, who does not appear in the text, indeed appears in the icon. The text, furthermore, makes a distinction between Satan and Hades that the icon does not, but does not mention that Hades is trampled, which is then again depicted in the icon.

The Orthodox Resurrection Icon was inspired by the Scriptures, the liturgy and apocryphal sources.[215] Although notorious as a *locus obscurantissimus,* 1 Pe 3.19-20 makes clear that the Resurrection is even proclaimed to sinners: 'He went and made a proclamation to the spirits in prison, who in former times did not obey.' The biblical foundation of the belief in the descent into hell thus already leaves the possibility of universal salvation open.

Other important sources of inspiration for the Resurrection Icon were undoubtedly liturgical texts. Melito of Sardes testifies in his Easter sermon from the second half of the 2nd century, 'I have freed those condemned and given life to the dead. I awoke those who were buried, vanquished death and triumphed over the enemy. I descended into hell, where I bound the mighty one and raised men up to heaven!' A hymn by Ephraim the Syrian reads, 'Glory to you who came down and plunged into the depths to seek Adam who you freed from Hades in order to lead him into paradise.'

---

215   For this section I rely heavily on Quenot, Michel: *The Resurrection and the Icon.* New York 1997, pp. 73-81.

Texts from the Orthodox Easter liturgy also emphasise that through his Resurrection Christ opened the gates of the underworld. Thus it is sung in the vespers of Holy Saturday, 'Today hell groans and cries aloud: '"My power has been destroyed. I accepted a mortal man as one of the dead; yet I cannot keep Him prisoner, and with Him I shall lose all those over whom I ruled. I held in my power the dead from all the ages; but see, He is raising them all."' The Easter matins reach their climax in the frequent repetition of the sixth century *troparion*, 'Christ is risen from the dead, trampling down death by death, and upon those in the tombs bestowing life.' And the so-called Paschal Canon of John of Damascus (8th century), in the sixth ode, presents events as follows:

> Thou didst descend, O Christ to the depths of the earth. Thou didst break the everlasting bars which had held death's captives, and like Jonah from the whale on the third day, Thou didst arise from the grave. O my Savior, as God Thou didst bring Thyself freely to the Father, a victim living and unsacrificed, resurrecting Adam, the father of us all, when Thou didst arise from the grave.

Besides the liturgical texts, the iconographers undoubtedly found inspiration in the apocrypha and in the views of the church fathers. A good example is the following catechesis by Cyril of Jerusalem (313-387):

> Death was afraid when it saw this New Man descending unfettered into hell. Why does the sight of him make you afraid, o guardian of hell? What unwonted fear has come upon you? Death has fled and this flight only betrays its fear. The holy Prophets come to meet him, Moses, the Law-Giver, Abraham, Isaac, Jacob, David, Solomon, Isaiah, and John the Baptist, the witness who had asked: "Are you the one who is to come or should we await another?" He redeemed all the righteous ones that death had swallowed up … Then all the righteous said: "O Death, where is your victory? Hell, where is your sting? The Conqueror has set us free!

The apocryphal Gospel of Nicodemus, which also bears the name The Acts of Pilatus, is from a later date (5th-6th century). The second part thereof describes Christ's descent into hell. The following is a particularly striking quotation:

While Satan and Hades were speaking thus to one another, there sounded a loud voice like thunder: "Lift up your gates, O rulers, and be lifted up, O everlasting doors, and the King of glory shall come in." When Hades heard this, he said to Satan: Go out, if you can, and withstand him. So Satan went out. Then Hades said to his demons: Close the bronze gates tightly, set the iron bars, double the locks, and maintain a constant watch. For if He enters here, He will become our Master. When the forefathers heard that, they all began to mock him, saying: "O all-devouring and insatiable one, open, that the King of glory may come in." The bronze gates were broken in pieces and the bars of iron were snapped; and all the dead who were bound were loosed from their chains, and we with them. And the King of Glory entered like a man, and all the dark places of Hades were illumined. Then the King of Glory seized the chief ruler, Satan, by his head and handed him over to the angels, saying: Bind his hands and his feet and his neck and his mouth with iron fetters. The King of Glory stretched out his right hand and took hold of our forefather Adam and raised him up. Then He turned to the rest and said: Come with me, all you who have suffered death because of the tree which this man touched. For behold, I raise you all up again through the tree of the cross.

The Message of the Icon

How is the motif of the decent into hell visually portrayed by the iconographer?[216]

The Lord of Life reveals himself, bathed in light, to the dead, just as he had shown his solidarity with the living during his earthly life. He does it by penetrating the depths of the underworld, where only darkness rules. The mandorla makes it clear that Christ enters the realm of the dead not as a human being but as the Glorified One. Part of Christ's long gown waves in the direction of heaven, to where he will lead the departed. The descent carries the beginnings of the Ascension within it. With his feet, Christ flattens the gates of hell.

When Christ takes Adam firmly by the hand, the raising of Adam becomes symbolic of the raising of all the saved. Adam's sleeve is sometimes portrayed as being lighter than the rest of his clothing and his hand is usually depicted within the mandorla. Christ's touch, after all, constitutes the beginning of Adam's sanctifi-

216 For some excellent studies of this icon see: Schulz, Hans J.: 'Die Anastasis-Ikone als Erlösungsaussage und Spiegel des sakramentalen Christusmysteriums'. *Der Christliche Osten 36 (1981)*, pp. 3-12, 39-46 and by the same author: 'Die "höllenfahrt" als "Anastasis"'. *Zeitschrift für Katholische Theologie 81 (1959)*, pp. 1-66 and Kartsonis, Anna D.: *Anastasis. The Making of an Image*. Princeton 1986.

Fig. 1: Christ's Descent into Hell, Beginning of the 16ᵗʰ century, Ikonen-Museum Recklinghausen.

cation, but not yet his complete salvation. After Christ's descent, death remains part of life, but he becomes a passover, a crossing, a means of reaching new life. Before the definitive achievement thereof, is the waiting for Christ's Second Coming.

Eve is either placed on the same side as Adam, who alone is taken by the hand, or on the other side, in which case Christ takes both by the hand. Sometimes Eve lifts her hands, partly concealed in the folds of her cloak, modestly upwards. This humble gesture of welcome harks back to a custom of the Byzantine court, where those of lower status had to conceal their hands in the presence of their rulers as a sign of submission. Nevertheless, Eve's presence as the only woman is virtually constant in the iconography of the *Anastasis*. She is thus the mother of all the living. Because she was seduced, her responsibility for original sin was deemed less weighty by the church fathers than that of Adam. It is thus normal that she, like Adam, should participate in the Resurrection.

Aside from Adam and Eve, a number of other Old Testament figures or deceased contemporaries of Jesus are also portrayed in the icon. Some are identifiable. Abel, as the first victim of human iniquity, is a prefiguration of Jesus' sacrifice on the cross. John the Baptist, by baptising Jesus and pointing him out as the Lamb of God, prefigured the sacraments of Baptism and the Eucharist. Family ties with Christ are given as an explanation for the almost constant presence of David and Solomon. Even the *Anastasis*, an outstanding portrayal of Christ's divinity, contains in this way a reference to Christ's humanity.

Death can be depicted in various ways. Sometimes it is an old man lying submissively under Christ's foot. At others, in place of this figure, just the broken gates to the underworld are shown, or their locks and keys. And sometimes, the observer only gets to see the complete darkness of the underworld. In Western portrayals and Eastern portrayals of a later date it is emphasised that the realm of the dead is a place of torment and punishment.

Finally, on the icon there are usually two rocks visible. The Resurrection of Christ, according to the tradition, is concurrent with miraculous natural phenomena such as the shaking of the earth. Due to this, the original monolith broke in two.

On the basis of the depiction of the *Anastasis* alone, we can neither deny nor affirm that God will save the whole of humanity at the end of time. Therefore, further theological reflection on the significance of Jesus' salvific acts appears necessary.

What do Eastern and Western Theologians have to say about the connection between the descent into hell and the deliverance of the whole of humanity?
In Western theology, it is especially Hans Urs von Balthasar and Jürgen Moltmann who devote attention to this topos.[217] Moltmann does this, firstly, in his principal

---

217 For further literature on this topic see a.o.: Connell, Martin F.: 'Descensus Christi ad Inferos: Christ's Descent to the Dead', *Theological Studies* 62. Washington D.C. (2001), pp. 262-282 and Herzog, Markwart: 'Descensus ad inferos: eine religionsphilosophische Untersuchung der Motive und Interpretationen mit besonderer Berücksichtigung der monographischen Literatur seit dem 16. Jahrhundert'. (*Frankfurter theologische Studien*, 53). Frankfurt 1997.

work on Christology.[218] For this theologian the descent into hell of the Second Person of the Trinity makes it clear that God himself revealed himself to the dead. This mythological scene indicates, according to him, that death cannot call a halt to the universal love of God. The dead too may henceforth know themselves 'in Christ', but the eschatological constraint compels him to underline that the end of the dominion of death will only occur with the definitive return of Christ. For this reason, Moltmann raises this subject anew in his primary eschatological work.[219] In his suffering and death, he argues, 'Christ suffered the true and total hell of God-forsakeness for the reconciliation of the world.' His work of salvation forms the foundation upon which we can trust, 'that nothing will be lost but that everything will be brought back again and gathered into the eternal kingdom of God.' Formulated as a thesis, 'The true Christian foundation for the hope of universal salvation is the theology of the cross, and the realistic consequence of the theology of the cross can only be the restoration of all things'. The definitive end of the world will certainly be accompanied by a judgement, but, thanks to Christ's death on the cross, it will not be terrible: 'It is a source of endlessly consoling joy to know, not just that the murderers will finally fail to triumph over their victims, but that they cannot in eternity even remain the murderers of their victims'. While Moltmanns's theological imagination connects the descent into hell with faith in a universal reconciliation, the Catholic theologian Von Balthasar, in his contemplation of Holy Saturday, is more conscious of the limitations of theological imagination. In his opinion, one ought to find a middle-way between a literal interpretation of Christ's descent into hell – Christ underwent, in his opinion, a *Gang zu den Toten*, not a descent into hell – and a radical demythologising of it that would lead to the rejection of the theologoumenon. This piece of tradition reveals important insights, such as the solidarity of the Crucified One with all the dead. Because the Son of God experienced the reality of death, the dead cease to be without hope. The significance of the salvation that is offered through Jesus' encounter with the realm of the dead may however not be objectified.

Von Balthasar warns us not to derive any systematic theory about universal salvation from expressions of Christian piety, even though they may be legitimate in themselves, such as those specifically represented in the Orthodox Resurrection Icon. Furthermore, for his tastes, the triumph of the Pascal events in this icon is too strongly anticipated by inserting it into the reality of Holy Saturday:

---

218 Moltmann, Jürgen: *The Way of Jesus Christ. Christology in Messianic Dimensions.* London 1990.

219 See especially the section on 'Christ's Descent into Hell and the Restoration of All Things' in Moltmann, Jürgen: *The Coming of God: Christian Eschatology.* London 1996, pp. 250-255.

The dramatic portrait of the experience of triumph, of a joyful encounter between Jesus and the prisoners, and in particular between the new Adam and the old, is not prohibited as a form of pious contemplation, but it does go beyond what theology can affirm. It is here most particularly that the exigence for system-building must be checked. Otherwise it would move forward unhindered to the construction of a doctrine of apokatastasis.[220]

Faith in universal salvation likewise has its advocates and opponents in Orthodox theology. John Meyendorff is himself well aware of the limitations of theological imagination:

Byzantine theologians seldom devote much explicit attention to speculation about the exact fate of souls after death. The fact that the Logos assumed human nature as such implied the universal validity of redemption, but not the *apokatastasis*, or universal salvation, a doctrine which in 553 was formally condemned as Originistic. Freedom must remain an inalienable element of every man, and no one is to be forced into the Kingdom of God against his own free choice; the *apokatastasis* had to be rejected precisely because it presupposes an ultimate limitation of human freedom – the freedom to remain outside of God.[221]

A contemporary Orthodox advocate of the belief in the salvation of all is Bishop Kallistos Ware, who turns to tradition to support this belief.[222] First, this theologian considers the thinking of Origen. Origen was himself very well aware of the speculative character of eschatology, the theological discussion of the final future with God. Only with a lot of hesitation was he prepared to make any pronouncements in this regard. His belief in universal salvation was above all based on 1 Cor 15.28: 'When all things are subjected to him, then the Son himself will also be subjected to the one who put all things in subjection under him, so that God may be all in all'. However, this is not about an undertaking characterised by necessity, which would not do justice to human freedom. At the same time, Origen does not want to deny God the possibility of punishing people. It is,

220 My translation from von Balthasar, Hans Urs: 'Mysterium Paschale'. *Mysterium salutis: Grundriss heilsgeschichtlicher Dogmatik*, vol. III/2. Einsiedeln, Benziger 1969, pp. 254-255 (part of a larger section on 'Der Gang zu den Toten' pp. 227-255). For an English summary of Balthasar's view, see his article on 'The Descent into Hell'. *Chicago Studies* 23 (1984), pp. 223-236.

221 Meyendorff, John: *Byzantine Theology. Historical Trends and Doctrinal Themes*. New York 1974, p. 163.

222 Ware, Kallistos: 'Dare We Hope for the Salvation of All? Origen, St Gregory of Nyssa and St Isaac the Syrian'. *The Inner Kingdom* (The Collected Works, 1). Crestwood N.Y. 2000, pp. 193-215.

nevertheless, his conviction that God's punishment will be therapeutic and will come to an end when purification has occurred. Ware asks, moreover, whether the condemnation that was pronounced in the margins of, rather than during, the Fifth Ecumenical Council does not have more to do with the fact that Origen tied his eschatological vision to the belief in the pre-existence of souls than to his views on universal salvation as such. Another church father Gregory of Nyssa, who opposed Origen's speculations on the state of the soul before the beginning of creation but shared his belief in the eventual restoration of the cosmos, was after all not condemned. Ware calls attention to yet a third universalist, Isaac the Syrian, who is convinced that the pain of those in hell consists of the understanding that they have rejected the love of God. God lets them experience pain out of love and has thus not broken all ties with the punished. Furthermore, at the end of time, his endless mercy will put an end to their pain, because 'love no flood can quench' (Song of Songs 8.7). His consideration of the tradition brings Kallistos Ware to the following conclusion:

> Our belief in human freedom means that we have no right to categorically affirm, "All *must* be saved." But our faith in God's love makes us dare to *hope* that all will be saved.[223]

I believe that the distinction that the British Catholic theologian James Alison makes between apocalyptic and eschatological imagination can offer us a way out of the one-upmanship in the arguments pro and contra that we have heard. Alison values the qualification that is made by Hans Urs von Balthasar, but believes that contemporary theology must defend the possibility that hell will turn out to be empty. The classical vision of the definitive separation of the sinners and the righteous on the day of judgement continues the spiral of violence. In his opinion, a theologian should cultivate an eschatological imagination rather than an apocalyptic. That implies an acceptance of the idea of universal salvation, but 'not as a system', rather as 'a story already told, with its beginning, its moment of high drama, and its happy ending'.[224] 'Would God that Origen's profound intuition turns out to be right, and that at the end all manner of things are well for everybody and that even the most obstinate of Cains have learned to accept the forgiveness of our Abels. But there is a great difference between hoping in this possibility and suppressing hope by taking it for granted'.[225]

---

223 Ware 2000, p. 215.

224 Alison, James: *Raising Abel. The Recovery of the Eschatological Imagination.* New York 1996, p. 175.

225 Alison 1996, p. 177.

The Isenheimer Altar Lends Itself to Contemplation of the Significance of Salvation History

Christians believe that God's relationship with humanity is not arbitrary, but rather proceeds according to a specific plan. From the moment of Creation, God entered into a covenant with humanity. He continuously invited human beings to the good, but in the light of human failing God decided, at the high point of salvation history, to completely reveal himself in the form of his Son. Through his undeserved death, the power of death was definitively broken so that we too could be granted hope in eternal life. In an era in which doubts about grand narratives are taking root, questions often arise concerning the legitimacy of theological discourse on salvation history. Fortunately there exist timeless artworks in which the coherence of salvation history is displayed and defended. In the second part of this contribution, I dwell upon the the Isenheimer Altar by Matthias Grünewald and its theological significance.

Some Background to the Artist, the Artwork and the Patrons
On the artist, we can be brief. He left very few traces, which is strange for an artist from the periods of the Renaissance and Humanism. There is even doubt as to his identity.[226] One researcher found details about a certain Mathis Gothart Neithardt who he identifies with Grünewald, another is convinced that there lived two artists in the same period, Nithart and Grünewald. People employ a margin of ten years – from 1470 to 1480 – to define his birth date in Würzburg. The oldest painting that has been preserved is a Crucifixion that he produced in 1502 for a patron in Basel. It would remain his favourite theme. For the largest part of his life, between 1505 and 1526, he resided in Aschaffenburg. A document from 1505 mentions the fact that he was working there as a master. From 1511 he worked in the service of the court of the archbishop of Mainz that was established in this town. Now and then he took on other commissions. One of these, the realisation of the Isenheimer Altar, took up the whole period from 1512 to 1516. It is not impossible that in 1520 Grünewald accompanied his master to the crowning of Charles V in Aachen, as it is mentioned in the travel journal of Albrecht Dürer. In the year 1526 he possibly went into voluntary exile in the free city of Frankfurt. After all, people wanted to condemn everybody from the archbishop's entourage who had sympathised with the Peasants' Revolt of 1525, and Grünewald had supposedly also done so. At least, the inventory of goods

---

226 Eloï Leclerc wrote a spiritual novel on the enigmatic painter. See Leclerc, Eloï: *La nuit est ma lumière: Matthias Grünewald*. Paris 1994. See also the interesting section on 'Grünewald: histoir d'une identité perdue'. Pantxika Béguerie and Georges Bischoff: *Grünewald, le maître d'Issenheim*, Townai, 1996, pp. 64-74.

that he gave to his adopted son testifies to this. Among other things, this included the so-called Twelve Articles from the creed of the peasants, sermons and a bible translation by Luther. Whether this could indicate that at the end of his life he was sympathetic to the Reformation cannot be deduced from his major work, in which so much attention is paid to Mary. Grünewald died in 1528 in Halle.

When admiring the artwork in the Musée d'Unterlinden in Colmar, it is important to be well aware of the originally intended position. The artwork formed the high altar for the church of a hospital for plague victims that was connected to the monastery of the regular canons of the Antonite Order in Isenheim. This order was founded in 1095 and, in Grünewald's time, widely distributed in Europe. The wealthy monastery of Isenheim, about twenty-five kilometres south of Colmar in Alsace, was the motherhouse of the German province of the order. For most of the liturgical year, the people who suffered from so-called St. Anthony's Fire and who had to attend the liturgy at a safe distance from the uninfected worshippers, were only able to see the closed altarpiece, which was raised metres high above the altar and depicted the crucified Christ. From the sight of his enormous suffering, the sick could draw comfort. People also became aware of their own sinfulness and the salvation made possible by Christ's Crucifixion.

During the Christmas and Easter cycles the worshippers got another view of the altarpiece to look at, in which the joyful mysteries of the Annunciation of God's intention to save humanity, the Incarnation and the Resurrection are portrayed.

From this second position, by opening the middle panel again and flipping the predella upwards, the altarpiece could be presented in still a third position. This happened during the octave of the feast of the order's founder. Now, some scenes from the life of the desert father St. Anthony, the driving force of the Antonite Order, were made visible. The message that this sends is that participation by the faithful in salvation history implies more than gratitude for Jesus' Incarnation, death and Resurrection. It also asks for imitation of and sharing in Christ's suffering. The dominant position that St. Anthony receives in the altarpiece is in my opinion not coincidental. In his life, Christian salvation history is concretised.

The advantage of the current position of the altarpiece in the museum is that the entire dynamics of salvation history are shown, unlike in its original position in the church where only the crucifixion scene was visible for most of the year. The great 20th century theologian Karl Barth, who refers to this work several times in his oeuvre, admitted at the end of his life that under the influence of, among other things, this work, he developed, perhaps even too one-sidedly, a theology of the cross and therefore suggests that images should rather always remain sub-

ordinate to preaching: 'We need make no images. However, when one nevertheless chooses in favor of an image, then that of the humiliated Son of Man. I was
at the time very much impressed by the Crucifixion by Grünewald. But perhaps
certain errors in my *The Epistle to the Romans* were caused by Grünewald. I would
not install that picture in a church. It would not be good for the congregation,
because the Resurrected One is not visible in Grünewald's piece. The Humiliated
One is actually also the Raised. For that reason alone, an image is not advisable,
because it cannot be complete'.[227]

With which sources did the artist inspire himself during the creation of his
artwork?[228] For the scenes from the life of St. Anthony he most probably inspired himself with the so-called *Legenda aurea*, a compilation of the lives of the
saints from the Middle Ages. In the literature, the possibility is also suggested
that Grünewald was influenced by the mystical visions of St. Birgitta of Sweden,
which were first published in German in Nuremburg in 1502. Birgitta, who lived
from 1303 to 1373, received a vision shortly before her death from the archangel
Gabriel in the church of St. Lawrence at the House of Damasus in Rome, a hymn
of praise to Mary that is still known as the *Sermo angelicus*.

The Message of the Artwork

I now want to examine the three ways of viewing the altarpiece and the representation of salvation history that these contain.

Those who look at the altarpiece in its closed position, spontaneously focus
their attention on the Crucified One, the depiction of whom dominates most of
the middle panel. The suffering of the Crucified One is reproduced with incredi-
ble realism, with a disfigurement of the feet like that seen in cases of St. Anthony's
Fire. The tableau of the Crucifixion has a pitch-black sky, without moon or stars,
as a background. The only other colours that break it up are the red cloaks of the
apostle John and John the Baptist and the white of the inscription on the cross,
the torn loincloth, the Lamb of God, the Baptist's book and Mary's cloak.

With this, three of the four other figures on the middle panel have already
been introduced.

On the right stands John the Baptist, who pointed to the coming of Christ
and identified him as the Saviour. It is also written in the book that he holds
in his hand, 'He must become greater and I smaller'. His presence indicates that

---

227 See Marquard, Reiner: *Karl Barth und der Isenheimer Altar (Arbeiten zur Theologie)*, Stuttgart 1995, p.
     59.

228 In the book by Nyssen, Wilhelm: *Choral des Glaubens. Meditationen zum Isenheimer Altar*. Freiburg
     im Breisgau 1983, the mystical texts which allow to be compared with Grünewald's masterpiece
     have been translated.

Fig. 2: The Isenheimer Altarpiece, first position. Musée d'Unterlinden Colmar, photo O. Zimmermann.

after Easter the disciples gradually began to see the salvific significance of this apparently senseless event. Jesus' death on the cross came to be understood as an offering of atonement for our sins, hence the symbolism of the innocent lamb. The blood of the animal is collected in a chalice, as a sign that the Church still commemorates the sacrifice of her Lord. The lamb also carries a victory cross.

On the left stand three figures. In the case of the kneeling Mary Magdalene, her contorted hands are especially striking. From her open mouth comes a lament, as if it were audible. Nevertheless, it is noticeable that earthly beauty still means something to her. Her blond curls hang over her magnificent dress. Perhaps she has the balm with her with which, shortly before, she had anointed the feet of her Lord. The Mother of Jesus, just as her son wrapped in a shroud, seems to follow her son in death and to undergo spiritual death throes. In contrast to Mary Magdalene, the colour has drained from her countenance. Compared with the manner in which the artist portrays her in the Annunciation and Nativity, Mary in her purity is perfectly detached from earthly beauty. The suffering Mary is only held upright by John.

The Crucifixion tableau finds its continuation below, in the predella. The deceased Christ is taken from the cross and mourned by the bystanders. The onlookers gaze at his open wounds, but they realise that an end has come to Christ's suffering. The landscape is a little bit lighter and already allows one to sense something of Easter morning. Indeed, in the bare trees it can be seen that even 'all creation is groaning in labor pains' (Rom 8.22). Mary's sorrow is greater still. Her white headscarf has come down over her eyes. Her hands are contorted from the grief. Mary Magdalene too appears to be in an ecstasy of grief, while John slightly raises the body of his master.

With regard to the two saints on the left and right side panels of this first position, one notices that Grünewald has depicted Abbot Anthony far larger than St. Sebastian. St. Anthony is represented, as the tradition prescribes it, with a cross ending as the Greek letter Tau. St. Sebastian is represented here because during the Middle Ages one believed that he could relief the pains of those suffering from the plague.

The second view of Grünewald's masterpiece depicts the glorious events of salvation history. The middle panel is a diptych, with music-making angels in the temple of the Old Covenant on the left and the birth of the Son on the right, the beginning of the New Covenant. This symbolic representation of the Old and New Covenant is flanked by two side panels. On the left, the Annunciation to Mary is depicted, on the right, the Resurrection. The proclamation of the coming of salvation and the fulfilment of salvation thus frame the Incarnation, which constitutes the beginning of our salvation. Half of the scenes take place in a church building, half of them in the open air.

The commentators differ most in their opinions over the interpretation of the left half of the middle panel. The angels express their joy with their music because God has provided for Mary in his plan for salvation and has thus made the Incarnation possible. Amidst the angels there is a winged being wearing a crown of peacock's feathers. Some interpretations see in this figure in the shadows of the piece, Eve, the ancestress of all the living.[229] Another interpretation sees in it the figure of Lucifer, the fallen angel through whom, according to many medieval theologians, evil came into the world making salvation necessary.[230] His face and hands are painted in the same colours as Christ's dead body in the Crucifixion and the laying in the tomb. The peacock's feathers reflect his arrogant attitude.[231] By depicting Lucifer with a violin, thus allowing him to pay homage to the newborn child, Grünewald alludes to a popular theory concerning salvation. Since the sin of Adam and Eve, Satan had acquired the right to keep all human beings in hell

---

229 Nyssen 1983, pp. 33-35.

230 Mellinkoff, Ruth: *The Devil at Isenheim. Reflections of Popular Belief in Grünewald's Altarpiece*. Berkeley 1988, pp. 19-31.

231 Possibly Grünewald was inspired by the representation by Adam and Eve which Albrecht Dürer realised on copperplate in 1504. For further comments and a picture of Dürer's representation see Béguerie & Bischoff 1996, p. 33.

Fig. 3: The Isenheimer Altarpiece, second position. Musée d'Unterlinden Colmar, photo O. Zimmermann

upon their death. God decided to mislead Satan and to present himself in human form before the gates of hell. Because Satan, who was mistaken about the identity of Christ, assaulted a sinless person, he had to give up his unlimited power.

The most important figure on the left half of the middle panel is depicted in the right bottom corner, near the temple door. The figure is kneeling, but has a halo around its head. Most commentators see Mary in it, as she was foreseen in God's plan for salvation before the creation of the world. She looks almost like a bride, as if she is depicted as the dearest creature, always open to God's plan for salvation.[232] Still, other scholars ask themselves if the occurrence of a double depiction of Mary in the same painting is not an unnecessary complication.[233] Could it not rather be about a personification of the Church? On the threshold of the temple of the Old Covenant, she is the witness to the birth of the Saviour. We see her, as it were, being born out of the temple. Her body is still shrouded in the darkness of the temple, while her head already bathes in the light of the New Covenant. Above the young Church, two angels, barely visible, hold a staff and a tiara. They are the symbols of the triumphant church, which shall only belong to her after the completion of Christ's work of salvation. The crown on the head of this woman also looks a little bit like the flames of Pentecost. In Grünewald's production, the birth of the Saviour is at the same time the birthplace of the Church.

232   Nyssen 1983, pp. 34-35.
233   Mellinkoff 1988, pp. 77-82.

We next consider the panel in which the mother with her child is depicted amidst a renewed creation. As a recollection of Paradise, exactly on the borderline between this panel and the one previously discussed, a pomegranate tree grows heavenward. In the distance, one sees the construction of a small church on a rock. Mary looks like a rose in bloom. Her child has clearly already got a will of his own. He holds in his hands a rosary with large beads. A bridegroom in the German empire gave this to his bride as a gift on the morning of the wedding. The child is thus presented as the bridegroom who comes into the world to get engaged to his bride, Creation. At the same time, Grünewald indicates the future suffering of the child. The gate of a house at the foot of the mountain is shaped like a cross. The baby's clothes are torn indicating the way in which Jesus will be the Messiah.

The three objects that are placed at the bottom of both central panels by the artist, beg explanation. The bathtub could be a reference to the sacrament of baptism, through which all who believe that this child is the Saviour will be saved. The full glass jug on the threshold could contain the holy oil that is added to the water of baptism. In Grünewald's time, people also believed that the anointing with oil protected them against the attacks of the devil. The chamber pot with Hebrew lettering could symbolise the wickedness of those who did not recognize the Saviour, primarily the Jews, as well as the transience of the Old Covenant. Grünewald probably shared his contemporaries' aversion to the Jews, which, among other things, is shown in the order that Kaiser Maximilian I had issued in 1510 to drive the Jews out of Colmar. Here, in a less beautiful way, the humanity of Grünewald's presentation of salvation history reveals itself.[234]

Now, a short observation on the two side panels of this second position. While a nearly invisible dove hovers in the middle of the room, an angel appears to Mary in the panel of the Annunciation. Mary draws back before the radiant apparition, but keeps her ear turned towards the angel. The early church thought for a long time that Mary had received the Word by hearing it. In the open book, Isaiah's prophecy of the Saviour born to a virgin is written (Is 7.14v). In her dark green dress, Mary seems to represent the whole of creation.

In the panel of the Resurrection, the completion of Christ's first coming is depicted. The sleeping guards represent those who do not want to see how the world is already saved. The wonder of the Resurrection is further strengthened by the fact that one of the guards, just like the immense boulder, appears to float. Christ is no longer depicted with his wounded body. Rather, his limbs and countenance are of an unnatural beauty. The wounds on his hands and feet are the last

---

234 Mellinkoff 1988, pp. 59-67.

Fig. 4: The Isenheimer Altarpiece, third position. Musée d'Unterlinden Colmar, photo O. Zimmermann

signs of his humanity, but he is surrounded by a bright halo. The light of heaven transforms the shroud into a robe fit for a feast. The Son presents himself to the Father to show, with his glorified wounds, what he has suffered for the world. Christ is clearly depicted as the Pantocrator who will come again to pronounce his judgement on humankind and the world. The gracious benevolence that radiates from his eyes and the smile with which he looks at creation allow the faithful to look forward to that moment, full of confidence.

The difficult path of being a disciple is ultimately illustrated by means of two scenes from the life of the patron saint, the only panels from the third position that are by Grünewald. In the left scene, Anthony, in his ninetieth year, visits the one hundred and thirteen year old hermit Paul. His shabby dress shows that a Christian should not cling to earthly things. The hermit sits by a life-giving well. The herbs that grow there would be used in treatments against St. Anthony's Fire. Above, the raven is visible, which according to legend brought bread to both of them. Art experts suspect that Grünewald, in the figure of Anthony, depicted the superior of the monastery of Isenheim, Guido Guersi, because his coat of arms is depicted at the foot of the stone on which he sits. Some suspect that the sinewy old man on the right is Grünewald himself. If in the conversation between the two elders about eternal life the peaceful character of salvation is expressed, then the other panel depicting the temptation of St. Anthony conveys the message that the followers of Christ will share in his Passion. The terrible monsters around the abbot represent different vices. Some are attacking his house. In the corner lies someone who looks a lot like one of the plague victims of Isenheim itself. It is true that the glory of the Lord appears in the clouds, but it is a distant apparition, indicating that the world will still be subject to the power of evil for quite some time before the Second Coming of Christ definitively breaks the power of the devil. The face of the abbot is still barely a human face. The saint stands on the verge of succumbing, as is also expressed in the lament on the piece of paper, which is taken from the *Legenda aurea*, 'Where were you, good Jesus, where were you, why were you not there to heal my wounds?' Only if a person, when faced with trials, keeps his eyes directed towards the Son of Man and becomes like him in his Passion, can he know that participation in the suffering of the Lord will lead to participation in his Resurrection. In the laugh of the abbot, it nevertheless becomes clear that he, by the power of his faith, has won the battle against the powers of evil.

Is the Isenheimer Altar more than a Traditional Presentation of Salvation History?
Grünewald has undoubtedly portrayed a classical theological presentation of salvation history. Sometimes the critique is offered against this presentation that there is no room for any form of human involvement in the events of reconciliation.[235] In my opinion the artist has however demonstrated that the Christian faith, on the contrary, promotes active human involvement. The artist certainly does not call into question that salvation is a divine salvific offer in the first place, not a work of humans. Still, in Grünewald's altarpiece, at least an equal emphasis is placed on the human being.

In human existence, suffering is a daily reality. Only on feast-days is the altarpiece opened so that the glorious intervention of God through the Incarnation and Resurrection is visible. During the week, the faithful are only confronted with the realistic depiction of the Crucifixion and a few saints that one can call upon to help to relieve human affliction.

The artwork also pays attention to the importance of the human assent to the divine offer of salvation. The artist is attentive to Mary's joy at the birth of her Son and her untold sorrow at the foot of the cross, in which John and Mary Magdalene also share. When we observe the incongruous picture of John the Baptist pointing to the suffering Jesus as being the Lamb of God, he becomes a model for all believers. Christians are asked to believe in Christ as the Saviour, even if his identity seems to be hidden in the event of the cross.

So too, the representation of Jesus' Resurrection does not exclude us. Bathed in light the Resurrected One shows his wounded hands to those standing before

---

235 This opinion is defended in Wiersinga, Herman: *Geloven bij daglicht. Verlies en toekomst van een traditie.* Baarn, 1992, p. 104.

the altarpiece and looks at each of them personally. Thanks to Christ's Resurrection the believer may hope that eternal life may also become a reality for him or her. The believing viewer is furthermore invited to follow Christ's way of life, as is illustrated in the depiction of Anthony's struggle with the demons.

In the Isenheimer Altar, Matthias Grünewald has negated the main criticism of the Christian account of salvation history by depicting the human person as a full participant in the divine drama of salvation.

Conclusion

In the East as well as the West, the Christian churches in general stimulated the aesthetic expression of the content of the faith. Indeed, Christian art has had catechetical value for centuries. However, it is especially the heart that was and is moved. The artworks that are discussed in this contribution seek to fill the heart of the believer with the hope that God is preparing a future for humanity that surpasses death. The believer knows that he belongs to the human race, which since Adam has needed salvation to come from elsewhere. The situation of need is particularly acute when it involves the suffering person, the Abel of the Resurrection Icon and the Anthony of the tempation scene by Grünewald. The believer also finds consolation in the idea that Jesus himself could only become the Christ, the bringer of salvation, through the cross. It is the Crucified One who breaks the power of death in the Resurrection Icon and the reality of Jesus' suffering and death is nowhere made so clear as in Grünewald's Crucifixion and laying in the tomb. The Crucified One is actually also the Glorified One who takes Adam and Eve, and with them the whole of humanity, by the hand and gives them a future, and who in Grünewald's Resurrection tableau promises each believer in person an everlasting future with God. Through this, the trust of the human being can be so strengthened such that he or she, even in the harshest trials, does not lose his or her good dispostion. Yet perhaps that is only reserved for the saints. The presence of the saints in the Isenheimer Altar nevertheless reminds every believer of the fact that the offer of salvation can only become reality if he or she is prepared to walk in the footsteps of the Saviour. The Christian narrative of salvation, however, insists that salvation is not something to be acquired but remains a divine gift. Could God's love not ultimately touch the heart of every Adam and every Eve of the Resurrection Icon, and even that of the most arrogant fallen angel of the Isenheimer Altar? This was in every sense the message that both of these artworks had in store for the eschatological imagination of this theologian.

Sepolcro:

Musical Devotion of the Passion in 17th-18th Century Austria[236]

Nils Holger Petersen

The aim of this essay is to give a brief introduction to a musical genre intimately tied to the devotions for Holy Week in baroque Vienna. The *sepolcro* was well-defined, geographically, chronologically, and in terms of its devotional context and characteristic features. Above all, it was connected to the Imperial Court in Vienna in the second half of the 17th and the first half of the 18th century. It is my further intention to put the mentioned practices into a larger perspective of music history: Wolfgang Amadeus Mozart (1756-91) grew up in a Salzburg where offshoots of such traditions were still alive; he composed one of his earliest pieces of music drama in such a context. The extent to which such early Salzburg experiences and practices are important for the understanding of his later work – and thus for the understanding of the musical heritage of Mozart – is a matter of interpretation; I shall end this essay with a brief reflection on this question with its implications for the question of the significance of a heritage of medieval rituals for modern music history by way of their baroque receptions and transformations.

236 It is gratefully acknowledged that research for this article has been supported by the *Danish National Research Foundation* which funds the *Centre for the Study of the Cultural Heritage of Medieval Rituals* at which the work has been carried out.

I. The *sepolcro*: a general introduction

The term *sepolcro* – in its modern use – denotes a kind of oratorio written for a staged performance at a replica of a holy sepulchre in connection with a devotional ceremony during Holy Week. In a *sepolcro*, some narrative related to the Passion of Christ – often with a specific theological theme rather than a straightforward representation of (a part of) the biblical Passion narratives – was represented and staged (in costumes) in a church in front of a so-called Easter sepulchre. At the time, several terms could be used for such devotional music dramas (the texts of which were mostly Italian but occasionally German): *sepolcro*, *azione sacra*, *azione sepolcrale*, and *rappresentazione sacra*. The oratorio genre itself had only just developed at the time where this new – related but in certain ways also quite different – practice was initiated at the Viennese Court.

Whereas the oratorio had its origin in the Catholic reform movement of the 16th century in Rome where the Florentine priest Philip Neri (1515-95) founded a confraternity, the *congregazione dell'oratorio* (in English usually referred to as the *Oratorians*), with the general intention to promote devotion through spiritual music, inspired by the religious song of the Florentine confraternities (the so-called *lauda*), the origin of the *sepolcro* is specifically connected to the devotional activities of the Viennese court under Leopold I (1658-1705).[237] In Rome, biblical or biblically inspired musical dialogues in the devotional services of the Oratorians gradually led to the establishing of a particular musical genre of such large-scale spiritual musical works – which in terms of musical means (the so-called *stile rappresentativo* or *recitativo*, the new musical technology developed in the Florentine academies of the last decades of the 16th century) were almost indistinguishable from the opera which developed during the same time first in Florence and then in other Italian cities to become a public genre in Venice a few decades into the 17th century. The word oratorio – the Italian word for prayer hall – became a term for the new genre toward the middle of the 17th century. Oratorios were often performed in connection with preaching at musical devotions. In the early formative period, such works could also be staged and performed in costumes, as it seems to have been the case with one of the first larger music dramatic works performed at the oratory of the Oratorians (in February 1600): Emilio de Cavalieri's *Rappresentatione de anima, et di corpo*. It is a matter of definition whether to regard this devotional music drama as an early oratorio or opera. Neither of the two genres can be said to have been defined at this point although one usually points to courtly music dramas (1598 and 1600) by Jacopo Peri

---

237 Throughout this article, I refer to Smither, Howard E.: *A History of the Oratorio*. Chapel Hill 1977, vol I, esp. Part I, sections ii–iv and Part III, section viii for general information about the early history of the *oratorio* and the *sepolcro* (unless otherwise indicated).

(1561-1633) and Giulio Caccini (1551–1618) as the first 'real' operas. Tradition-ally, opera and oratorio have been treated apart from each other in music history; recent scholarship, however, seems to indicate a closer relationship between the origins of these genres than hitherto generally acknowledged.[238]

In Vienna, the Italian oratorio was also introduced in the mid-17th century. However, the *sepolcro* became a more significant – and moreover specifically Vien-nese – contribution to the history of spiritual music drama. Emperor Leopold I had been educated by Jesuits and – as a child – destined to an ecclesiastical career. However, because of the sudden death of his older brother in 1654, plans were changed and four years later, he became Roman-German emperor for almost half a century. Leopold had been trained musically; he wrote and continued to write music also as an Emperor, he wrote several *sepolcri* himself (see below). Differ-ently from the Italian tradition, the sacred music dramas in Vienna were often directly integrated into liturgical ceremonial during Lent.

In the 17th century, Vienna and the Austrian hereditary lands had become a stronghold for the Counter-Reformation. The Habsburg emperors and their courts had been defenders of the Catholic Church against the Protestants also during the 16th century. However, at the time of Leopold I, the activities of the Counter-Reformation had successfully changed the balance between Protestants and Catholics (not the least through the efforts of the Jesuits) and the reign of Leopold I not only emphasized Catholic beliefs and devotions but also in a more overt political sense constructed itself as a Catholic regime par excellence. The devotional practices at the Imperial court during Holy Week including the men-tioned performances of sacred music dramas at an Easter sepulchre should be seen in the context of other public Imperial devotional practices at this time.[239]

In modern times, only few *sepolcri* have been re-performed (and recorded) although the genre has been generally described and discussed from a music his-

238 See Petersen, Nils Holger: 'Intermedial Strategy and Spirituality in the Emerging Opera: Gagliano's *La Dafne* and Confraternity Devotion'. *Cultural Functions of Interart Poetics and Practice*. Ulla-Britta Lagerroth and Erik Hedling (eds.). Amsterdam 2002, pp. 75-86 as well as Østrem, Eyolf and Pe-tersen, Nils Holger: 'The Singing of *Laude* and Musical Sensibilities in Early Seventeenth-Century Confraternity Devotion'. *Journal of Religious History* 28:3. 2004, pp. 276-97 and 29:2. 2005, pp. 163-76, both giving further references. For a discussion of Cavalieri's *Rappresentatione* as a 'border-line opera', based on a non historical concept of 'opera', see Donington, Robert: *The Rise of Opera*. London 1981, pp. 126-28.

239 See Smither, vol I, pp. 371-73. Concerning the vast amount of Habsburg involvement in public de-votional activities, including the promotion of Eucharist devotions (for instance the so-called forty hours devotion, see below at n. 28), the Marian cult, as well as of new saints with roles concerning National protection and involving pilgrimages to holy sites, public processions, the erection of columns in Vienna and elsewhere in connection with prayers for Divine help against the plague and as an expression of gratitude for such alleged help but also connected to the propagation of the idea of the Habsburg Emperors as champions of the Catholic faith against heresy, see Winkelbauer, Thomas: *Ständefreiheit und Fürstenmacht: Länder und Untertanen des Hauses Habsburg im Konfessionel-len Zeitalter*. von Herwig, Wolfram (ed.): *Teil 2, Österreichische Geschichte, 1522-1699*. Wien 2003, esp. pp. 185-223.

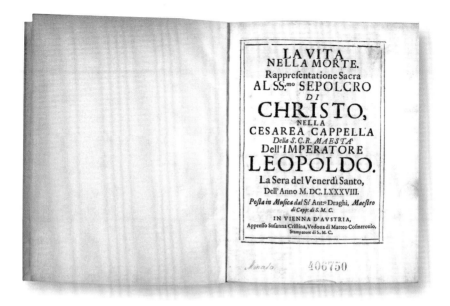

Fig. 1: Front page of the printed libretto for La vita nella morte, by Antonio Draghi. Musiksammlung, Österreichische Nationalbibliothek, Vienna. With kind permission of the Musiksammlung.

torical point of view. To my knowledge, the practice has never been scrutinized as a devotional, liturgical practice and a vast material of such devotional music dramas is still completely unknown today. The *Musiksammlung* of the *Österreichische Nationalbibliothek* in Vienna preserves many scores of *sepolcri*. The main composer during the reign of Leopold I was Antonio Draghi (1635–1700) who was employed variously at the Court since 1658 and from 1682 to his death occupied the highest musical position in Vienna as *maestro di cappella* at Leopold's court. He wrote (at least) forty sacred music dramas (among them 26 *sepolcri*) and many more secular music dramatic works. The main librettist in Vienna at the time was Nicolò Minato or Minati (c.1630–1698).

To give a small impression of the kind of themes met with in the *sepolcri*, I shall give a few examples of titles for Draghi's and Emperor Leopold's *sepolcri*: *Il epitafio di Christo* (1671) by Draghi was sung at the holy sepulchre of Christ during Holy Week, the poetry was written by Nicolo Minati.[240] Another *sepolcro* by Draghi is *La vita nella morte* (1688), sung at the Holy Sepulchre on Good Friday

---

240 *Musiksammlung, Österreichische Nationalbibliothek*, Mus.Hs. 18888. On f. 2r, the heading indicates: 'Al Epitafio di Christo: Sonata auanti Il santiss.ᵐᵒ sepolcro. Musica d'Antonio Draghi. Poes: di Nicolo Minati' and refers to the orchestral introduction as 'sonata'. I thank the staff of the *Musiksammlung* for kind help during my visit to the library in February 2006.

Fig. 2: Page from the partiture to the sepolchro La vita nella morte, p. f 10r. Musiksammlung, Österreichische Nationalbibliothek, Mus.Hs. 18870. With kind permission of the Musiksammlung.

1688, again with poetry by Nicolo Minati (fig. 1).[241] This *sepolcro* will be discussed in some detail below.

Il Sagrifizio d'Abramo (1660) by Emperor Leopold I was as it seems performed at the Holy Sepulchre on Good Friday with a text by Count Caldana.[242] The emperor also wrote music for some German *sepolcri*: *Die Erlösung des Menschlichen Geschlechts In der Figur des aus Egipten geführten Volcks Israel* (1679),[243] and *Sig des Leÿdens Christi über die Sinnlichkeit* (1682).[244]

---

241 *Musiksammlung, Österreichische Nationalbibliothek*, Mus.Hs. 18870. The heading on f. 2r gives: 'La vita nella morte: Rapresentatione per il s. sepolcro L'Anno 1688. Poes: di Nicol: Minati. Mus d'Ant. Draghi. Sinfonia a 6.' *Sinfonia* is here the heading given for the instrumental introduction to the work. See also the printed libretto (also preserved at the *Musiksammlung* at shelfmark 406750-B.Mus): Nicolo Minato, *La Vita nella morte. Rappresentatione sacra al SSmo sepolcro di Christo, nella Cesarea cappella della S.C.R. Maestà dell'Imperatore Leopoldo. La sera del Venerdì Santo. Posta in musica da Antonio Draghi*. English translation of the title: 'Life in Death. Holy Representation for the Most Holy Sepulchre of Christ in the Imperial chapel of his Holy Imperial Royal Majesty Emperor Leopold. Evening of Good Friday. Set to music by Antonio Draghi'.

242 *Musiksammlung, Österreichische Nationalbibliothek*, Mus.Hs. 16596. After the title, the heading continues: 'Musica Dell'Augustiss:mo Imp:re Leopoldo; al sepolcro del Giovedi – the last word, however, corrected by a different hand to Venerdi Santo – dell'Anno 1660.'

243 *Musiksammlung, Österreichische Nationalbibliothek*, Mus.Hs. 16529. The heading continues after the title: 'In Ihrer Erz-Fürstlichen Dyrchleücht Erzherzogin Maria Antonia Hoff-Capellen Am H: Grünen Donnerstag 1679. Teutsch gesungener Vorgestelt. Die Music componirt von ihro keyserl.-königl. Mayestät [...] Die Poesie von Hans Albrecht Ruedolf.'

244 *Musiksammlung, Österreichische Nationalbibliothek*, Mus.Hs. 16897. After the title the heading goes on: 'beÿ dem heiligen Grab in Ihrer Erz-Fürstlichen Durchleücht Erzherzogin Maria-Antonia, Hoff-Cappellen Dem h. Grünnen Donnerstag 1682. Teütsch gesungen Vorgestellt. Die Music von ihro keÿsl: Maiest. [...] Das Gedicht von Johan Albrecht Ruedolf.'

II. *La Vita nella morte*: Life in Death

Aside from a clear reference to the Holy Sepulchre, unfortunately no information is given about the surrounding ceremonial of the score of this work. This is so also for the other scores of *sepolcri* mentioned here. On the other hand, the score contains some information about the staging. Immediately after the *Sinfonia* for 6 string instruments (and organ),[245] the following heading and directions for the ensuing staged representation appears:

> The Holy Sepulchre is revealed.
>
> A view of harsh, arid, thorny ground. In the distance is the Earthly Paradise, with the Angel standing at the entrance, armed with a flaming sword. Enter those representing Sin, Toil, Death and Humanity. Humanity arrives first hoeing the ground. The others follow.[246]

The roles of the *sepolcro* are – as evident from this description – to a large extent allegorical figures (Fig. 2).

The protagonist – with regard to the performance – is the figure of Humanity (*Humanità*), who, as the play begins, is weighed down by work, unhappiness, and – more than anything else – his consciousness of guilt and his sorrow at having lost God: 'I lament my guilt and not my suffering' and 'I weep only because I have lost God.'[247] The musical opening of this 'scene' underlines the ritualized context of the music drama. The figures of Sin, Toil, and Death all emphasize how Humanity is tied to his sinfulness and that there is nothing he can do about it. Their lines – and arias – underline this aspect with keywords such as suffering, hardship, death, and guilt (*pena, stento, morte, colpa*), they very soon join each other in a refrain: 'Suffering, wear yourself out, then die.'[248] This item, in its compact and very recognizable musical setting, is repeated a number of times between the following lines for all the four roles (including Humanity), these are mainly recitatives but also include an aria with an instrumental *ritornelle* for Humanity. In all, the refrain is given four times during the short opening scene establishing

245   Antonio Draghi/Niccolò Minalti: *La vita nella morte* (1688). Musical score (manuscript). Musiksammlung, Österreichische Nationalbibliothek, f. 2r–9v.

246   I quote the English translation by Mary Pardoe from the booklet for the CD-recording of *La Vita nella morte* conducted by Christophe Coin (Auvidis France 1998), p. 24. Original text: 'Scopertosi Il SS^mo Sepolcro: Si uede l'Aspetto d'una Campagna sterile, aspra, spinosa, e più in lantano il Paradiso Terrestre, con l'Angelo su l'Ingresso, armato di spada di Fuoco. Comparisce chi rappresenta Il Peccato. La Fatica. La Morte. l'Humanità. Viene l'Humanità zappando la terra. Li altri la seguono' Draghi: *La Vita nella morte*, f. 10r.

247   CD-booklet, *La Vita nella morte*, pp. 30 and 32. Original text: 'Io lagrimo la colpa e non la pena' and 'Lagrimo sol perchè perduto ho Dio', Draghi: *La Vita nella morte*, f. 18v and 22v.

248   CD-booklet, *La Vita nella morte*, p. 24. Original text: 'pena, stenta, e poi morrai', Draghi: *La Vita nella morte*, f. 10v.

in this way a musical equivalent of the mentioned basic point of view concerning the impossibility for Humanity to change his situation.[249]

The drama – as all *sepolcri* – is in one part without other divisions than those provided by the stage directions when new roles come onto the stage. These divisions, however, also mark the dramatic course of the action quite clearly. The first change is due to the arrival of the figure of Hope in God.[250] Hope in God immediately introduces the idea not only of hope but of compassion, referring, of course, to Jesus. When Humanity exclaims: 'My offence to the Lord is too great and I dare not hope for his forgiveness', Hope answers: 'What you deserve not, he may bestow upon you.'[251] Hope introduces a more florid style of singing,[252] and Hope and Humanity join each other in praising the name of Jesus, 'Sweet name, pious name', as a refrain connected to Humanity's recitative 'Jesus, the name of my God!' and aria 'Sweet name, pious name, the soul's contentment'.[253]

The next step in the course of events is the arrival of two even more important figures that do not only give hope but actually carry out what was prophesied by Hope: 'Enter the representation of Divine Love and, beside him, the Angel who was guarding the earthly paradise with his flaming sword.'[254] Divine Love, as the central allegorical figure, directly announces the redemption to Humanity in accordance with Hope and the Angel:

> Hope: 'Rejoice',
>
> Angel: 'Be joyful',
>
> Divine Love: 'For you are redeemed!'[255]

This very short tripartite (but monophonic) refrain in its brevity seems to form a counterpart to the aforementioned refrain at the beginning of this *sepolcro*. Death, Sin, and Toil who have become weakened during the scene with Hope in God, have now vanished and never make an appearance again throughout the play.

---

249 Draghi: *La Vita nella morte*, f. 10v, 12r (twice), and 15v-16r.

250 'Viene chi rappresenta la Speranza in Dio', Draghi: *La Vita nella morte*, f. 27v.

251 CD-booklet, *La Vita nella morte*, p. 34. Original text: 'Humanità: Il signor troppo offesi: e non ardisco Di sperarne il perdono. Speranza: Quel, che non merti, egli può darti in Dono.' Draghi: *La Vita nella morte*, f. 28v.

252 See especially Hope's aria, 'Del Dio, che ti creò' [God who has created you], f. 29r-v with an instrumental *ritornelle* f. 30r.

253 'Nome dolce Nome pio', f. 34r-v. For Humanity's recitative 'Giesù, nome del mio Dio!' and aria, 'Nome dolce Nome pio che dell'Alma sei contento', see f. 32r-34v.

254 CD-booklet, *La Vita nella morte*, p. 40. Original text: 'Viene chi rappresenta l'Amor Divino e s'accosta chi rappresenta l'Angelo che con spada di Foco custodiua il Paradiso Terrestre.' Draghi: *La Vita nella morte*, f. 36v.

255 CD-booklet, *La Vita nella morte*, p. 40. Original text: 'Speranza: Godi, Angelo: esulta, Amor Divino: Sei redenta.', f. 36v.

Fig. 3: *La vita nella morte, p. f. 52v – 53r. Musiksammlung, Österreichische Nationalbibliothek, Mus.Hs. 18870. With kind permission of the Musiksammlung.*

The new refrain is repeated twice and then repeated once more in a musically extended version where the three voices which the first two times follow upon each other now sing in polyphony, partially imitating each other unfolding in florid melodies with word repetitions to provide a somewhat longer and more jubilant element.[256] After this, Divine Love and the Angel explain the love of Christ – rendering a traditional account of the redeeming quality of the crucifixion which also includes an anti-Jewish statement when Divine Love concludes his account of the sorrowful death of Christ 'Amidst the abuse and insults of the Jews'.[257]

This section can be understood to constitute a dramatic highpoint. It manifests the reversal of the human condition through the redemption. This comes to the fore also in the way the figure of Humanity in his reaction to the crucifixion narrative brings out the words of the title of the *sepolcro* as part of a line: 'Destiny

---

256 f. 37r, then f. 38r–v. The extended version follows on f. 40r–v.

257 CD-booklet, *La Vita nella morte*, p. 48. Original text, '[...] e dei Giudei tra le bestemie e l'onte', f. 48r.

in the cross! Life in death!'[258] The calmly ascending melody of the last part of this statement – and the halt to which the musical flow comes at its cadenza – makes it stand out in a marked way. It is followed up by a concluding statement by the Angel and Divine Love about Christ's wounds as the 'gateway to heaven'.[259]

Music dramatically, however, the most stunning effect comes in the next musical item, an aria sung by the Angel after a short recitative in which he draws attention to what was already mentioned in the stage directions, namely that he is the Angel who previously guarded the gates of paradise. He no longer does so – obviously – but after stating that he cannot do so because Christ has re-opened the gates, he sings an aria in which the Italian poetry (to which the English translation does not do justice) and the music together creates not only a jubilant conclusion to the scene – although Humanity does give a short recitative response afterwards before the next person arrives on stage – but an unprecedented expression of energy and newness in a musical representation of words which strongly emphasize ascending directions as well as large-scale (mythological and cosmic) dimensions of the text in melodic movements characterized by ascending figures and by a huge melodic range (an octave plus a fifth) which is already manifested within the first two bars of the aria. A florid instrumental refrain also marked by ascending figures is attached to the aria which in each stanza repeats the first line at the end, textually, thereby musically adding to the excitement (Fig. 3):

A la vita, al Cielo, al Ciel	Your rebellious sin against God
Soura gl'Astri la salita	no longer excludes you
Non ti uedi più impedita	from life, from heaven,
Dal peccato à Dio ribel.	from rising above the stars.
A le stelle, al Ciel, sù, sù!	Come to the stars, to heaven!
De le squadre, che rubelle	Jesus in his bounty makes you heirs
Cader già da l'altre celle	to the rebellious legions
Ti fà herede il pio Giesù.	that did fall from the high spheres.[260]

The two last divisions of the *sepolcro* introduce first the Good Thief (from Golgotha) and then Adam and Eve.[261]

---

258 CD-booklet, *La Vita nella morte*, p. 48. Original text, 'Ne la Croce la sorte, la vita Ne La morte', f. 51r.

259 CD-booklet, *La Vita nella morte*, p. 48, 'del Ciel le Porte', f. 51v.

260 CD-booklet, *La Vita nella morte*, pp. 48–51, original Italian text, f. 52r–53r, the instrumental refrain f. 53r-53v.

261 On f. 54r and 60r.

In both cases, the point seems to be to have a kind of 'eye witness' report from a mythical event from salvation history. Through the Good Thief we are brought to be 'present' at the crucifixion, not just to hear about it through theological discourse, and we are – similarly – brought to the actual event of the Fall through the accounts of Adam and Eve and we even get representations of the redemption of the Good Thief and of confessions of sin by Adam and Eve in their own words.[262] Such ritual representational technology had (among other medieval representational liturgical ceremonies) been fundamental for medieval memorial Passion devotions to which 17th-century *sepolcro* devotions in some ways seem to be counterparts. The so-called forty hours devotion with its keeping watch over a replica of Christ's sepulchre for forty hours in which the host is exposed (a tradition introduced in the 16th century with obvious parallels – as well as differences – to medieval Passion practices) has features in common with the practice of the *depositio hostiae*, the liturgical memorization in the form of a burial of the consecrated host (occasionally the cross) after the veneration of the cross on Good Friday afternoon.[263]

After the mentioned representations of elements from the Passion and Fall narratives, all figures (except for the three from the beginning of the piece, Sin, Toil, and Death, who are no longer part of the drama, and the Good Thief who is no longer mentioned on the stage after his 'scene') join in the final praises and expressions of thanks to God.[264]

III. Salzburg traditions and Wolfgang Amadeus Mozart

Staged performance practices for *sepolcri* seem to have diminished during the early 18th century in Vienna where the main composers of such devotional works were Johann Joseph Fux (c. 1660-1741) and Antonio Caldara (1671-1736). The musical pieces became increasingly difficult to distinguish from the general Italian oratorio.[265] However, as late as 1767, the eleven year old Wolfgang Amadeus Mozart composed his – short – *Grabmusik* (K. 42), *eine Cantata zum hl: Grab Christi, von 2 singenden Personen*, 'a cantata for the holy sepulchre of Christ with two roles', as

---

262 It should be mentioned that Humanity's aria after the presentation of the Good Thief is marked in the score as having been composed by Emperor Leopold: 'Aria di S.M.C' (S.M.C. short for Sua Maestà Cesarea, i.e. His Imperial Majesty), see f. 57v.

263 For the forty hours devotion and the complex relationship to medieval ceremonial, see Petersen, Nils Holger: 'Renaissance Rituals in a Florentine Lay Confraternity: *Compagnia dell'arcangelo Raffaello'. Analecta Romana Instituti Danici* 2004, pp. 153–60.; for the idea of presence at the mythical events and medieval representational liturgy, see Petersen, Nils Holger: 'The Representational Liturgy of the *Regularis Concordia'. The White Mantle of Churches: Architecture, Liturgy, and Art Around the Millenium*. Nigel Hiscock (ed.). Turnhout 2003, pp. 107-17.

264 f. 65-79, in various combinations and musical forms, beginning with Adam and Eve after their confession, recitatives, and arias, and tutti choruses.

265 Smither 1987, vol. I, pp. 408-9; vol. III, p. 35.

his father, Leopold Mozart, entered it into his catalogue of Wolfgang's compositions, the *Verzeichniss alles desjenigen was dieser 12jährige Knab seit seinem 7ten Jahre
componiert und in originali kann aufgezeichnet werden*, the 'catalogue of everything
this twelve-year old boy has composed since his seventh year and which can be
shown in original [manuscripts]', written in Vienna 1768.[266]

The Archiepiscopal Court of Salzburg where Wolfgang's father Leopold Mozart was employed and where Wolfgang was to live and function for most of
his childhood and youth had – since the Middle Ages – been an independent
principality within the Holy Roman Empire of the German Nation, ruled by an
archbishop who in addition to being the ruling prince of the territory also carried the title *Primas Germaniae*. Performances of German oratorios for Lent were
part of the archiepiscopal court traditions; some of these 'were probably sung
before a model of the holy sepulchre erected in the cathedral.'[267] Indeed, an or-
nate so-called *Grab-theater* (sepulchral theatre) – in existence during the reign of
Archbishop Siegmund Christoph, Graf von Schrattenbach (1753-1771) – seems
to have been replaced by a simple sepulchre (with only four candles) during
the reforms of his Enlightenment successor Hieronymus, Graf von Colloredo
(1772-1803).[268] Nothing is known about contemporary performances of the
Grabmusik,[269] but it is intriguingly possible – both from the title, from Leopold's
short description, and the contents of the short dramatic dialogue – to read it as
belonging to some late Salzburg tradition of a devotional Passion practice which
may not necessarily have been equivalent to the Imperial practices in Vienna, but
nevertheless seems to have had something in common with them. The modern
editor of the *Grabmusik* has raised the question whether this piece could have
been given a staged performance with costumes. In view of the lack of extant
documentation, he – and we – can get no further.[270]

We know that the Mozart family – at least occasionally – practiced individual
visits to holy sepulchres. In 1771, Leopold Mozart – during one of his trips to
Italy with Wolfgang – mentioned a planned visit to a holy sepulchre in a letter

---

266 See Giegling, Franz: 'Zum vorliegenden Band'. *W.A.Mozart: Grabmusik*, Giegling (ed.), pp. vii–ix.
     Neue Mozart Ausgabe, Geistliche Gesangswerke, Werkgruppe 4, Band 4. Partitur, BA 4507. Kassel
     1957. The young Mozart also wrote other devotional or educational music dramas (in what seems
     to be a Jesuit tradition of school music dramas at the time). For Leopold Mozart's entry, see Bauer,
     Wilhelm A. and Deutsch, Otto E. (eds.): *Mozart, Briefe und Aufzeichnungen* Gesamtausgabe, 7 vols.
     Kassel 1962-75, vol. I, pp. 287-89.

267 Smither 1987, vol. III, p. 342. For Salzburg at the time of the young Mozart, see in Sadie, Stanley:
     Mozart: The Early Years, 1756-1781. New York 2006.

268 Smither 1987, vol. III, p. 342, esp. n. 39.

269 See, however, the anecdotal (possible) information about the composition of the *Grabmusik* in
     Sadie 2006, pp. 118-19. Sadie also indicates the *Grabmusik* to have been performed in front of a
     holy sepulchre in the cathedral or some other Salzburg church.

270 Giegling 1957, 'Zum Vorliegenden Band', p. viii.

to his wife shortly before Easter (14th of March), and in 1779, Wolfgang's sister Nannerl makes a similar note in her diary.[271]

It seems that the – aforementioned – *depositio hostiae* ceremony was still performed in the cathedral of Salzburg during Wolfgang's Salzburg years.[272] The dramatic construction of the *Grabmusik* would fit perfectly as a music dramatic continuation after the end of the *depositio hostiae* where the Latin verse *Christus factus est pro nobis usque ad mortem* and its response *mortem autem crucis* (Christ has sacrificed himself for us unto death; even the death of the cross, cf. Phillipians 2.8) were sung and a silent prayer followed. It is not difficult to imagine the *Grabmusik* beginning at this point – on the Grab-theater in front of the holy sepulchre – with no overture, starting with a simple recitative where *Die Seele* (the Human Soul) asks 'where am I' continuing with a lament on Christ's death and the question of why. The cantata further unfolds as a dialogue in recitatives, arias and a final duet between the Soul and an Angel. The – traditional – theological point of the piece is that the Human Soul is co-responsible for the death of Christ; this insight leads to his contrition and the forgiveness of his sins, and to his redemption (in the duet). The work concludes in a praising chorus – probably written or re-written some years later (1775-76)[273] – indicating that the piece had not become obsolete for him at that time. The point in this – much too brief – discussion is simply to make it clear how the very young Mozart did – serious – musical work in the context of baroque devotions (with medieval backgrounds). The uses of liturgico-musical techniques in Mozart's representations of the supernatural in his mature operas *Idomeneo* (1781) and *Don Giovanni* (1787) may be taken as an indication that the liturgical influence of his youth had lasting consequences for his musical work – and therefore for European music history at large.[274]

271   Bauer und Deutsch 1962-75, vol. I, pp. 425 and 542, see also the commentary in vol. V, pp. 300 and 584.

272   See the list of liturgical sources from Salzburg mentioned in Lipphardt, Walther (ed.): *Lateinische Osterfeiern und Osterspiele*, 9 vols. Berlin 1975-90, vol. IV, pp. 1309-1313, and the comments in vol. VIII, pp. 599-603; see especially the ceremony in the *Rituale Salisburgense* of 1640 and 1686 (sources 716 and 717 in Lipphardt's list), pp 1309-10 and 1312, and cf. Fellerer, Karl Gustav: *Die Kirchenmusik W.A. Mozarts*. Laaber 1985, pp. 31-46.

273   Giegling 1957, 'Zum Vorliegenden Band', p. ix; Fellerer 1985, p. 116.

274   See Petersen, Nils Holger: 'Time and Divine Providence in Mozart's Music'. *Voicing the Ineffable*. Siglind Bruhn (ed.). Hillsdale – New York 2002, pp. 265-86, esp. pp. 272-80, and Petersen, Nils Holger: 'Søren Kierkegaard's Aestheticist and Mozart's Don Giovanni'. *Interarts Studies – New Perspectives*. Ulla-Britta Lagerroth, Hans Lund, and Erik Hedling (eds.). Amsterdam 1997, pp. 167-76 and Petersen, Nils Holger: 'The *Trump of God*: Musical Representations of Divine Judgment in Mozart Works, 1767-1791'. *Transfiguration: Nordic Yearbook for Religion and the Arts* 2007 (forthcoming).

19th Century Devotional Medals

Eli Heldaas Seland

> Collecting devotional medals can have few material advantages; what can
> be gained by collecting them is of a purely spiritual value. […] We look at
> a devotional medal with different eyes; while silver and money value does
> not dazzle us, the simplest devotional medals can, by means of their spi-
> ritual meaning and its representation delight us immensely.
>
> *Leo Kuncze, Systematik der Weihmünzen, 1885.* [275]

Neither to us are 19th century devotional medals primarily interesting because
of their material or artistic value. They are interesting because Leo Kuncze and
others cherished these objects highly in the 19th century, whereas others criticized
or simply dismissed them as simple and uninteresting. My ongoing study aims
to discuss the role and importance of these objects in pious life in the 19th century. They existed in millions, but have left few marks in art historical or other
research. This article is a presentation of the group of objects known by the name
of (religious or) devotional medals, the aim of which is to define the objects,
outline their history and describe some central features.

Religious medals and devotional medalets

The term *religious medal* is rather imprecise, but it is the one most frequently used
to denominate the objects in question. These objects are often hard to place in
a systematic order with chronology and geography as structuring principles, and

---

275 Kuncze, Leo: *Systematik der Weihmünzen: Eine ergänzende Studie für alle Freunde der Numismatik.*
Raab 1885, pp. 26-27. My translation, from the original: 'Das Sammeln der Weihmünzen kann nur
von ferneher einen materiellen Vortheil bringen, der eigentliche Nutzen des Sammelns ist lediglich
ein geistiger […] Wir sehen eine Weihmünze mit andern Augen an; nicht Silber und Geldwerth
blendet uns, sondern es kann uns die einfachste Weihmünze nach ihrer geistigen Bedeutung und
ihrer Darstellung hoch entzücken.'

they tend to show up towards the end of catalogues and collections. Therefore, in the ears of those familiar with the world of numismatics and/or the daily life in a collection of coins and medals, the term has connotations such as 'other', 'miscellaneous' and 'difficult to systematize' clinging to it.

The origin of the word *medal* is the Latin word for metal: *metallum*. Many European languages have similar words for it, e.g. German *Medaille*, French *médaille*, Italian *medaglia* and Scandinavian languages *medalj/e*. Other variants of the same word are also in use, such as *medallion*, which means large medal, but which is also given less precise meanings, and even used about jewellery and/or amulets which are not strictly medals. The English term *medalet* nominates small medals,[276] and devotional medals are often, though not necessarily, medalets. (The term *medalet* will be used in this article when reference is made specifically to small, mass produced objects, otherwise the more general *medal* will be used). Medalets more often than medals have hoops. The German word *Anhänger*, and the English *pendant* are used about hanging jewellery and, mounted adequately any medal or medalet can be a pendant.

There are different ways of defining 'medal'. A dictionary has this general definition:

> '...' a piece of metal, usually in the form of a disc, struck or cast with an
> inscription or device to commemorate an event etc., or awarded as a dis-
> tinction to a soldier, scholar, athlete etc., for services rendered, for profi-
> ciency, etc.[277]

The definition given by R.N.P. Hawkins, a numismatist, gives more specialized details about some technical aspects:

> '...' normally featuring portraiture and/or pictorial matter, metallic, circu-
> lar. Traditionally struck by repeated blows giving higher relief to the im-
> agery than is practical for coins, and customarily of larger diameter than
> normal coinage.[278]

---

276 Medalets have often been produced as smaller, cheaper variants of medals, for instance in the occasion of royal and national events. Hawkins, R.N.P.: *A Dictionary of Makers of British metallic tickets, checks, medalets, tallies, and counters 1788-1910*. London 1989, p. v.

277 *The Concise Oxford Dictionary of Current English, 8th ed.* Oxford 1990.

278 Hawkins 1989, p.v.

Hawkins further distinguishes medalets from medals, by stating that medalets have the same function as medals, but are normally smaller and in normal relief. Neither of these definitions are invalid for devotional medals, but both are inadequate. The Catholic Encyclopaedia lists the typical motifs in an article under the entry *devotional medals*, in which it is stressed that the article is concerned 'only with *religious* [my italics] medals', which:

> are produced not only to commemorate persons (e.g. Christ, the Blessed Virgin, and the Saints), places (e.g. famous shrines) and past historical events (e.g. dogmatic definitions, miracles, dedications etc.) as well as personal graces like First Communion, Ordination, etc., but they are also often concerned with the order of ideas (e.g. they may recall the mysteries of our Faith, such as the Blessed Sacrament or the Divine Attributes), *they are used to inculcate lessons of piety, are specially blessed to serve as badges of pious associations or to consecrate and protect the wearer, and finally are often enriched with indulgences.*[279] [My italics]

They are often, as here, mentioned together, and sometimes confused; religious and devotional medals are not always the same thing. All devotional medals are religious, but not all religious medals are devotional. There are religious medals which have as their primary function to commemorate historical persons, places or events, and which therefore function exactly the same way within the Christian universe as secular medals do outside. Devotional medals have other, or additional, functions, but what exactly separates the devotional medals and medalets from other religious medals? In the following we will illuminate this topic, by considering the historical use of terms for the relevant objects, the history of the objects and their forerunners, and some different functions and ways in which they have been used.

The collector Franz Töply von Hohenvest wrote a booklet in 1893, called *Numismatik. Miscellen. Die Weihmünzen für Sammler,* in which he defines 'Weihmünzen' as metallic pieces with representations of places of pilgrimage or saints.[280] He further refers to a priest and collector in Hungary,[281] and undoubtedly means Leo Kuncze, who was responsible for the only attempt to systematize (Catholic) devotional medals, in the years prior to 1885, when his catalogue of about

---

279 *New Advent*: http://www.newadvent.org/cathen/10111b.htm accessed 09.13.05. The article also provides a good survey of the history of devotional medals.

280 'Unter der Benennung "Weihmünzen" sind in meiner numismatischen Sammlung alle metalloglyptischen Stücke verstanden, welche sich auf Wallfahrtsorte oder auf Heilige beziehen.' von Hohenvest, Franz Töply: *Numismatik. Miscellen. Die Weihmünzen für Sammler.* Graz 1893, p. 1*.

281 '[…] ein Sammler in Ungarn, ein Priester'. von Hohenvest 1893, p. 1*

8000 devotional medals *Systematik der Weihmünzen: Eine ergänzende Studie für alle Freunde der Numismatik* issued. Kuncze means, by the term *Weihmünzen*, medals that are consecrated or could be so.[282] He does not specify the criteria for consecration, but refers to motifs to which we are religiously attracted.[283] When Kuncze uses *Münzen*, coins, rather than *Medaillen*, it is to clarify the relationship to *Denkmünzen*, which are commemorative coins and medals without a religious motif or function. He explicitly rejects the terms *Jetons* and *Pfennige* because of their devaluating implications.

The term *Wallfahrtspfennige* is, however, used by other authors writing in German to describe medals which are sold or given out to pilgrims visiting a shrine.[284] And whether or not we are comfortable with just this term, a terminology which says something about the context of devotional medals and medalets can be very convenient. Kuncze systematizes according to motifs in a hierarchical, theological order, and though his effort is impressive, the result has clear practical limitations.

Historical forerunners and similar objects

Excavations in the catacombs outside Rome have brought forth medals with, as shown by de Rossi,[285] Christian motifs; motifs which are also found in funerary paintings, on sarcophagi and in monumental variants in basilicas from the period of Early Christianity. As this is not an essential point to this study we shall leave discussions concerning the exact dates and the question whether the particular objects are original medals or converted coins in peace, and content ourselves with stating that the history of devotional medals is probably no younger than the history of Christian images in general, or even than Christendom itself. De Rossi points to the contemporary existence of 'Gnostic and superstitious medals' and it is likely that the early Christians simply Christianized the already existing customs related to amulets.

The origin of *Agnus Deis* – wax discs impressed with the figure of a lamb and blessed at stated seasons by the Pope – is uncertain.[286] Originally, however, they were probably made using wax from the previous year's Easter candles in Roman

---

282 '…' der Ausdruck "Weihe-Münze" passe für a l l e Medaillen diese Art, da alle, wenn sie auch nicht geweiht sind, doch geweiht werden k ö n n e n, und geweiht zu werden p f l e g e n.' Kuncze 1885, p. 8.

283 '…' zu denen wir uns religiös hingezogen fühlen'. Kuncze 1885, p. 7.

284 E.g. in Pachinger, Anton M: *Wallfahrts- und Weihemünzen des Erzhertogtums ob der Enns*. Linz 1904; Pachinger, A.M: *Wallfahrts-, Bruderschafts- und Gnadenmedaillen des Herzogtums Salzburg*. Wien 1908.

285 de Rossi, Giovanni Battista: 'Le medaglie di devozione dei primi sei o sette secoli della chiesa'. *Bullettino di Archeologia Cristiana*, Anno VII 3 & 4. Roma 1869.

286 *New Advent*: www.newadvent.org/cathen/01220a.htm accessed 10.05.05.

Fig. 1: The Agnus Dei motif, here used on a silver reliquary of unknown origin from the 15th century. Portable reliquaries of this kind also have much in common with medals, being round, made of metal, decorated with reliefs on both sides and designed to be hung around the neck. Bergen Museum, MA 167.

churches. Being consecrated, *Agnus Deis* enjoy the special status that this implies in the Catholic Church. Historically, they have been used for devotional purposes; thus they have much in common with modern medals in function, and, the material taken aside, the relationship with regard to form is obvious (Fig. 1).

Another forerunner, perhaps more directly so in terms of form than in terms of function, though both aspects are relevant, is *ecclesiastical seals*. Seals have been used from medieval times to the present day to authenticate documents, and norms and standards have of course changed over time. Common for most ecclesiastical seals, however, particularly older ones, is the vesica-shape, the pointed oval.[287] Interestingly, the oval – pointed or not – is a much used form in the modern medalets, and the visual parallel is obvious.

Pilgrims' badges were much used in medieval times and have been subject to several studies. Among the earliest known variants are scallop shells, sold by licensed vendors to pilgrims visiting the shrine of St. James the greater in Santiago de Compostela. In time, natural shells were replaced by shells made of metal, and eventually other metal badges, too, and the use was spread all over Europe.[288]

---

287 *New Advent*: www.newadvent.org/cathen/07243a.htm. accessed 10.05.05.

288 von Wilckens, Leonid: 'Die Kleidung des Pilger'. *Wallfahrt kennt keine Grenzen. Themen zu einer Ausstellung des Bayerischen Nationalmuseums und des Adalbert Stifter Vereins, München*. Kriss-Rettenbeck, Lenz and Gerda Möhler (eds.). München 1984, p. 175.

Fig. 2: Pilgrim's badge from Rocama-dour, France, 14ᵗʰ century. This leaden badge is an offprint of a seal, and the inscription reads: SIGILLUM: BEATE MARIE:DE ROCAMADOR. Bergen Museum, B.6242a.

The most commonly used materials were lead, pewter or an alloy of these, but occasionally badges were made from more valuable materials such as (gilt) silver. The shape and form varied, but the badges were as a rule one-sided and equipped with hoops or similar devices to facilitate the attachment of the badges to the pilgrims' clothes or hats (Fig. 2).

It was important that the badges be visible if they were to fulfil their function of identifying and protecting the bearer. Kurt Köster points to the abuse of pilgrims' badges by beggars, frauds and vagabonds, soldiers and spies in disguise as proof of their importance to real pilgrims on their way to or from their goal; seeking on the one hand *charities* such as food, drink and housing, and on the other hand *protection* travelling dangerous roads.[289] The badges were taken home as souvenirs, which would in turn inspire prayer and devotional practices. They could for instance be used as votive gifts. Pilgrims' badges were not a legally valid proof of having visited a shrine and performed the appropriate rituals; only written certificates were. However, the notion that the badge bore some of the holy power of the shrine or the place visited was widespread. Badges would be

289 Köster, Kurt: 'Mittelalterliche Pilgerzeichen'. *Wallfahrt kennt keine Grenzen. Themen zu einer Ausstellung der Beyerischen Nationalmuseums und des Adalbert Stifter Vereins, München.* Lenz Kriss-Retten-beck and Gerda Möhler (eds.) 1984, p. 207.

brought in direct contact with a cult object, and became a vehicle for holy power. A telling expression of this belief is the tradition of including a small mirror in the badge, a mirror which was understood to capture holy rays issuing from the object of veneration in question. Badges having been bestown with such a power have been called representative relics, and they were used for pious purposes, in what Kurt Köster calls 'superstitious, magical and popular medical practices'.[290] This somewhat condescending way of referring to popular practices is common, but perhaps not just. It is often hard to see what separates superstition from piety. So called popular medicine has also been performed with holy water transported from shrines in miniature ampullae.[291] The tradition of attaching pilgrims' badges to church bells, in order to strengthen their capacity to keep Evil at a distance, has been helpful to the research concerning such badges.

Other objects which have certain similarities with devotional medalets are tokens and jetons. Jetons were used in the Middle Ages as a means of counting, and later they became popular as representation gifts.[292] They often had a stamp identifying the person or institution they were made for, and therefore some have religious motifs though their function was highly profane. Tokens are of a later origin, and have been in use from the 17th century onwards, primarily as a means of compensating for lack in supply of ordinary coins. They could be issued by official suppliers such as (the equivalent of) national banks, or by private persons and companies; trading houses etc. Tokens made as substitutes for coins would normally be metallic and have a set nomination. However, with the industrial era tokens came to be produced from other materials such as 'brass, copper, lead, plastic and card embossed, incised or printed with an astonishing variety of designs and wording [...]',[293] and used for different purposes, such as advertising and signs of admittance. There are also specifically Christian uses of tokens: After the Reformation so called 'community tokens' came into use in non-catholic contexts. They were particularly popular in the Presbyterian Church, where the church elders would hand out communion tokens which permitted those found worthy to receive communion.[294]

---

290 Köster 1984 p. 207, in original language: 'aberglaubische, magische und volksmedisinische Praktiken.'

291 Mitchiner, Michael: *Medieval Pilgrim and Secular Badges*. London 1986, p. 8.

292 Mitchiner, Michael: *Jetons, Medalets & Tokens*, Vol.I: *The Medieval Period and Nuremberg*. London 1988, p. 17. The etymological origin of the word *jeton* is disputed, see Rouyer, Jules and Hucher, Eugène: *Histoire du jeton au moyen age*. Paris 1858, p. 15, who claim that the word comes from the old French verb *jetter/getter*, which signifies *compter* (i.e. count) in modern French, whereas others mean the origin is the French word *jeter* (i.e. throw).

293 Fletcher, Edward: *Tokens & Tallies 1850-1950*. Witham 2004, p. 5.

294 Mitchiner 1988, p. 620. *The Material History of American Religion Project*: www.materialreligion.org/documents/aug98doc.html; *Coin Library*: www.coinlibrary.com/wpns/club_wpns_pr_communion.htm accessed 22.11.05.

It is not always easy to distinguish at first glance between mass produced medalets, jetons and tokens from the 19th century, but as a rule the medalets are more elaborately executed even though they are normally not classified as 'high' art. In the case of devotional medalets, their expression is generally reminiscent of other religious images belonging to the same visual culture. Most devotional medalets have images on one or both sides, and on some, presumably Lutheran prayer medals, miniature texts, e.g. the Creed or Our Father fill one side. Tokens and jetons can have text, numbers and images, but as a rule the images are simpler, and less important to the total expression than in the case of the medalets.

The origin of medals

It is commonly agreed that medals, unlike coins, did not exist in the Middle Ages; but as we have seen there were several forerunners, at least in the world of devotion. Medals are, in the numismatic literature and generally, understood to have originated in the early Renaissance, around 1400, with Italian artists as the primary executors and foremost among them Pisanello. Many see them as a specific Renaissance phenomenon, inspired by the example of ancient Rome and Greece, but also clearly a product of contemporary society: 'Medallic art [...] can be seen as the ultimate celebration of the individual. As such it could have been produced in no other society and at no other time'.[295] Such a view on medals as the one expressed here by Mark Jones, clearly favouring one particular kind of medals and practically discarding all others, is widespread, and that is one reason why it can be difficult to talk about the devotional objects with which we are concerned as *medals*. In terms of function they are often more closely related to their medieval forerunners than to the modern medals, but still they are normally classified as medals, or medalets. This is perhaps best understood in light of the die hard conception of the Renaissance as Humanity's liberation from the dark Middle Ages which stood strong in the 18th, 19th and to some extent the 20th centuries. The achievements of Pisanello and other 14th and 15th century medallists have been seen to represent a great qualitative improvement with respect to the medieval forerunners, often perceived as crude and artless. Even though influential currents, e.g. within the Romantic Movement have appreciated medieval art and artefacts, pilgrims' badges and similar objects have also been devalued and efficiently kept out of discussions to which they belong.[296]

---

295 Jones, Mark: *The Art of the Medal*. London 1979, p. 6.

296 As an example, see Kurt Köster's citation of a leading French archaeologist objecting to the aquisition, on part of Musée de Cluny, of a great find of pilgrims' badges from Loire: 'Diesen Ankauf nannte er öffentlich "un malheur pour tout le monde et une calamité pour ceux qui aiment les choses intéressantes, belles et authentique"; er meinte, diese armselige Objekte habe man besser erst gar nicht aus dem grund der Flüsse ans Licht gezogen.' Köster 1984, p. 204.

Leo Kuncze sees the coming into being of that which he calls *Weihmünzen* as a process which stretches over centuries, but he points to some important events. The first one he refers from Domenico Magri's *Hierolexicon*, which first issued in 1677. According to this source the holy virgin appeared to a man in 1183, leaving him a medal with a portrait of the Saviour and the inscription 'Agnus dei, qui tollis peccata mundi, dona nobis pacem' which means 'Lamb of God, who takes away the sin of the world, give us Peace' and is part of the standard Catholic Mass liturgy,[297] and told him to take it to his bishop to have it copied and distributed, so that it may bring peace to those carrying it. Kuncze uses the word *Medaille* for this object without further reflection, Magri names it *sacrum numisma*.[298] What this actually was, and what it would have been, seen and understood as in the 12th century, *if the story really is that old* (further investigation into this matter will have to be carried out) is hard to tell.

Kuncze also points to the importance of the rosary for the popularity of devotional medals. One common way of carrying medalets has been attached to rosaries. The rosary too has medieval origins, and was officially approved by Pius V, in his bull *Consueverunt Romani Pontifices* of 1569. In 1572 the Feast of Our Lady of Victory was instituted to celebrate the victory of the Spanish and Venetian fleet over the Turks at Lepanto the previous year, and the following year Gregory XIII altered it to the Feast of Our Lady of the Rosary.[299] Perhaps as important as the direct link between rosaries and medalets, is the preoccupation with devotional instruments in this period. At about the same time, a new practice which is of interest to us surfaced: blessing and attaching of apostolic indulgences to coins and medals. This may be seen as a development of the already established practice connected with the *Agnus Deis*, but for metallic objects such as medals and coins it was probably new.[300] One of the first known occasions is when Pius V granted indulgences to Spaniards in Flanders who, during the revolt of Gueux in 1566 wore a medal with an image of Our Lord on one side, Our Lady of Hal on the other.[301] The practice was formalized by Sixtus V in the bull *Laudeamus*

---

297   Originally, *miserere nobis* was sung at the end of the phrase three times. Gradually, beginning in the 10th century, it was replaced by *dona nobis pacem* the third time. Jungmann, Joseph A.: *The Mass of the Roman Rite: Its Origin and Development (Missa Solemnis)*. Francis A. Brunner (transl.). Dublin 1986, vol. II, p. 339.

298   Magri, Domenico: *Hierolexicon sive Sacrum Dictionarium in quo Ecclesiasticæ voces, earumque Etymologiae, Origines, Symbola, Cæremoniæ, Dubia, Barbara Vocabula, atque Sac.Scripturæ & SS.PP.Phrases Obscuræ elucidantur*. Rome 1677, p 407. Online at www.uni-mannheim.de/mateo/camenaref/magri/magri1/books/magrihierolexicon_13.html accessed 18.11.05.

299   Miller, John D.: *Beads and Prayers. The Rosary in History and Devotion*. London 2001, p. 29.

300   According to Herbert Thurston's article under the entry *Devotional Medals* in *New Advent*, no example of a blessing for numismata is found among medieval benediction forms. *New Advent*: www.newadvent.org/cathen/10111b.htm accessed 23.11.2005.

301   Ball, Ann: *Encyclopedia of Catholic Devotions and Practices*. Huntington IN 2003, p. 348.

viros gloriosos of 1ˢᵗ December 1587,[302] where it is recounted that in tearing down old walls in the Lateran workmen carrying out restoration works had discovered ancient coins with portraits of the early Christian emperors on the obverses and crosses on the reverses. The pope granted a number of indulgences, on the performance of certain pious works, to those who came to possess the old coins enriched with the new blessing. The coins were richly mounted and sent to persons of distinction.[303]

The new praxis of blessing and/or attaching indulgences to such objects can perhaps be said to mark the coming into being of medals as devotional objects. It certainly must have altered their status markedly, making them more attractive to own, not so much for their material, as for their spiritual value. In the years to come, renowned artists in many Europeans cities made devotional medals, but often the medallist, the date and the place of issue are unknown. As a rule, it is probably right to say that specifically devotional medalets have had less in common with medals traditionally classified as art than with the great and varied flora of popular images, tokens etc. In the years following the Reformation, satirical medals, with motifs ridiculing the antagonist, were popular.[304] In plague years the production of certain medalets and amulets reached peaks. Such objects have probably been available to large segments of the people, whereas beautifully executed silver medals which were given as presents for baptisms and weddings, sometimes with a personal motif or inscription, were for the very few. In modern times artful and materially valuable devotional medals are still made, but it seems that as of the 19ᵗʰ century they have been outnumbered by small, mass produced medalets which are not distinguished by particular artistic quality, but which have nevertheless been so popular that church authorities have found it necessary to *warn* the public against excessive use of them.[305]

---

302 *New Advent*: www.newadvent.org/cathen/07788a.htm accessed 23.11.2005.

303 *New Advent*: www.newadvent.org/cathen/10111b.htm accessed 23.11.2005.

304 Laugerud, Henning: 'Mali Corvi Malum Ovum: Reformasjonstidens satiriske medaljer'. *Biblioteca Obskura. Festskrift til Torstein Arisholm på 30-årsdagen.* Laugerud, Korslund , Emberland (eds.). Bergen 1996.

305 The Norwegian bishop Johannes B. Fallize said in 1892 (my translation): 'We cannot but warn here against the overflowing of devotionals, such as medals, which tends to get out of control and leads only to disdain of these venerable objects'. ('Vi kan ikke her unlade at advare mod den formelige oversvømmelse af devotionalier, som f.eks. medaljer, der stedse tager mer overhand og kun fører til ringeagt for disse ærverdige gjenstande'). Fallize, Johannes B.: *Kirkelige bekjendtgjørelser for Norges apostoliske vikariat*, nr. 7, 10/9. 1892.

The 19ᵗʰ century

The Sammlung Rudolph Kriss in Bayerisches Nationalmuseum in Munich and the Cribb Collection in British Museum in London both contain numerous devotional medalets from the 19ᵗʰ and 20ᵗʰ century, and some, though comparatively few, earlier ones. Though not all-comprehensive or entirely representative, these collections give an indication of the size and variety of this material. There appears to be a predominance of 19ᵗʰ century objects, or more precisely: objects which originated in the 19ᵗʰ century. The relative scarcity of older material may be a result of the interests of the respective collectors, it may be a consequence of practical matters such as immediate availability at the time of collecting; earlier samples may have disappeared in different ways and for different reasons, and finally it probably reflects the historical situation that greater numbers of these objects circulated in the 19ᵗʰ than in earlier centuries. Some medalets have been in continuous production up to the present day, and others originate in the 20ᵗʰ or 21ˢᵗ century. Devotional medals are not, as we see, exclusively a 19ᵗʰ century phenomenon, but the assumption that they are somewhat more representative of a widespread phenomenon in the 19ᵗʰ than in other centuries, and therefore have a great potential for interpretation, makes them interesting, and the availability of objects and source material from this period makes them relatively accessible, as objects of study.

Obviously, new technology available for manufacturers in the 19ᵗʰ century made mass production of medalets easier and cheaper than it had been before; infrastructure made distribution simpler; i.e. the supply was facilitated. This would typically stimulate the demand for such objects somewhat, but there are other and probably better ways of explaining the increase in demand. One sees, particularly in the Catholic Church in the 19ᵗʰ century, an offensive strategy of defence from the influence of the modern world. This strategy consisted in not only approving of, but encouraging, popular pious practices to which the Church had been indifferent or reluctant earlier. Hugh McLeod characterizes the result as 'an emphatically supernaturalist Catholicism, dedicated to alliance with what was seen as the faith of the common people against the false hopes of rationalism, scientism and liberalism.'[306] Particularly important in France was the movement called Ultramontanism – which combined 'a highly dogmatic and anti-rationalist theology with a warmly emotional piety, and a preference for a life within a catholic ghetto.'[307]

In the 19ᵗʰ century unusually many apparitions of Mary were acknowledged by the Catholic Church authorities, and whole industries were created around them

---

306 McLeod, Hugh: *Religion and the people of Western Europe 1789-1989*. Oxford and New York 1997, p. 47.

307 McLeod 1997, p. 47.

Fig. 3: Obverse and reverse of The Miraculous Medal. Bergen Museum, Coins and medals collection.

and the pilgrimages that followed. The most famous is probably Bernadette Soubirous' visions at Lourdes and the healing miracles that followed. Another example is the vision of Catherine Labouré in Paris which led to the production of the Miraculous Medal (Fig. 3), in connection with which, in turn, miracles took place.

Numerous new pious organizations were established, e.g. l'Enfance Missionnaire, many cults like that of the Sacred Heart of Jesus and the Holy Family were nurtured, and many new religious orders saw the light in this period.

The functions and use of devotional medals

In this article, objects of Catholic, Protestant, Presbyterian and secular origin have been discussed. This proves that devotional medalets and similar objects have played roles in different settings; nonetheless they are considerably more widespread in a Catholic context than in any other. Why? First and foremost because the veneration of Holy persons, above all Christ and Virgin Mary but also saints, carried out in the presence, and with the aid of images, plays such an important role in Catholic culture. The fact that the Catholic Church went particularly far in the 19th century in their attempt to answer the challenges and threats they felt exposed to in contemporary society, is probably also a part of the explanation. Medalets and other mass produced imagery clearly had a potential for playing roles within the development outlined above. Out of sight, out of mind is a saying with high relevance for the 19th century, a time when the visual surroundings changed, for many people rapidly and drastically, and when new popular cultures arose, inside and outside church milieus. We can identify at least three basic functions of images in Christian contexts of relevance in this discussion: Images can have a normative function, presenting the *Civitas Dei* – the objects of faith with those aspects and ideals one chooses to emphasize. They can have a formative function, in shaping a *sensus fidelium* – a sort of identity, in the form of a common sense of what it means to be a part of a community of believers, either in particular groups or in the Church as such. A third function can be that of making *the holy* present, providing what we may call a *praesentia sacri et genius loci*.

Documentation of the actual, practical *use* of devotional medals in the 19th century is not abundant, probably because in the relevant environments the practices concerned with such objects have been a natural part of daily routine, not something seen as requiring much reflection, at least not in writing. However, some practices have survived, probably practically unaltered, until the present day. Catholic devotional medalets are for instance still consecrated by an authorized person. 'It belongs to the nature of practical piety that it is not just a question of pious thought, but also of something done in a certain way to evoke and structure such thoughts. A living religion "of interest to the heart" must express itself in devotional practices […].'[308] The practices surrounding the medalets are probably essential to understanding them, their way of making meaning to people, and their mode of operation. For instance, we cannot judge them valueless because they are mass produced. They are not exclusive works of art, because the idea of them are to be inexpensive objects; money should not be relevant for one's opportunity to obtain medalets; the decisive factor was whether one went to the right places and did the right things.

As mentioned earlier, there is a word in German for medals acquired in connection with pilgrimages; Wallfahrtsmedaillen. The thousands of medalets from European shrines which are preserved in collections and listed in catalogues indicate that this is probably the one single kind of medal that has been most widespread. Medals taken home from pilgrimages became materialized memo-

---

308   The charter of *ENID: European Network on the Instruments of Devotion*: www.enid.uib.no/html/network_charter.htm accessed 23.01.06.

ries, comparable to today's mass tourism's souvenirs, and were proof of having reached one's goal. The actual use of such medals upon return home is hard to trace, but it is likely that they have been seen as a vehicle of holy power; a means of transporting the *genus loci* of a particular place. The small size of the medalets of course makes them particularly suitable for this purpose.

Another characteristic of medalets is their two-sidedness. The possibility of coupling e.g. a holy place on one side with a representation of a saint or a theological concept on the other side, or indeed two saints, two concepts, a text and a place etc. gives unlimited opportunities for creating objects which become clear statements or encouragements to reflect or meditate on particular issues. Medalets have clearly been used as inspiration for personal meditation and prayer. For that purpose too, it can be practical to carry a medalet on you at all times, either on a separate chain, or attached to your rosary. There are however, other, more probable and immediate reasons for just that. Images of saints have been used to visualize the person or power which is addressed in prayer, and sometimes this prayer will have been of a rather urgent nature. If one believes the medalet as such will provide protection, or that the saint depicted would be more liable to help someone with a medalet, it must of course be carried. The Benedict medal (Fig. 4) has a special status and can, provided it is legitimately blessed, be used to give the blessing of St. Maur over the sick. It also has the prayer *May we be strengthened by his presence in the hour of our death*, written on it, so ideally the owner of such a medal should probably wear it at all times, in order to be prepared for what might come.

It has often been stressed from Church authorities that medals must not be conceived as 'mere charms'[309] that can work more or less mechanically, to give good luck etc. Amulets are seen as superstitious, but the line between piety and superstition is a fine one; it is not always easy to see or define, and in our context it is not necessarily of particularly high relevance.

Some medals may be worn as substitutes for scapulars, and they have been used as proofs of membership in pious organizations. The leap from this to medalets used to identify oneself and/or signal one's position or values more generally, is short. One could however not wear unlimited amounts of medalets. As referred to above (note 305), a Norwegian bishop in 1892 warned against 'the overflowing of devotionals, such as medals'. It is likely that many devotional medalets were not worn at all, but simply kept, and perhaps even collected much in the same manner people might collect stamps. If this was the case, and people valued the medalets as such, the bishop's objection was probably based on an

---

309 *The Order of Saint Benedict homepage*: www.osb.org/gen/medal.html accessed 24.01.06.

Fig. 4: Obverse and reverse of The medal of Saint Benedict. This version is also known as the Jubilee Medal of Montecassino; it was struck under the supervision of the monks at Montecassino in Italy in 1880, to commemorate the 1400th anniversary of the birth of St. Benedict. Bergen Museum, Coins and medals collection.

understanding that the value of devotionals must lie not in the objects themselves, but in their function as instruments of devotion.

The motivation for medal production has of course varied, depending where the initiative came from. One aspect it is important to be aware of in the medalets, is their propaganda potential. Medalets were used by missionaries e.g. in China,[310] but also served the purpose of propagating views in more homely contexts. Production of The Miraculous Medal (Fig. 3) started in 1832, after the French novice (now Saint) Catherine Labouré had a vision in 1830, in which the Holy Virgin told her to see to that such a medal was made. By 1840 millions of exemplars of medalets, with the Immaculate Conception as the central motif, inscribed in several different languages, had been distributed across the world. It has been suggested that the existence, the specific design, and the immense popularity of this medal, all may have to do with a desire to promote the concept of the Immaculate Conception, prior to the declaration of the dogma in 1854.[311]

---

310   Cribb, Joe: 'Medaglie cristiane e croci usate in Cina'. *Medaglia* no.15. Milano 1978, pp. 21-37.

311   Ajmar, Marta and Sheffield, Catherine: 'The Miraculous Medal: An Immaculate Conception or Not'. *The Medal* 24. London 1994, pp. 37-51.

Conclusion

Devotional medals and medalets are a group of objects which have not previously been subject to much academic interest. This presentation has shown that they have several historical forerunners and that they are no exclusively modern phenomenon, though the majority of the material known and accessible to us dates from the 19th century. Though often defined as and treated alongside medals, being first and foremost instruments of devotion (and in the Catholic Church sometimes sacramentals), not works of art, they have a somewhat particular status. Like many secular medals they can be commemorative and they play a role in defining a community and distinguishing its members. When seen as in themselves miraculous or as capable of transporting holiness, they gain a supernatural aspect which the secular medals lack, and which gives them a position on the very verge of magic. Being so closely attached to religious institutions, they must be assumed to reflect as well as influence the ideals of the members and participants in those institutions. The church in the 19th century is characterized by an intense struggle against the competition from the outside world and the increasingly modern society. My research, anchored in the study of devotional medalets, will investigate the ideals, the mechanisms and the impact of the visual culture which was sanctioned and actively nurtured by the church in this period, when the status of the popular piety was elevated and medalets 'overflowed' the market.

Visuality and Devotion in the Middle Ages

Henning Laugerud

> O foolish Galatians! Who has bewitched you,
> before whose eyes Jesus Christ
> was publicly portrayed as crucified.
>
> Gal 3.1

Introduction

Images played an important part in both private and public medieval devotions. Two well known examples are the crucifix in St. Damian that spoke to St. Francis of Assisi and St. Catherine of Alexandria's conversion in front of a panel depicting the Virgin and the Child.[312] The examples are many and the sheer amount of pictorial representations of all kinds, both for public and private use from the Middle Ages, illustrates this. The question one could ask, then, is: why is this so, what did medieval men and women see in these images? To answer this question we must look closer into the subject of sight and vision which was thought of in rather different terms than today. The importance of images had to do with the importance of sight and vision, and the close connections between sight, knowledge and understanding.

Theories of vision

In the lavishly illustrated English manuscript *Omne bonum*, probably made between 1360 and 1375, we find an interesting illumination showing the three

---

312 According to tradition that was well established by the 13th century, see Varnhagen, Herman: *Zur Geschichte der Legende der Katharina von Alexandrien*. Erlangen 1891. I will return to St. Francis later in this article.

Fig. 1: Illumination from the 14ᵗʰ century manuscript Omne bonum. © British Library Board. All rights Reserved MSS Royal 6 E VI, fol. 16.

stages, or levels, of vision according to St. Augustine (354-430).[313] The image is divided into three hierarchical levels (Fig. 1).

On the first, lower level we can see a man and a woman kneeling in prayer on each side of a schema of the Universe with the terrestrial Paradise and the Fall of Man in the centre. On the second level, above this, St. Paul and St. Benedict are pictured kneeling in prayer. St. Benedict is pointing downward and St. Paul is raising his hands. They are both gazing upward to the next level where we can see a large face with no body, the Godhead, surrounded by angels. One of the angels is holding a soul.[314] Each level is clearly separated from the next, but the rays that are emitting from the face of God, even though diminishing from level to level in a downward movement, connect them all.

This is an illustration of St. Augustine's theory of vision as we find it in the twelfth chapter of *De Genesi ad litteram*.[315] Here St. Augustine takes as his point of departure St. Paul's reference to a visionary experience in the 2 Corinthian where St. Paul speaks about the man who was 'caught up to the third heaven', into Paradise.[316] St. Augustine explains that the three heavens refer to three kinds of human sight. The first is corporeal or optical vision, where one sees the incorporeal through natural optical perception. The second is spiritual or imaginative vision where one sees incorporeal shapes as in dreaming. The third is intellectual vision, where one has a direct sight of incorporeal beings and the Divine truths.[317] Here we find a theory of sight, or vision, where optical and physical vision is intimately connected to spiritual and 'visionary' seeing.

This theory of sight and visual cognition became the common ground for all theories of vision in the middle ages. Sight was considered to be the most important of all the senses and the foremost way of cognition. St. Augustine says in his *Confessiones* about the longing for knowledge and learning that: 'This longing – since its origin is our appetite for learning, and since the sight is the chief of our senses in the acquisition of knowledge – is called in the divine language "the lust of the eyes".'[318] In the 13th century the Oxford philosopher Roger Bacon (c. 1214-

---

313   British Library MSS Royal 6 E VI – 6 E VII. The illuminations is in 6 E VI, fol. 16. See Sandler, Lucy Freeman: *Omne bonum. A fourteenth-century encyclopedia of universal knowledge*, 2 vols. London 1996.

314   The reference here is to St. Pauls vision of the Deity on the road to Damascus and St. Benedict's vision when he saw the soul of bishop Germanus being raised to heaven.

315   On the facing page (fol. 15v) of the illumination the text in question is an explanation of the visions of Saints Paul and Benedict, and all the relevant passages from St. Augustine's *De Genesi* are quoted.

316   2 Cor. 12.2-4.

317   See St. Augustine: *De Genesi ad litteram*, Chapter 12, 7. I am here referring to *On Genesis. The Works of Saint Augustine*. I/13. New York 2002, p. 471.

318   St. Augustine: *Confessiones*, Book 10 chapter 35. Here cited after *The confessions of St. Augustine*. New York 2002, p. 203. The citation from the Gospels is 1 John 2.16.

c. 1292) writes in his treatment of optics that it is necessary for all things to be known through the science of optics.[319] In his *Opus Majus* he states that: 'In God's Scripture nothing is so much enlarged upon as those things that pertain to the eye and to vision'.[320] The same way of thinking is central to St. Thomas of Aquino (c. 1226-1274), who regards sense-perception as the starting point of knowledge, pointing out that sight is the chief sense for acquiring knowledge.[321]

This way of thinking is based on optical theories of the Middle Ages founded on the concept of a kind of physical connection between the seer and the seen, the eye and what the eye was looking at. There are two main theories: The extramission theory and the intramission theory. The first theory states that the eye *sends out* 'rays' or 'sense-particles' towards an object and these 'rays' or 'particles' are then reflected back to the eye. The intramission theory states in contrast that the eye *receives* 'rays' or 'sense-particles' that the object of the gaze *emits* towards the eye. This is of course a very brief and simplified version of the optical theories, but it will suffice for now.[322] The main point here is that central to both theories is the idea that there is a physical connection between the person that sees and that which is seen. One could say that the eye in some sense 'touches' the object of the gaze.[323]

Sight as Knowledge

As we have seen, already St. Augustine emphasised that 'sight' was 'knowing'. To see was to understand. Seeing was not only a metaphor for understanding or knowledge. Optical sight took part in a process of understanding, and the spiritual or intellectual 'sight' was an extension of the optical or physical. All these levels of visions were modalities on the same hierarchical scale, where one moved from the 'lower to the higher'. This is something we recognize as an anagogical perspective, and Cynthia Hahn has characterised St. Augustine as: 'the foremost theologian of vision'.[324] But this understanding of sight was not particular to him.

319 Roger Bacon in *Opus tertium* here cited after Lindberg, David C.: *Theories of Vision from Al-Kindi to Kepler*. Chicago 1976, p. ix.

320 Roger Bacon: *Opus Majus*. 5, III, dist. 3, kapt. 1. Here cited after *The Opus Majus of Roger Bacon*. R.B. Burke (transl.). Philadelphia, London and Oxford 1928, vol. 2, p. 576. To Bacon optics was the fundamental basis for all human knowledge, as Lindberg states: 'Even the briefest perusal of Bacon's works cannot fail to reveal that optics was one of the central elements in his planned synthesis of all human knowledge', Lindberg 1976, p. 108.

321 'It is natural to man to attain to intellectual truths through sensible objects, because all our knowledge originates from the senses.' *Summa Theologica* I, Q. 1, art. 9. Here cited after Thomas of Aquino: *Summa Theologica*, vol. 1. Allen Texas 1981 (1911), p. 6.

322 To this see Lindberg 1976.

323 This does of course make the object of sight less an 'object' and more of a 'subject' since it is actively participating and communicating in the process of sensing. This is a kind of 'optics of dialogue'.

324 Hahn, Cynthia: '*Visio Dei*. Changes in Medieval Visuality'. *Visuality Before and Beyond the Renaissance*. Robert S. Nelson (ed.). Cambridge 2000, pp. 169-196.

St. Thomas was also, along with all the rest of the theologians and philosophers in the Middle Ages, of the opinion that the sight is the most important and noblest of the senses.[325] The Thomistic theory of knowledge is based on this. A central epistemological point by St. Thomas is his use of *visio* – vision, sight or gaze – as a metaphor for understanding and knowledge, but not only as a metaphor: 'All science is derived from self-evident and therefore *seen* principles; wherefore all objects of science must needs be, in a fashion seen.'[326] Sight is knowledge also in a psychological way because we understand, according to St. Thomas, through inner images or 'phantasms'. We think with images. Our intellectual concepts are images stored in our minds.[327] This is also how we remember. Our memory is the storeroom of all these images, and the fact that they are mental images makes it possible for the ideas to be remembered and contemplated. To see is to understand – an etymological connection which we can still find in most European languages.

These concepts were, among other things, based on the pseudo-Dionysian concept of knowing the higher through what is lower. In *The Ecclesiastical Hierarchy* we read that: 'it is by the way of the perceptible images that we are uplifted as far as we can be to the contemplation of what is divine.'[328] This was a key concept in the theology of pseudo-Dionysius (late 5th century) which was directly related to church decorations and the sacred vessels. Later in the 12th century Abbot Suger of St. Denis (c. 1081-1151) writes in his *De administratione*:

> Thus, when – out of my delight in the beauty of the house of God – the loveliness of the many-colored gems has called me away from external cares, and worthy meditation has induced me to reflect, transferring that which is material to that which is immaterial, […], then it seems to me that I am dwelling, as it were, in some strange region of the universe which neither exists entirely in the slime of the earth nor entirely in the purity of Heaven; and that, by the grace of God, I can be transported from the inferior to that higher world in an anagogical manner.[329]

---

325 See for instance *De veritate*, Q. 12, art. 3, ad 2 see St. Thomas of Aquino: *Truth*, vol I-III. (*Quaestiones disputatae de veritate.*) Indianapolis and Cambridge 1994 (1954). See also: *Summa Theologica* I, Q. 1, art. 9, and particularly: Q. 67, art. 67.

326 *ST* II-II, Q. 1, art. 5. Here cited after *Summa Theologica* 1981, p. 1166.

327 For a short introduction to St. Thomas' philosophy of mind and theory of knowledge see: Kretzmann, Norman: 'Philosophy of mind' and MacDonald, Scott: 'Theory of knowledge' both in Kretzmann, Norman and Stump, Eleonore (eds.): *The Cambridge Companion to Aquinas*. Cambridge 1994. See also: Gilson, Etienne: *The Philosophy of St. Thomas Aquinas*. Cambridge 1929.

328 Pseudo-Dionysius: *The Ecclesiastical Hierarchy*, Chapter 1, 2. here cited after: *The Complete Works*. New York 1987, p. 197. For other statements on the role of perceptible symbols see for instance: *The Divine Names*, Chapter 4, 9 or *The Celestial Hierarchy*, Chapter 1, 3 and several other places in the pseudo-Dionysian corpus.

329 *De administratione*, chapter XXXIII, here cited after Panofsky, Erwin (Ed. & Transl.): *Abbot Suger on the Abbey Church of St.-Denis and its art treasures*. Princeton NJ 1979 (1946), pp. 63-65.

This is a kind of anagogical optics. Such an anagogical sight provided an opportunity to proceed from the pictorial programme to the spiritual realities for which they stood. This gives the three well known functions ascribed to images in the Church-teachings from St. Gregory onwards a different momentum. The argument that images should serve three purposes: didactic, commemorative and to kindle religious feelings or emotions are thus far more complex than they might look at first glance.[330] The commemorative aspect was underlined as one of the three functions of images. This was connected to the image aspect of the psychology of memory. This means both the mnemotechnical aspect of images and memory understood in terms of the psychology of knowledge, that is, the image as a model and some kind of physical equivalent to the inner images in the mind. Memory is therefore an important part of this 'culture of visuality'. The art of memory is not only concerned with the more instrumentalistic aspect of memory, but also with how the human brain works and how knowledge and understanding are attained. Memory can be individual as well as collective or social, and these two 'spheres of memory' are constantly interacting.

St. Bonaventure (c. 1221-1274) expresses the same tenets in his *Itinerarium Mentis in Deum*:

> [...] since the creation of the world His invisible attributes are clearly seen
> ... being understood through the things that are made [...] Thanks be to
> God [...], who has called us out of darkness into His Marvellous light,
> when through these lights externally given we are led to re-enter the mirror of our mind in which divine realities are reflected.[331]

Here St. Bonaventure expresses another influential concept related to the importance of sight; namely the Platonizing metaphysics of light that is also central to the thinking of pseudo-Dionysius. In this view light was the noblest natural phenomenon because it was the least material and therefore the closest approximation to pure form, one of Gods attributes. Light was also a prerequisite for physical optics as well as the spiritual. What you see is light.[332]

---

330 For a discussion of the thinking of St. Gregory in these matters see: Duggan, Lawrence G.: 'Was art really the "book of the illiterate"?'. *Word and Image* 5:2 London 1989 and Chazelle, Celia M.: 'Pictures, books and the illiterate: Pope Gregory I's letters to Serenus of Marseilles'. *Word & Image* 6:2. London 1990.

331 St. Bonaventure: *Mystical Opuscula, I.* Paterson NJ 1960, p. 27.

332 See *ST* III, Q.45, art. 2. Gods word of creation was 'fiat lux', and Christ is light out of light, 'lumen de lumine', as we read in the Nicene Creed. To this point see for instance the discussion in von Simson, Otto: *The Gothic Cathedral. Origins of Gothic Architecture and the Medieval Concept of Order.* Princeton 1988 (1954), chapter 2, particularly pp. 50-58. For a short introduction see also Eco, Umberto: *Art and Beauty in the Middle Ages.* Yale 1986 (1956).

As we can see there was a relation between optical sight and spiritual seeing, between knowledge and vision. This emphasis of vision or sight can also be seen in other aspects of medieval devotions, perhaps most significantly in the cult of Corpus Christi where the 'sighting' of the Host was a central element. The Elevation of the Host was an important part of the Eucharistic celebration because people believed that seeing the Host had a special saving effect.[333] This way of thinking became increasingly important during the late medieval period. Eamon Duffy points out that:

> [...] the reception of communion was not the primary mode of lay encounter with the Host. Everyone received at Easter, and one's final communion, the viaticum, or 'journey money' given on the deathbed, was crucially important to medieval people [...] But for most people, most of the time the Host was something to be seen, not to be consumed.[334]

To see the Host: 'was a privilege bringing blessing.'[335]

The gaze could be instrumental to attain salvation. This was not new to the Middle Ages but was part of a long tradition originating in the Old Testament, as the example with the brazen serpent and the story of Job shows. These episodes from the Old Testament books were in the Middle Ages seen as prefigurations of the seeing of Christ. St. Paul himself stresses the importance of the gaze in his epistles, for instance in the Galatians 3.1, where he says: 'O foolish Galatians! Who has bewitched you, before whose eyes Jesus Christ was publicly portrayed as crucified' (Fig. 2).

From the 13th century onwards it became increasingly common among theologians to speak about 'spiritual communion' as something that could be achieved by seeing and contemplating the body of Christ. Angela of Foligno (ca. 1248-1309) says for instance in one of her *Instructions*:

> The more perfectly and purely we see, the more perfectly and purely we love. As we see, so we love. Therefore, the more we see of Jesus Christ, God and man, the more we are transformed into him by love. And to the extent that we are transformed into him by love, we will in turn be transformed into the suffering which the soul sees in Jesus Christ, God and man.[336]

---

333 See Rubin, Miri: *Corpus Christi. The Eucharist in Late Medieval Culture*. Cambridge 1994. On this topic see particularly chapter 1, pp. 49-82 and chapter 5, pp. 288-297.

334 Duffy, Eamon: *The Stripping of the Altars. Traditional Religion in England 1400-1580*. New Haven and London 1992, p. 95.

335 Duffy 1992, p. 101.

336 Angela of Foligno: *Instructions*, book 3. Here cited after: Angela of Foligno: *Complete Works*. New York 1993, p. 242.

Fig. 2: 'O foolish Galatians! Who has bewitched you, before whose eyes Jesus Christ was publicly portrayed as crucified'. Detail of the 14th Century frescoes on the North Wall of the Chapter House of the Dominican convent Santa Maria Novella in Florence. The citation is inscriped above the Crucified Christ. The frescoes were executed by Andrea di Bonaiuto (c. 1320-1379).

There is an exchange between Christ and the one who seeks Him, an interaction where the believer, through prayer, contemplation and seeing, is spiritually consumed into the sacred body of Christ. But despite of this: Gods real nature is still veiled behind the physical appearances as bread and wine. As St. Thomas puts it in his hymn *Adoro Te Devote*: 'Devoutly I adore You, hidden Deity, Under these appearances concealed' and in the last verse: 'Jesus, Whom now I see enveiled, What I desire, when will it be? Beholding Your fair face revealed, Your glory shall I be blessed to see.'[337] We do not of course see His 'fair face revealed' in the Eucharist, but perhaps as close as possible in our fallen state.

The act of seeing had both a sacramental aspect and an aspect of identification. The significance of the visuality of images lay in their spiritual importance, not only as 'instruments of piety', but also in the transference of grace. Images seem to have had a 'quasi-sacramental' character in the late middle ages, due

337 Here cited after *The Aquinas Prayer Book*. Manchester, New Hampshire 2000, pp. 69-71.

to the significance of sight and vision in gaining knowledge of God. The cult of Corpus Christi, with its emphasis of the visibility and the seeing of the host, is another expression of the same attitude and devotional thinking and practice.

Images and Visions

The mystical experience was closely linked to the visual culture of the Middle Ages, as the word *vision* itself clearly points out. We can find numerous examples of the close connection between images and mystical visions, where mystics recognize Christ or Saints from images they have seen in the churches, or actively contemplate images in an effort to seek a mystical experience. Images themselves could also 'become' visions in a sense; as in the well known episode where the miraculous crucifix in the church of St. Damian spoke to St. Francis and gave him his sanctifying command.[338] Legends about miraculous paintings and sculptures were many and popular in the 13th century, but stories of this kind are also well known from the 12th century. Caesarius of Heisterbach (c. 1170-c. 1240) narrates several such stories in his *Dialogus miraculorum*.[339]

Some of the central visions of St. Thomas took place in front of a crucifix. Bernhard Gui narrates in his *Legenda S. Thomae* about a vision St. Thomas had when working on the subject of the eucharistic theology. St. Thomas placed the sheets of paper with his text on the altar, and with uplifted hands prayed to the crucifix and asked for a judgement of his text:

> Suddenly the *socius* of Thomas and other brethren there present saw Christ Himself appear! He stood on the altar, above the sheets of paper, and spoke to His servant in these words: You have written well, Thomas, of the sacrament of my Body; you have answered the questions put to you as well as it can be answered, in human language, by man still living in mortal life.[340]

The way in which he was praying resembles the descriptions and illustrations in *The Nine Ways of Prayer of St. Dominic* (Fig. 3). An interesting aspect of this illumination, as with many other medieval illuminations, is that the depicted crucifix is

---

338 The story is recorded in *The Second Life*, Chapter VI. It is also referred in *Legenda Aurea*. See for instance: Thomas of Celano: *Saint Francis of Assisi. First and Second Life of St. Francis*. Placid Herman OFM (ed. and transl.). Chicago 1988 (1963), p. 144.

339 See Caesarius of Heisterbach: *The Dialogue on Miracles*, vol. 1-2. Henry von Essen Scott & C.C. Swinton Bland (transl.). London 1929.

340 Bernhard Gui: *Legenda S. Thomae*, Chapter 24. Here cited after Foster, Kenelm O.P. (Ed. & Transl.): *The Life of Saint Thomas Aquinas. Biographical Documents*. London 1959, p. 43-44.

Fig. 3: Illumination from a 14ᵗʰ century manuscript of The Nine Ways of Prayer of St. Dominic, prayer VII. Codex Rossianus 3, Vatican Library.

presented as seen to be alive. Here image and vision are being merged together. In fact, as we shall see, most mystics of the Middle Ages saw visions in what we might call conventional picture terms.

An illustrative example is the German visionary Gertrude of Helfta (1256-1301/02). In her description of one of her visions in *The Herald of Divine Love* there are some interesting passages. On one occasion she had prayed and asked the Lord to pierce her heart with the arrow of His love:

> After I had received the life giving sacrament, on returning to my place, it seemed to me as if, on the right side of the Crucified painted in the book, that is to say, on the wound in the side, a ray of sunlight with a sharp point like an arrow came forth and spread itself out for a moment and then drew back.[341]

Gertrude states here rather bluntly that an image played an instrumental role in her vision. It is also significant that Communion and vision are connected.

---

341 Gertrude of Helfta: *The Herald of Divine Love*. New York 1993, p. 102. Book II, Chapter 5.

The corporeality of the Host lends credibility and virtue to the corporeal images. Gertrude had several visions of this kind connected to crucifixes and in Book 3 of *The Herald* she recounts an incident where Christ spoke to her from a crucifix, and later, when holding one in her hand she was given the understanding of how one should gaze at a crucifix in a devout manner so that Christ would look back at the beholder. According to *The Herald* she received, on another occasion, an instruction of what one was to consider in ones heart when looking at a crucifix:

> See how I hung upon the cross for love of you, naked and despised, my
> body covered with wounds and every limb pulled out of joint. And now
> my heart is moved with such sweet charity toward you that, if it were ex-
> pedient for your salvation, and if you could be saved in no other way, I
> would bear it for you alone all that you may imagine I bore for the whole
> world.[342]

This is very similar to the words of the 'Man of Sorrows' in an illuminated manuscript from c. 1300, showing the three stages of the devout soul (Fig. 4).[343] In this illuminated scene the optical and the devout, mystical vision are merged.

In one of Gertrude's visions Christ even explained the reason why He showed himself in corporeal visions. Christ told her that spiritual and invisible things could only be explained for the human intellect through *similitudes* of things perceived by the mind. Therefore no one ought to despise what was revealed through bodily things. On the contrary, one should study anything that made the mind able to taste the 'sweetness of spiritual delights through the likeness of bodily things'.[344] This is in complete accordance with what St. Thomas writes in his *Summa theologica*.[345]

A famous late medieval example which clearly shows the relationship between physical images and mystical vision is St. Catherine of Siena (c. 1347-1380). There are many references to easily identifiable images or image types in her visions, and in the earliest known biography of her life the references to images are particularly explicit. In this *Miracles of the Blessed Catherine* we can read a description of what was probably her first vision. Here she saw Christ dressed in white as a bishop, smiling to her, and behind him a host of saints among whom

---

342 *The Herald*, p. 210. Book III, Chapter 41.

343 The 'Troiz estaz de bones ames', from *La sainte abbaye*, Yates Thompson MS 11. See Rouse, Richard H. & Rouse, Mary A.: *Manuscripts and their Makers. Commercial book producers in Medieval Paris 1200-1500*. Turnhout 2000, p. 155-157.

344 Hamburger, Jeffrey: *The Visual and the Visionary*. New York 1998, p. 147.

345 Se for instance *ST,* I. Q. 1 art. 9.

Fig. 4: Illumination from the late 13th century manuscript: Li liures de lestat de lame, showing the vision of the 'Man of Sorrows' as a motif in the lower left part. La sainte abbaye. © British Library Board. All Rights Reserved Yates Thompson MS 11, fol. 29.

she recognized the Saints Peter, Paul and John: 'as she had seen them painted in the church.'[346] At another occasion, when St. Dominic came to speak to her, she saw him in the same form as she had seen him painted in the church.[347] Interestingly enough her stigmatisation vision is 'modelled' on the stigmatisation of St. Francis; *not* as it is described in his *Vitae*, but according to the pictorial conventions of the stigmatisation.[348]

During her last dramatic days in Rome in 1380 something happened which serves as yet another example of how an image became, or became part of, a vision. She was praying beneath Giotto's mosaic of the *Navicella*, a symbolic image of the Church, in the old St. Peter's. This was a motif she had seen before, in the Chapter Hall of the Dominican convent of Santa Maria Novella in Florence (Fig. 5). While she was thus lying in prayer on the floor, she saw and felt how Christ lifted the whole ship, the bark of St. Peter, unto her shoulders and trying to raise she collapsed under its weight.[349] Placing the whole Church upon her shoulders was Gods 'response' to her desire to become a sacrificial victim for the renewal of the Church. The physical image steps outside its frame and in a way 'comes alive'.[350] Again we see how images and visions merge, more literally than in most other cases.

The recognition of, and the possibility to identify what she saw was dependent on physical painted images she had seen before. And it was exactly this relation that gave her visions credibility. This was in the minds of the medieval women and men, as we have already seen, the only way God and spiritual truths could be explained to the human intellect: Through bodily things and recognizable forms.

---

346 *I miracoli di Beata Caterina* was written around 1374 by a close follower of her circle. See Fawtier, Robert: *Sainte Catherine de Sienne. Essai de critique des Sources. Sources Hagiographiques*. Paris 1922, p. 218. This vision is also recounted by Raymond of Capua in his *Legenda maior*, in a slightly altered version. See Raymond of Capua: *The life of Catherine of Siena*. Conleth Kearns OP (transl.). Washington D.C. 1994, p. 29.

347 Fawtier 1920, p. 222.

348 See: Meiss, Millard: *Painting in Florence and Siena after the Black Death. The Arts, Religion, and Society in the Mid-Fourteenth Century*. Princeton 1978 (1951), pp. 117-121.

349 See the letters number 371 and 373 in Caterina da Siena: *Epistolario*. Rome 1979.

350 There are many legendary examples of all kinds of images that come alive from the medieval period. Caesarius of Heisterbachs *Dialogus miraculorum* is already mentioned, important is also Gautier de Coincy's *Miracles de Nostre Dame*. A famous example is the lavishly illustrated *Cantigas de Santa Maria de Alfonso X, el Sabio* from the end of the 12th century. For an overview of this material see for instance: Mussafia, Adolfo: 'Studien zur Mittelalterlichen Marienlegenden. I.' *Sitzungsberichte der Phil.-Hist. Classe der Kaiserliche Akademie der Wissenschaften*, b. 113. Wien 1886, pp. 917-994. For an art-historical discussion of this see Freedberg, David: *The Power of Images. Studies in the History and Theory of Response*. Chicago 1989, and Belting, Hans: *Bild und Kult: eine Geschichte des Bildes vor dem Zeitalter der Kunst*. München 1990.

Fig. 5: The Navicella motif in the Chapter House of the Dominican convent of Santa Maria Novella in Florence. The 14th Century frescoes by Andrea di Bonaiuto (c. 1320-1370).

Modes of vision and the familiarity of Images

To return to the question posed in the introduction of this article, what medieval women and men saw in their images, I would answer: Immensely much more than we do, as Carolly Erickson puts it in her classical study from 1978: 'Their sight was different from ours in kind; accepting a more inclusive concept of reality, they saw more than we do. From a modern point of view, the visionary is a person who sees what isn't there; his or her visions separate him or her from reality. In the middle ages visions defined reality.'[351]

What we can literally *see* here are people living within a visual culture far more complex and advanced than ours. The frescoes on the church walls, illuminations, altarpieces and sculptures; all kinds of physical images could be the beginning of the beholder's journey from mere sight to vision. Any work of art could prompt a vision. Images should lead the gaze of the beholder to a reality beyond this one, towards Heaven and the Divine:

> Whether calmly contemplative or ecstatically rapturous, all such devotional images were intended, in their very exemplariness, to elevate the spirit, to absorb the worshiper's mind in God, to direct the devout beholder's gaze toward a realm ultimately beyond what can be seen corporeally in nature, to the divine truth, which can only be apprehended (as the church fathers thought) with spiritual eyes.[352]

The references to physical images by visionaries were quite explicit and functioned as a way of giving their mystical visions credibility. How do you recognize that which you have never seen? This means that the Divine shows itself in recognizable forms, as Christ Himself told Gertrude of Helfta.

But it was also emphasised that this human gaze was far from perfect. The kind of vision that the believer could obtain in the human state was an obscured and reflected glance or a temporary glimpse, seen as through a darkened glass or mirror, as in an enigma, whereas the ideal kind of vision that the illuminated seer would enjoy in the future state of Salvation was fully revealed as a stable, fixed gaze, face to face with God. As St. Paul says: 'We see now in a mirror dimly, but then face to face.'[353]

The border between seeing a physical image, a phantasm and a visionary image were blurred. In a way we could say that there was a *familiarity* between all

---

351 Erickson, Carolly: *The medieval vision. Essays in History and Perception*. New York 1978, pp. 29-30.

352 Barolsky, Paul: 'Naturalism and the Visionary Art of the Early Renaissance'. *Gazette des Beaux-Arts*, 6ᵉ periode, tome 129, Paris 1997, p. 63.

353 1 Cor.13.12.

these images. This gives for instance the late medieval 'andacthsbild' a somewhat more potent devotional power. The medieval images, then, can be seen as windows through which one could, if properly prepared, look into the realm of Heaven. Not face to face, but as in a 'mirror dimly'. Sight was connected with knowledge and understanding. All these ways of seeing, through images, to inner images and intellectual reasoning and knowledge, and mystical vision are in a sense just different modes of seeing, that is, attaining knowledge of the Divine and finally; Salvation. It is all different modalities of vision on a scale with escalating perfection. Painted and sculpted images were physical starting points of the anagogical process towards understanding, or rather seeing the Divine. Contemplation of, and devotions to images were means used to reach a higher level of understanding and knowledge of the Divine truths – the ultimate aim of which was the 'seeing' of the Godhead 'face to face'.

'the solace of his image':

Images and Presence in Late Medieval Devotional Practice

Laura Katrine Skinnebach

Introduction

In the gospel according to Matthew (28.6) the three Marias are confronted with Christ's absence from the grave: 'He is not here; for he has been raised, as he said. Come, see the place where he lay'. The passion and death of Christ, culminating with the resurrection three days later, is the most important event in Christianity and its influence on the development of Christian faith and religiosity cannot be underestimated. If Christ had not been raised, all proclamation and all faith would have been in vain.[354] The ascension of Christ was, however, also the beginning of physical absence. One of the central aspects of ritual and devotional practise became the attempt to make up for this 'loss of body'.[355]

The desire for *realis praesentia* has been strong in Christian cultural history and this is clearly reflected in the cultural products of the Christian Church and its devotional life, but perhaps it reached its most vivid and visual peak in late medieval Catholicism. During this period the Church and devotional life was preoccupied with divine *presence* to the extent that it seems like it had become one of the focal points of religious thought and practice. It is reflected in the numerous ways the body of Christ was celebrated with the *Corpus Christi* feast as a

---

354 '… and if Christ has not been raised, then our proclamation has been in vain and your faith has been in vain […] But in fact Christ has been raised from the dead, the first fruits of those who have died.' 1 Corinthians 15.14 and 20.

355 Pranger, Burcht: 'Images of Iron: Ignatius of Loyola and Joyce'. *Religion and Media*. Hent de Vries (ed.). Palo Alto CA 2001, p.183. The concept of 'loss of body' is quoted from Cramer, Peter: *Baptism and Change in the Early Middle Ages ca. 200-ca.1150*. Cambridge 1993, p. 221.

particularly strong feature. It is also reflected in the staging of liturgy, the earliest example being the *Quem Queritis* performed together with the symbolical burial of Christ – in the form of a Crucifix or a consecrated host or even a small statue – on Good Friday in the Easter Liturgy.[356] But one of the most obvious signs of the desire for real presence is perhaps reflected in the field of the visual. During the late Middle Ages images reached major importance as instruments for obtaining or experiencing different kinds of divine presence. The following essay will attempt to give some examples of medieval ideas of divine presence and in particular how it was reflected in and associated with the field of the visual in northern Europe.

Images as presence: the Veronica-legend as an introductory case

In the late Middle Ages the legend of Veronica was regarded as an authoritative account of how Christ had instituted images as mediators of divine presence.[357] The legend existed in different variants whereof two will be dealt with here. The most well known one (today) tells that Veronica dried the face of Christ with a piece of cloth when he was on his way to Calvary and, miraculously, the face of Christ was imprinted on the cloth. After the Crucifixion of Christ, Emperor Tiberius was cured from a deadly illness upon showing devotion to the image in the cloth. In spite of the physical absence of Christ, the imprint on the cloth had the same powers as if the Lord had been present himself. The alternative version was recorded in the extremely popular *Legenda Aurea*. The collection was originally made in the 13th century but copied in numerous editions around Europe, even in the 15th century. This version has a detailed description of how Veronica received the imprint. Emperor Tiberius, who was incurably ill, sent a messenger to Jerusalem to find Jesus who was said to be able to cure all illnesses. The messenger met a woman, Veronica, who reported of the tragic death of Christ but comforted him by telling about an image that had been handed to her by Christ:

356 Further descriptions and references about medieval Easter liturgy can be found in Grinder- Hansen, Poul: 'Public Devotional Pictures in Late Medieval Denmark'. *Images of Cult and Devotion. Function and Reception of Christian images in Medieval and Post-Medieval Europe*. Søren Kaspersen (ed.). Copenhagen 2004, esp p. 233ff.

357 One indication of this is that the Legend of Veronica was referred to numerous times in the Reformation debate about images as one of the first believable examples of Christ himself having favoured images as an instrument of devotion. See for example the treatises by Hieronymus Emser 'That One Should not Remove Images of the Saints from the Churches nor Dishonour Them, and that They are not Forbidden in Scripture' and Johannes Eck 'On not Removing Images of Christ and the Saints' both in *A Reformation Debate: Karlstadt Emser, and Eck on Sacred Images. Three Treatises in Translation*. Translated with introduction by Bryan D. Mangrum and Guiseppe Scavizzi. Toronto 1998.

When the teacher was going about preaching and I, to my regret, could not be with him, I wanted to have his picture painted so that when I was deprived of his presence, I could at least have the solace of his image [*solaciu imagines sue figura*]. So one day I was carrying a piece of linen to the painter when I met Jesus, and he asked me where I was going. I told him what my errand was. He asked for the cloth I had in my hand, pressed it to his venerable face, and left his image on it. If your master looks devoutly upon this image, he will at once be rewarded by being cured.[358]

Deprived of the presence of Christ, Veronica wanted an image of him because she believed it would give her solace: she believed that an image could be a substitute for the presence of Christ. A middle English translation of the *legenda* has Veronica uttering that if she has a painted image she would 'have always with me his presence'.[359] According to that particular translation, an image *is* presence.

Of course the image produced on the piece of cloth by Jesus himself preserves a different and much more miraculous kind of presence; it is in fact able to transcend the boundaries between heaven and earth and perform the same wondrous acts as the living Christ, provided that it is approached with proper devotion. The legend thus links images to devotion and presence, in particular regarding the 'true image' on the cloth, but also, in some form, applying to other kinds of images. The *Legenda Aurea* version of the Veronica legend was perhaps not the authoritative version in the Middle Ages[360], but it still reveals some very central ideas and ideals regarding medieval images.

The devotional and visual tradition that developed in relation to the legend, illustrates how devotion related to images was connected to presence. It developed from sometime in the late 12th century when it was related to an actual object, the Suidarium, a piece of cloth kept in St. Peters in Rome.[361] According to the chronicles of Matthew Paris it was annually displayed by Pope Innocens

---

358 *Legenda Aurea Readings on the Saints*, 2 vols. William Granger Ryan (transl.). Princeton NJ 1993, vol. I, 'On the Passion of the Lord', p. 53. This particular translation is very close to a selection of Latin texts which can be found on the online library *Verteilte Digitale Inkunabelbibliothek*: http://inkunabeln.ub.uni-koeln.de/. It lists 5 versions of the *legenda aurea sanctorum, sive Lombardica historia* from 1480, 1481, 1482, 1483 and 1478. Four of them have similar text 'solaciu imagines sue figura'.

359 The full quote is; 'My lord and my master when he went preaching, I absented me oft from him, I did do paint his image, for to have alway with me his presence, because that the figure of his image should give me some solace'. *Legenda Aurea. Medieval Sourcebook Online*: 'The Passion of the Lord'. www.fordham.edu/Halsall/basis/goldenlegend/GL-vol1-passionofourlLord.%20html

360 It would be interesting to discuss this matter in more detail. Medieval images depicting the Suidarium seem to be following both traditions. Some are clearly inspired by the legend of Veronica wiping the face of the Lord but others seem to be following the parallel *Legenda* tradition.

361 Belting, Hans: *Bild und Kult. Eine Geschichte des Bildes vor dem Zeialter der Kunst*. München 1990, pp. 233-252 and Freedberg, David: *The Power of Images. Studies in the History and Theory of Response*. Chicago and London 1989, pp. 207-210. According to both, the Veronica tradition might have been linked to the *Abgar-mandylion* tradition.

III (1198-1216) and carried around the streets of Rome in order to cure the ill of the city. The pope also wrote a popular prayer which instructed the beholder to commemorate the Lord when meeting him 'face to face' and recommended the public to memorize the prayer and carry it around with them and, to arouse more devotion in them, it was illustrated with images showing the face of Christ.[362] Images, and not only the Suidarium itself, thus held an important position in the practice of prayer as an instrument that evoked devotion. Images depicting the Suidarium were reproduced in numerous copies and functioned as devotional objects in churches all over Europe. It seems to have been extremely popular in Northern Europe after 1400. In Denmark it is commonplace to find it painted on altarpiece predellas and murals and here we also find a prayer to the face of Christ in the Prayer Book of Anna Brade;

> We salute you, the face of our redeemer, which shines with divine clarity imprinted in a piece of cloth [...] and given to a woman, Veronica, as a token of love [...][363]

If the prayer was read together with a *pater noster* and one *ave* in front of an image showing the face of Christ, the devotee would be entitled to 17 years and 36 days of indulgence. The instructions for this particular prayer do not specify if it had to be directed towards the original Suidarium located in Rome – such information is usually noted in the instructions to the prayers in Anna Brades Prayer Book – so most likely, a painted reproduction of the Suidarium in the local church would have sufficed.

The ideas regarding images as reflected in the legend of Veronica are to some extent the prototype of the medieval *use* of images. All images represented some kind of (potential) presence, or, at least, gave some solace for the absence of Christ. But it was all a matter of approach; to meet the image with proper devotion, such as a prayer, a bodily posture and a mental disposition. The connection between image, devotion and presence will be further exemplified in the following.

---

362 A German translation of this passage from Matthew Paris' chronicle can be found in Belting 1993, *Anhang* p. 604.

363 My translation. The Danish text reads; 'Heelseth være tw vor genløsers anledhe i huilket ther skyn guddomens clarhedz skapnet instryct i eth clæde/ I hwidhedz eller sneæss fæyrendæ/ oc guiffuet een qwinnæ veronica for kerlighetz tegn'. Nielsen, Martin Karl: *Middelalderens danske bønnebøger*, 5 vols. Copenhagen 1946, vol II, p. 65.

Real presence: Eucharistic vision

The concept of real presence is of course closely linked to the Mass and the celebration of the Eucharist. When the celebrant utters the words of institution, bread and wine are transformed into the body and blood of Christ and from this moment Christ is present on the altar. It is a physical presence, yet invisible; bread and wine still appear as bread and wine after the transformation has occurred.

In late medieval imagery there are numerous depictions of Eucharistic transformation. It seems as if 'this invisible moment of sacramental change triggered a wealth of images visibly expressing the Christ who failed to be visible in the sacrament itself'.[364] One of the most common Eucharistic iconographies was without doubt the Mass of Gregory. According to legendary tradition, Christ appeared to Pope Gregory one day when he was celebrating Mass in order to prove that the wine and bread really *was* his flesh and blood. One example is found in the high-altarpiece in the Church of Mary in Bergen, Norway, most likely made in northern Germany around 1480 (Fig. 1). The depiction of the Mass of Gregory is positioned on the outside of the wings of the triptych with three other images which I will return to shortly. This particular depiction shows the Pope kneeling before the altar, surrounded by representatives of the ecclesiastical hierarchy, while Christ appears on the altar-table. He is depicted as the suffering Christ, the Man of Sorrows, with the signs of the Passion on his body. Blood run directly from his side-wound and wounds in his hands and into the chalice on the altar table, and thus makes visually manifest to the Pope and the beholder of the image, that the transubstantiated wine *is* the blood shed by the suffering Christ. What the beholder of the image sees is a linkage between the invisible divine presence in the Eucharist and the historical Christ made visible by a visual representation. The invisibility of the Eucharistic transformation is thus suspended by showing Christ as actually visible; the invisible body and blood of Christ in the Eucharist might thus be experienced as visible as well.[365]

The depiction of the Mass of Gregory is also a depiction of devotional practice directed towards the Eucharist. The image depicts the Pope kneeling in adoration of Christ and his miraculous presence on the altar. The three other images of the wings (see Fig. 1) circle around a similar double reference; the Eucharist and devotion. The motifs on the northern wings show the Nativity and the Ado-

364 Pranger 2001, p.183

365 In 1993 a large exhibition in Westfälisches Landesmuseum Münster was dedicated to the theme *Imagination des Unsichtbaren*. The two-volume catalogue shows numerous examples of how Christian religious culture, in different historical periods, has attempted to visualize the invisible. *Imagination des Unsichtbaren. 1200 Jahre Bildener Kunst im Bistum Münster*, 2 vols. Münster 1993. Se also Ganz, Davis and Lentes, Thomas (eds.): *Kultbild. Ästhetik des Unsichtbaren. Bildteorie und Bildgebrauch der Vormoderne*. Berlin 2004.

Fig. 1: High-altarpiece from the Church of Mary in Bergen, Norway, dating from the last part of the 15th century. The painted images dealt with in the article are visible when the wings of the Triptych are closed. Photo: Henrik von Achen.

Fig. 2: The Seven Sacrament Altarpiece by Rogier van Der Weyden commissioned in 1441 by the Bishop of Tournai, Jean Chevrot for his private chapel. The central painting show the sacrament of the Eucharist while the wings depict 3 sacraments each. To the left (bottom to top of the image: baptism, confirmation and confession. To the right (top to bottom of the image): ordination, marriage and extreme unction. The altarpiece is now in Musée Royal in Antwerp. Copyright: Reproductiefonds Vlaamse Musea NV.

ration of the Magi. The main theme of the Epiphany scene is Virgin Mary and St. Joseph's adoration of the Child; Virgin Mary is kneeling with folded hands while St. Joseph, positioned behind the Virgin, is holding a rosary and thus performing a devotional practice that was not 'invented' until centuries after the birth of Christ. The Epiphany is central because it depicts the first visual and physical appearance of Christ. The Adoration of the Magi depicts the first public physical appearance of Christ as well as a public acknowledgement of his sanctity. Below the Mass of Gregory, the depiction of the Presentation in the Temple shows the Christ Child standing on the altar-table just as in the scene above and thus prefiguring the sacrifice of Christ and his sacramental function; he is already the living bread and wine. All three scenes refer to historical events in the childhood of

Christ where he was alive and walked the earth, but with reference to the Mass of Gregory they serve as clarification of the content of the mass and the miraculous sacramental presence of Christ.

The devotional practices performed in all four images are exactly the same; Gregory's kneeling position is similar to the poses performed by the Virgin and the King. The combination of these four images constructs a close relation between the Eucharist, devotion and presence. In order to experience real presence, the devotee has to articulate the euchanistic event – and perhaps also the images with it – according to the universal tradition of devotional practice.

The linkage between Eucharist, devotion and presence is perhaps even more clearly spoken in the *Seven Sacrament* altarpiece by Flemish artist Rogier van Der Weyden (Fig.2). The central panel of the Triptych depicts the sacrament of Holy Communion. The priest is celebrating Mass inside a spacious Gothic church at an altar positioned in front of a rood screen dividing the nave from the choir. He is depicted at the exact moment when he utters the words of institution and elevates the transubstantiated Host to make the body of Christ visible to the congregation. There is in fact no congregation to witness the transformation besides one man kneeling between the pillars dividing nave and aisle (and is he even looking at the celebrant?) and then, of course, the beholders of the image. The altarpiece thus creates an intimate contact with its beholder; a meeting between the visual articulation of the Eucharist established in the image and the devotional approach made by the beholder. What the beholder meets in this image is of course the sacramental ritual but it is first and foremost the scene in the foreground; a large Crucifix from floor to ceiling of the enormous nave. Four women and St. John, positioned directly on the church floor, laments the death of the crucified Lord. The juxtaposition of the ritual practice and the historical scenery is an illustration of *Anamnesis*; that the sacrament is both a commemoration of the Crucifixion of Christ (then) and a recalling of His divine presence (now). The invisible presence of Christ in the elevated Host is supplemented with a visual presence (now) represented by the historical event, the Crucifixion, and thus suspending time and space to create a new and actualized presence. To the beholder, the eucharistic presence in the background of the image is as real as the Crucifixion was to the beholders in the historical past and the eucharistic presence is, in spite of its invisibility, potentially visible if it is approached with proper adoration.

Another kind of visual manifestation of eucharistic presence, was the decoration of the Host, a common practice in the late Middle Ages. When the Host was elevated the beholder saw both the body of Christ and the image of Christ and the wafer became in itself the prototype of the merging of Christ and the image of Christ. Such a wafer is depicted in the Epitaph of Konrad Zingel painted in 1447 for the Church of St. Egidius in Nürnberg which by the way is another iconographic version of the Mass of Gregory than the one depicted in Church of Mary (Fig. 3).[366]

A prayer from a Danish book written by Christiern Pedersen printed in 1514, divides the mass into 33 articles, each supplied with a short prayer. Article 19 mentions the Elevation of the Host and the prayer to go with it is as follows;

> Blessed Lord, Jesus Christ, I thank you for the time you suffered heavy pains here on earth that you let yourself be nailed to the cross with nails which were punched through your hands and feet and be erected at the cross from earth to heaven with great pain. I ask you humbly, dear Lord, that you will erect my heart to heavenly things and pleasures [...][367]

The prayer displays a similar link between past and presence and its description of the crucifixion echoes the Seven Sacrament altarpiece.[368] Emperor Tiberius was, according to the Veronica legend, cured of his maladies only because he showed proper adoration to the image; the miraculous powers of the image were activated by his devotional approach. The experience of divine presence in the Eucharist followed a similar pattern; Christ's presence in the Eucharist was an undeniable fact, and the visual presence was provided for by the images, but the visionary and spiritual experience of divine presence could only be actualized by showing proper adoration to the body of Christ. Such as performing a prayer as the one mentioned in Christian Pedersen's book.

---

366 Similar motives are depicted on the Epitaph from 1481 belonging to one of the members of the family Hehel or Höhel in Nürnberg St. Lorenz and the epitaph from 1475 over Dorothea Schürstab from the Dominican nunnery St. Katharina in Nürnberg as well as the Epitaph of Henrich Wolf von Wolfenstahl 1500, now in Germanisches Nationalmuseum Nürnberg. See Streider, Peter, *Tafelmalerei in Nürnberg 1350-1550*. Nürnberg 1993.

367 My translation from Danish 'O velsignede herre ihesu criste Jeg tacker dig ath den tiidh dw hagde lidet megen swar pine her paa iorden ath du daa vilde lade sig negle til det hellige korss met stompede nagle som slagne vaare gennem dine hender och føder oc opregse dig paa korsset fra iorden i lucten met stor pine Jeg beder dig ydmigelige kere herre at dw vilt opløffte mit hierte til hiemmelske ting oc begerelser [...]'. This particular prayer is to be said during Elevation of the bread. There is a separate prayer for the Elevation of the wine. Pedersen, Christiern: *Bog Om Messen*. Published by Brandt and Fenger: *Christiern Pedersens Danske Skrifter*. Copenhagen 1851, p. 438.

368 Various examples are found in the Danish Prayer Books, see Nielsen 1946. See also Brandt and Fenger 1851. Vol 2, p. 437ff and Rubin, Miri, *Corpus Christi. The Eucharist in Late Medieval Culture*. Cambridge 1994. Esp. the chapter on 'Exchange and Encounter: Prayer at the Elevation and Communion', pp. 155-163.

Fig. 3: The Epitaph of Konrad Zingel and his two wives and their offspring, painted in 1447. It was most likely intended for the Church of St. Egidius in Nürnberg where it is still positioned today. Note the image depicted on the Host. Copyright: Germanisches Nationalmuseum, Nürnberg.

Physical presence: close encounters with the Holy

Images played a prominent role in obtaining experiences of physical divine presence.[369] Examples of such experiences are numerous in biographic and autobiographic medieval literature. St. Francis had an experience early in his life when he, according to his hagiographer Thomas of Celano, was praying in front of a crucifix in the Church of St. Damian and 'the painted image of Christ moved its lips and spoke' and encouraged him to rebuild the Church.[370] Experiences of divine presence mediated by images were according to the studies on *Frauenmystik* by Peter Dinzelbacher, rather commonplace among nuns in certain German monasteries.[371]

Today, our view of divine presence is that it mostly happened in monastic milieus and is associated with mysticism, and it is endeed often these 'professionals' we find in images and written source material. But perhaps the longing for divine visual presence was a much more general trend? In some rare cases we do in fact find indications of such visual experiences of divine presence happening to 'ordinary' people. Julian of Norwich, who was born sometime in the middle of 1300, experienced a crucifix coming alive and it revealed the Passion of Christ 'physically, yet obscurely and mysteriously'.[372] In *Dialogus miraculorum* a collection of tales written by the Cistercian monk Caesarius of Heisterbach (1180-1214) there is an account of a young man who visited a church and kneeled before the altar to repent that he had denied Christ. The altarpiece which depicted the Virgin and Child suddenly came to live. The Christ Child said that he could not forgive the young man, but the Virgin begged on his behalf. Christ was unrelenting, but the Virgin placed the Child on the altar table and kneeled before him, asking for forgiveness once again. At last the Christ Child granted the man pardon.[373]

In 'professional' milieus devotional practice was preoccupied with 'becoming one' with Christ. Through the practise of *Imitatio Christi* munks and nuns were

---

369 Henning Laugerud has made some interesting remarks on the connection between visions and images in his thesis; Laugerud, Henning: *Det Hagioskopiske Blikk. Bilder, syn og erkjennelse i høy-og senmiddelalder.* Avhandling for graden doctor artium, Institutt for Kunsthistorie, Det historisk-filosofiske fakultet, Universitetet i Bergen. Bergen 2005 (unpublished). The title in English is *The Hagioscopic gaze, Images, Sight and Knowledge.* Bergen 2005. Doctoral dissertation presented to the University of Bergen). See also the article by Laugerud in this volume.

370 Thomas of Celano: *Saint Francis of Assisi.* Placid Hermann OFM (transl. and ed.). Chicago 1988 (1963), p. 144.

371 Dinzelbacher, Peter: *Mittelalterliche Frauenmystik.* Paderborn, 1993 and Dinzelbacher, Peter: 'Religiöses Erleben vor bildener Kunst in autobiographischen und biographischen Zeugnissen des Hoch- und Spätmittelalters'. *Images of Cult and Devotion. Function and Reception of Christian Images in Medieval and Post-Medieval Europe.* Søren Kaspersen (ed.). Copenhagen 2004.

372 Julian of Norwich: *Revelations of Divine Love.* Harmondsworth 1966, chapter 10. According to the introduction by Clifton Wolters, Julian of Norwich was most likely living with her mother at the time when she received the revelations but they were not written down until later when she had become a recluse in Norwich.

373 McGuire, Brian (ed.): *Trivialliteratur og samfund I latinsk middelalderen.* Copenhagen 1982, 175ff.

aiming towards *conformitas Christi*: to imitate the life of Christ in order to reach a state of mind where one would be completely absorbed in His life and practice. Meditations on the life of Christ encouraged people to visualize themselves as present at major events in the life of Christ and to project themselves into history.[374] Visuals provided the devotees with images of Christ representing his history, attitudes, gestures, mimics, mental states and bodily postures,[375] and made internalization of his life more easily obtained.

The stigmatization of St. Francis was one of the most extreme examples of such a *conformitas Christi*. The event is depicted on a Pentateuch originally made for and positioned in Ulkebøl Church, Denmark. It was made sometime between 1515 and 1520.[376] When the wings are in a closed position, four paintings depicting important saints become visible (Fig.4). The two central images show Virgin Mary with the Christ Child and a crowned St. Katharina of Alexandria with a sword and a book. The two female saints are flanked by two male Franciscan saints; St. Anthony of Padua holding a cross in his right hand and a book in his left hand whereupon a naked Christ Child is seated; and St. Francis, who is receiving the stigmata on Monte La Verna from a seraph appearing in the sky. According to the legend, St. Anthony once had a vision of the Christ Child and the presence of the Child was so real that St. Anthony was able to kiss and communicate with it.[377] The event was witnessed by a third party from a hiding place, who nevertheless saw the Christ Child as clearly as St. Anthony. To St. Anthony, however, the experience was not just visual, it was also physical. St. Francis of Assisi's stigmata was of course the most radical experience of divine physical presence and a direct result of his imitation of the life of Christ. In his biography Bonaventura writes;

> Now after that the true love of Christ had transformed His lover into the
> same image, and after that he spent forty days in solitude, as he had deter-
> mined, when the Feast of Saint Michael Archangel came, this angelic man,
> Francis, descended from the mountain, bearing with him the likeness of
> the Crucified, engraven, not on tables of stone or of wood, by the crafts-
> man's hand, but written on his members of flesh by the finger of the Liv-
> ing God.[378]

374 Camille, Michael: *Gothic Art. Glorious Visions*. London 1996, p. 92.

375 Se Constable, Giles: *Three Studies in Medieval Religious and Social Thought*. Cambridge 1995, chapter II 'The ideal of the imitation of Christ' pp. 143-218.

376 For more information on the altarpiece see Plathe, Sissel F., Bruun, Jens (eds.): *Middelalderlige altetavler i Haderslev stift*. Herning 2003.

377 Liber Miraculorum from 1360 in *Acta Sanctorum*. Bollandus (ed.). Paris 1643, Venice 1734, Paris 1863, vol. 2, p. 724ff.

378 *The 'Little Flowers,' Life and 'Mirror' of St Francis*. Ernest Rhys (ed.). London 1912, p. 386.

Fig. 4: The Pentateuch from Ulkebøl Church, Denmark, ca. 1515-1520. Shown here is the second position with images of Mary, St. Katharina, St. Anthony and St. Francis. The altarpiece is most likely from an Antwerp workshop and made for a Franciscan house. Photo: Jens Bruun, www.altertavler.dk.

The wounds of Christ transferred to St. Francis body conforms him into the likeness of Christ. The cross he took when he began his lifelong imitation of Christ had been fixated to his body in the form of a true image, not engraven by man, but by the 'finger of the Living God'. St. Francis had become one with Christ as well as an image of Christ.

In devotional life, practised by ordinary people, there is no doubt that images and imitation of Christ was closely connected in the attempt to experience divine presence, even of a physical kind.[379]

In the presence of the divine: relations between man and the Holy in late medieval donator images

The merging of the above mentioned factors – imitation of the life of Christ, experiences of divine presence and visualizations of events in the life of Christ

379 Many examples of popular practises of imitation are given in Constable 1995, pp. 143-218.

– is found in medieval donator images. Making donations to the church in form of images in order to testify to one's devotion to God was a practice that received increased attention in the later middle ages. It was practised by lay and clergy alike, and the images depict devotees *in action*. Of course we do not know if the donated images represent the true devotional life of the donator or some ideal situation, but at least they give us a glimpse of what medieval people strived to accomplish.[380] In the following I will only refer to donator images commissioned by lay-people.

In the Church of St. Sebald in Nürnberg there is a small painted Epitaph for the Starck family from 1449 (Fig. 5). The top ¾ of the Epitaph is a cluster of smaller images within an extra ornamented painted frame. The central motif is a depiction of St. Joseph and the Virgin Mary's adoration of the Child in the centre. It is surrounded by four allegorical images all referring to the virgin birth and sacrificial death of Christ and four allegories referring to different biblical (Old Testament) accounts of adorations of God. The bottom ¼ of the image depicts both dead and living members of the Starck family. All depicted persons (Virgin Mary and St. Joseph, the biblical figures, and family members) are shown kneeling with folded hands. The devotional performance of the family members creates a linkage in time and space between past and presence, heaven and earth. The devout beholder of the image – be it the family members or other visitors to the church – would then, by miming the devotional (bodily and mental) position of the persons depicted, participate in the same timeless devotional practice and adoration of God as history prescribed.

Nevertheless, the relation between the Starck family and the Holy persons depicted in the upper part of the image is not direct; the family members are not included in the historical events depicted in the image such as we see in many other examples of late medieval imagery. The extra frame surrounding the upper cluster of images makes it a picture in the picture and the devotional practices performed by the family members are thus not turned directly towards the holy persons but towards *images* of the holy persons and historical event. The devotional experience of the family is not depicted as one of divine presence, but of images as communicators of divine presence. What the medieval beholder of the Starck epitaph would experience was a description of how to combine practice and image in daily devotion.

---

380 Donator images have on many occasions been interpreted for their intentional display of socio-economic power in medieval society. One example is Tuhkanen, Tuija: 'Retorisk analys i bild-tolkning. – att läse donatorernas intentioner i bilderna'. *Tegn, symbol og tolkning. Om forståelse og fortolkning av middelalderens bilder*. Gunnar Danbolt, Henning Laugerud and Lena Liepe (eds.). Copenhagen 2003, pp. 229-242.

Fig. 5: The Epitaph of the Starck family from 1449 in the Church of St. Sebald, Nürnberg. With kind permission of St. Sebald, Nürnberg.

A different example is the image usually referred to as *'Ecce agnus Dei'* painted by Dieric Bouts in 1462-64 (Fig.6). The image refers to John 1.29 and 36 which reads: 'The next day he [John] saw Jesus coming towards him and declared, "Here is the Lamb of God who takes away the sin of the world!"' and 'as he watched Jesus walk by, he exclaimed, "Look, here is the Lamb of God!" The two disciples heard him say this, and they followed Jesus.' The image shows John on the banks of the Jordan where he, according to the biblical text, was baptizing in the name of the Messiah to come. In front of him the donator is kneeling with folded hands. John's left hand is positioned on the shoulder of the donator and the right is pointing towards the opposite bank of the river where Jesus is walking as if he, John, was uttering the biblical words, 'Look, here is the Lamb of God!', in this very moment. John is – if we continue to follow the biblical text – encouraging the kneeling devotee to follow Christ as he encouraged the two disciples. John is in this context a kind of personal supervisor who guides the devotee towards Jesus and directs the devotional practice both physically and mentally. The donator does not seem to look at Jesus but gazes into eternity as if it was a mental gaze rather than a physical gaze. This might suggest that what this image depicts is not an actual experience of divine presence, but the inner meditation and vision of the donator. The image shows the beholder that by performing certain physical and devotional practices, the donator experiences an inner vision which almost resembles an actual presence of the Holy, in this case Christ.[381] If *Ecce Agnus Dei* depicts a devotional experience, an extreme capacity for imagining the holy in very clear visions would have been the criteria for such an experience. The river Jordan divides the image and, thus, the donator from Christ (who seems strangely inobtainable). However, a close physical connection is established between the donator and St. John, as if St. John has brought the devout directly to the banks of Jordan to show him Christ. The importance of saints as intermediators between Man and Christ is underlined, as well as Man's relations to Holy persons is clarified: saints were personal guides, wheras Christ could only be 'seen' or acknowledged.

Concluding remarks: representations versus experiences of presence

It has often been pointed out that medieval devotional experiences of presence were based on inner visualizations of Christ or the saints. Images such as *Ecce Agnus Dei* and the *Seven Sacrament* altarpiece would, then, be depictions of inner visualizations which offered the beholder the possibility of seeing, remembering and storing an image which they could later use in their private devotional practice. Or the devotional practice could be performed directly in front of the image which would, then, be the focus and fixation of meditation. It would be experienced within the imaginary space of the beholder. The presence of Christ was something that was experienced internally by the individual devotee.

---

381 Jørgensen, Hans Henrik Lohfert: *I kroppens spejl. Krop og syn I senmiddelalderens danske kalkmalerier.* Århus 2004, p. 52.

Fig. 6: 'Ecce agnus Dei' painted by Dieric Bouts in 1462-64 and commissioned by an unknown do-nator. Today it is positioned in Alte Pinakothek, Munich, Germany. Copyright Artothek.

But, as I have attempted to illustrate, presence could manifest itself in various ways. Presence could be an inner experience reached through devotional meditations before visual representations of the subject one wanted to experience (Christ or the Virgin). Presence could also be an in-between experience of presence and visual absence as in the transubstantiated Host, but the physical presence would be supplemented by images, not only painted or sculpted imaged, but an image printed directly on the Host itself. Furthermore, presence could be experienced as physical presence; that Christ or some saint actually appeared in front of the devotee. Such experiences of physical divine presence were reserved for the few, those who had devoted their lives completely to Christ to the degree that they were conformed to Christ, such as the case of St. Francis. But this did not prevent ordinary devotees to long or strive for experiences of divine presence, and this striving is in fact reflected in the material. One of the important ideals of devotion seems to have been the ability to reach a devotional level where God himself became present. The experience of divine presence was produced by performing some kind of devotional practice (prayers, meditations, imitations of the life of Christ) in front of a devotional fix-point; the image as an instrument of devotion.

But anticipation of experiences of presence was a delicate matter. Margery Kempe's biographer writes about how she took a step to far in striving to become a devoted Christian; 'She was smitten with the deadly wound of vainglory and felt it not, for she desired many times that the crucifix should loosen his hands from the cross and embrace her in a token of love.'[382] Medieval images testify to this longing for divine presence as well as the humbleness needed in the approach; presence could only be experienced if it was deserved and if the devotional approach was appropriate.

The visual representations of Christ and the saints clearly present them as being able to transcend from absence to presence or to move from heaven to earth in the same way as relics and holy locations functioned as exclusive spots, where the divide between heaven and earth was occasionally suspended. St. Thomas Aquinas wrote:

> The worship of religion is paid to images, not as considered in themselves, nor as things, but as images leading us to God incarnate. Now, movement to an image as image does not stop at the image, but goes on to the thing it represents.[383]

Images represented the target of devotion and channelled piety directly to God incarnate. Visual representations of Christ or the saints created a meeting point between the devotee and heaven and devotional practices actualized and articu-

---

382 Chapter 4 in *The Book of Margery Kempe*. Here quoted from *The Book of Margery Kempe*. Harmondsworth 1994, p. 48

383 *Summa Theologica* II-II, Q. 81, art 3 rep. to obj. 3. Quoted from *St. Thomas Aquinas Summa Theologica*. Fathers of the English Dominican Province (transl.). 1920. Online edition http://www.newadvent.org/summa/

lated an intercommunicative point where time and space was suspended Devotees could travel into the past and be part of historical events such as the donators in the Starck Epitaph or the donator in the *Ecce Agnus Dei,* or divine presence could occur in the very room where the devotee performed his or her devotional practises, such as it happened to St. Anthony of Padua.

Burcht Pranger has described the medieval devotional experience as 'the bliss of a devotional no-mans-land'[384], but perhaps we might have to take the medieval images more literally; that divine presence was experienced as real; that Christ or the saints sometimes overstepped the boundaries between heaven and earth and manifested themselves as sensual subjects or at least was experienced as such by the devout. In medieval images and the various devotional practices related to images, we find the idea that there is a relationship between image and divine presence. It is not a presence *ex opere operato* (to use a sacramental term) but a presence activated by devotion. Images communicated presence to those who longed for it; if approached in the right manner, images would mediate solace and presence.

---

384 Pranger 2001, p. 189.

Bibliography

A

des Abaux, Félibien: 'Description de l'Abbaye de La Trappe à Madame la Duchesse de Liancour'. *Reglemens de l'Abbaye de Nôtre-Dame de La Trappe*. Paris 1718, pp. 1-95.

von Achen, Henrik: 'Verdensbilde og billedverden. Menneskehjertet som religiøs figur og metafor: Et mottrekk mot sekulariseringsprosessen i nyere tid. En tentativ synsvinkel. *Mellom Gud og Djævelen. Religiøse og magiske verdensbilleder i Norden 1500-1800*. Hanne Sanders (ed.). Copenhagen 2001, pp. 17-40.

von Achen, Henrik: 'Human heart and Sacred Heart: reining in religious individualism. The heart figure in 17th century devotional piety and the emergence of the cult of the Sacred Heart'. *Categories of Sacredness in Europe, 1500-1800*. Arne B. Amundsen and Henning Laugerud (eds.). Oslo 2003, pp. 131-158.

von Achen, Henrik: 'The Sinner´s Contemplation'. *Images of Cult and Devotion. Function and Reception of Christian Images in Medieval and Post-Medieval Europe*. Søren Kaspersen (ed.). Copenhagen 2004, pp. 283-304.

Acta patris Ignatii scripta a P. Lud. Gonzalez de Camera: *Fontes narrativi de S. Ignatio de Loyola*, vol. 1, MHSI 66. Rome 1943.

Acta Sanctorum. Bollandus (ed.). Paris 1643, Venice 1734, Paris 1863.

Ajmar, Marta and Sheffield, Catherine: 'The Miraculous Medal: An Immaculate Conception or Not'. *The Medal* 24. London 1994, pp. 37-51.

Alison, James: *Raising Abel. The Recovery of the Eschatological Imagination*. New York 1996.

Amoris Divini et Hvmani Antipathia. Snyders (ed.). Antwerp 1629.

Angela of Foligno: *Complete Works*. New York 1993.

Andriotti, Fulvio: *Onderwys oft practycke om dickwils het H. Sacrament des avtaers*. Antwerp 1618.

Aquaviva, Claudio: 'De oratione et paenitentia'. *Epistolae Praepositorum Generalium ad Patres et Fratres Societatis Jesu*. Rome 1615.

Arendt, Hannah: *The Human Condition*. Chicago and London 1958.

St. Augustine: *On Genesis. The Works of Saint Augustine* I/13. New York 2002.

St. Augustine: *The confessions of St. Augustine*. New York 2002.

B

Bacon, Roger: *The Opus Majus of Roger Bacon*. R. B. Burke (transl.). Philadelphia, London and Oxford 1928.

Ball, Ann: *Encyclopedia of Catholic Devotions and Practices*. Huntington IN 2003.

von Balthasar, Hans Urs: *Herrlichkeit. Eine theologische Aesthetik*, 3 vols. Einsiedeln 1961-1967.

von Balthasar, Hans Urs: 'Mysterium Paschale'. *Mysterium salutis: Grundriss heilsgeschichtlicher Dogmatik*, vol. III/2, Einsiedeln, Benziger, 1969, pp. 254-255.

von Balthasar, Hans Urs: *Der antirömische Affeckt. Wie lässt sich das Papsttum in der Gesamtkirche integrieren*. Freiburg i.B. 1974.

von Balthasar, Hans Urs : 'The Descent into Hell'. *Chicago Studies* 23 (1984), pp. 223-236.

Barolsky, Paul: 'Naturalism and the Visionary Art of the Early Renaissance'. *Gazette des Beaux-Arts* 6e periode, tome 129. Paris 1997, pp. 57-64.

Bauer, Wilhelm A. and Deutsch, Otto E. (eds.): *Mozart, Briefe und Aufzeichnungen*. Gesamtausgabe, 7 vols. Kassel 1962-75.

Béguerie, Pantxika and Bischoff, Georges: *Grünewald, le maître d'Issenheim*. Tournai 1996.

Bell, Catherine: *Ritual Theory, Ritual Practice*. New York and Oxford 1992.

Bell, David N.: *Understanding Rancé: The Spirituality of the Abbot of La Trappe in Context*. Kalamazoo 2005.

Belting, Hans: *Bild und Kult: Eine Geschichte des Bildes vor dem Zeitalter der Kunst*. München 1990.

Belting, Hans: *Das echte Bild. Bildfragen als Glaubensfragen*. München 2005.

Benedict van Haeften OSB: *Schola Cordis*. Antwerp 1629.

Benjamin, Walter: *Ursprung des deutschen Trauerspiels*. Berlin 1928.

Berger, Peter L. (ed.): *The Desecularization of the World. Resurgent Religion and World Politics*. Washington D.C. 1995.

Beyer, Jürgen: *Lutheran lay prophets, c.1550-c.1700*. Leiden 2006.

Blume, Clemens and Dreves, Guido Maria (eds.): *Analecta hymnica medii aevi*. Leipzig 1886-1922.

Boetius a Bolswert: *Duyskens ende Willemynkens pelegrimagi tot haren beminden binnen Ierusalem … Bescreuen ende met Sin-spelende Beelden wtghegheven*. Antwerp 1627.

St. Bonaventure: *Mystical Opuscula, I*. Paterson NJ 1960.

Bouix, M. (ed.): *Oeuvres spirituelles du Père Jean-Joseph Surin: Traité inédit de l'amour de Dieu, précédé de la vie de l'auteur*. Paris 1890.

Bourdieu, Pierre: *Esquisse d'une theorie de la pratique*. Genève 1974.

Bunyan, John: *The Pilgrim's Progress*, 2 vols. London 1678 and 1684.

C

Cats, Jacob: *Proteus Ofte Minne-Beelden Verandert In Sinne-Beelden*. Rotterdam 1627.

Caesarius of Heisterbach: *The Dialogue on Miracles*, 2 vols. Henry von Essen Scott & C.C. Swinton Bland (transl.). London 1929.

Camille, Michael: *Gothic Art. Glorious Visions*. London 1996.

Caterina da Siena: *Epitolario*. Rome 1979.

Casanova, José: *Public religion in the modern world*. Chicago and London 1994.

Cavanaugh, William T.: *Theopolitical Imagination*. London 2002.

de Certeau, Michel: *Correspondance de Jean-Joseph Surin*. Texte établi, présenté et annoté par Michel de Certeau, Bibliothèque Européenne. Paris 1966.

de Certeau, Michel: 'L'illettré éclairé dans l'histoire de la lettre sur le Jeune Homme du Coche (1630)'. *Revue d'Ascétique et de Mystique* 44. Toulouse 1968, pp. 369-412.

de Certeau, Michel: 'Crise sociale et réformisme spirituel au début du XVIIe siècle'. *Revue d'Ascétique et de Mystique* 41. Toulouse 1965, pp. 339-386.

Chatellier, Louis: *The Europe of the Devout. The Catholic Reformation and the Formation of a New Society*. Cambridge 1991 (1987).

Chazelle, Celia M.: 'Pictures, books and the illiterate: Pope Gregory I's letters to Serenus of Marseilles'. *Word & Image* 6:2. London 1990.

City Archives at Rotterdam, archives of the Reformed consistory of Rotterdam, vol. 7, acta 4 October and 22 November, 1690.

Coin Library: www.coinlibrary.com/wpns/club_wpns_pr_communion.htm

Connell, Martin F.: 'Descensus Christi ad Inferos: Christ's Descent to the Dead'. *Theological Studies 62*. Washington D.C. (2001), pp. 262-282.

Constable, Giles: *Three Studies in Medieval Religious and Social Thought*. Cambridge 1995.

Costa, Eugenio: 'La tromperie, ou le problème de la communication chez Surin. Notes sur quelques textes de la "Science expérimentale"'. *Revue d'Ascetique et de Mystique* 44. Toulouse 1968, pp. 413-424.

Cramer, Daniel: *Arbor Haereticae Consanguinitatis*. Strassbourg 1623.

Cramer, Daniel: *Emblemata Sacra*. Frankfurt a.M. 1624.

Cramer, Peter: *Baptism and Change in the Early Middle Ages ca. 200-ca.1150*. Cambridge 1993.

Cribb, Joe: 'Medaglie cristiane e croci usate in Cina'. *Medaglia* 15. Milano 1978, pp. 21-37.

Cunningham, Bernadette and Gillespie, Raymond: *Stories from Gaelic Ireland: microhistories from the sixteenth-century Irish annals*. Dublin 2003.

D

Danielou, Jean, Honoré, Jean and Poupard, Paul (eds.): *Le catholicisme. Hier -- Demain*. Paris 1974.

Davies, Grace: *Religion in Modern Europe. A Memory Mutates*. Oxford 2000.

Deblaere, Albert: *Essays on Mystical Literature*. BETL 177. Leuven 2004.

Dictionnaire de Spiritualité VIII. Paris 1974, pp. 1308-1316.

Dimler, Richard: 'A Bibliographical Survey of Jesuit Emblem Authors in French Provinces (1618-1726)'. *Archivum Historicum societatis Iesu* 47. 1978, pp. 240-250.

Dinzelbacher, Peter: *Mittelalterliche Frauenmystik*. Paderborn 1993.

Dinzelbacher, Peter: 'Religiöses Erleben vor bildener Kunst in autobiographischen und biographischen Zeugnissen des Hoch- und Spätmittelalters'. *Images of Cult and Devotion. Function and Reception of Christian Images in Medieval and Post-Medieval Europe*. Søren Kaspersen (ed.). Copenhagen 2004.

Donington, Robert: *The Rise of Opera*. London 1981.

Douglas, Mary: *Natural Symbols*. Harmondsworth 1970.

Draghi, Antonio/Niccolò Minalti: *Il epitafio di Christo* (1671). Musical score (manuscript). Musiksammlung, Österreichische Nationalbibliothek.

Draghi, Antonio/Niccolò Minalti: *La vita nella morte* (1688). Musical score (manuscript). Musiksammlung, Österreichische Nationalbibliothek.

Duffy, Eamon: *The Stripping of the Altars. Traditional Religion in England 1400-1580*. New Haven and London 1992.

Duffy, Eamon: 'Elite and popular religion: the books of hours and lay piety in the later Middle Ages'. *Elite and popular religion: Studies in Church History 42*. Kate Cooper and Jeremy Gregory (eds.). Woodbridge 2006.

Duggan, Lawrence G.: 'Was art really the "book of the illiterate"?'. *Word and Image* 5:2. London 1989.

Durkheim, Emile: *Les formes élémentaires de la vie religieuse*. Paris 1912.

E

Eck, Johannes: 'On not Removing Images of Christ and the Saints'. *A Reformation Debate: Karlstadt Emser, and Eck on Sacred Images. Three Treatises in Translation*. Bryan D. Mangrum and Guiseppe Scavizzi (transl.). Toronto 1998.

Eco, Umberto: *Art and Beauty in the Middle Ages*. Yale 1986 (1956).

van Eijnatten, Joris: *Liberty and concord in the United Provinces. Religious toleration and the public in the eighteenth-century Netherlands*. Leiden 2003.

Eliade, Mircea: *Das Heilige und das Profane*. Hamburg 1957.

Emser, Hieronymous: 'That One Should not Remove Images of the Saints from the Churches nor Dishonour Them, and that They are not Forbidden in Scripture'. *A Reformation Debate: Karlstadt Emser, and Eck on Sacred Images. Three Treatises in Translation*. Translated with introduction and notes by Bryan D. Mangrum and Guiseppe Scavizzi (transl.). Toronto 1998.

ENID (European Network on the Instruments of Devotion) homepage: www.enid.uib.no

Erickson, Carolly: *The medieval vision. Essays in History and Perception*. New York 1978.

F

Fallize, Johannes B.: *Kirkelige bekjendtgjørelser for Norges apostoliske vikariat* 7:10/9 1892.

Fawtier, Robert: *Sainte Catherine de Sienne. Essai de critique des Sources. Sources Hagiographiques.* Paris 1922.

Fellerer, Karl Gustav: *Die Kirchenmusik W.A. Mozarts.* Laaber 1985.

Firth, Raymond: *We, the Tycopia.* London 1936.

Fletcher, Edward: *Tokens & Tallies 1850-1950.* Witham 2004.

Foster, Kenelm O.P. (ed. & transl.): *The Life of Saint Thomas Aquinas. Biographical Documents.* London 1959.

François de Sales: *Introduction à la vie devote.* Lyon 1608.

Freedberg, David: *The Power of Images. Studies in the History and Theory of Response.* Chicago and London 1989.

G

Ganz, David and Lentes, Thomas (eds.): *Kultbild. Ästhetik des Unsichtbaren. Bildtheorie und Bildgebrauch in der Vormoderne.* Berlin 2004.

Garelli, Franco: *Forza della religione e debolezza della fede.* Bologna 1996.

van Gennep, Arnoldus: *Onpartijdig en onzijdig opstel (…) over de zamenkomsten en oeffeningen der particuliere ledematen (…).* Dordrecht 1743.

van Gennep, Arnold: *Les rites des passages.* Paris 1981. (1909).

Georges, Dominique: 'Procès verbal'. *La vie du très-reverend père Armand Jean Le Bouthillier de Rancé.* Paris 1709, Book VI, pp. 251–274.

Gertrude of Helfta: *The Herald of Divine Love.* New York 1993.

Giegling, Franz (ed.): *W.A. Mozart: Grabmusik KV 42.* Neue Mozart Ausgabe, Geistliche Gesangswerke, Werkgruppe 4, Band 4. Partitur, BA 4507. Kassel 1957.

Giegling, Franz: 'Zum vorliegenden Band'. *W.A.Mozart: Grabmusik.* Franz Giegling (ed.). Kassel 1957. pp. vii–ix.

Gilson, Etienne: *The Philosophy of St. Thomas Aquinas.* Cambridge 1929.

Gijswijt-Hofstra, Marijke, Marland, Hilary and de Waardt, Hans (eds.): *Belief, trust and healing in Europe, sixteenth to twentieth centuries.* London and New York 1997.

Gluckman, Max: *Essays on the Ritual of Social Relations.* Manchester 1962.

Greeley, Andrew: *The Catholic Imagination.* Berkeley, Los Angeles and London 2000.

Grinder- Hansen, Poul: 'Public Devotional Pictures in Late Medieval Denmark'. *Images of Cult and Devotion. Function and Reception of Christian images in Medieval and Post-Medieval Europe.* Søren Kaspersen (ed.). Copenhagen 2004

Guillelmus Durandus: *Rationale divinorum officiorum* I-IV. CCCM 140. Turnhout 1995.

H

Hahn, Cynthia: 'Visio Dei. Changes in Medieval Visuality'. *Visuality Before and Beyond the Renaissance.* Robert S. Nelson (ed.). Cambridge 2000, pp. 169-196.

Hamburger, Jeffrey: *Nuns as Artists. The Visual Culture of a Medieval Convent.* Berkeley, Los Angeles and London 1997.

Hamburger, Jeffrey: *The Visual and the Visionary. Art and female Spirituality in Late Medieval Germany.* New York 1998.

Harms, W. and Freytag, H. (eds.): *Ausserliterarische Wirkungen barocker Emblembücher.* München 1975.

Hawkins, R.N.P.: *A Dictionary of Makers of British metallic tickets, checks, medalets, tallies, and counters 1788-1910*. London 1989.

Heckscher, William and Wirth, Karl-August: 'Emblem/Emblembuch'. *Reallexi-kon zur deutschen Kunstgeschichte*. Stuttgart 1959.

Hegel, Georg F. W.: *Theologische Jugendschriften*. Herman Nohl (ed.). Tübingen 1907.

Henkel, A. and Schöne, A.: *Emblemata. Handbuch zur Sinnbildkunst des XVI. und XVII. Jahrhunderts*. Stuttgart 1967.

Hennessy, William M. (ed.): *The annals of Loch Cé*, 2 vols. London 1871, reprint Dublin 1939.

Herzog, Markwart: *Descensus ad inferos: eine religionsphilosophische Untersuchung der Motive und Interpretationen mit besonderer Berücksichtigung der monographischen Literatur seit dem 16. Jahrhundert*. Frankfurter theologische Studien, 53. Frankfurt 1997.

Hilton, Walter: *The Scale of Perfection*, book I-II, 1380-96. Thomas H. Bestul (ed.). Michigan 2000.

Hindmarch, D. Bruce: *The Evangelical Conversion Narrative*. Oxford 2005.

Hoburg, Christian: *Lebendige Hertzenstheologie*. Leipzig and Frankfurt a.M. 1691.

von Hohenvest, Franz Töply: *Numismatikk. Miscellen. Die Weihmünzen für Sammler*. Graz 1893.

Höltgen, Karl J: *Faksimile. Henry Hawkins: The Devout Hart (1634)*. Ylkley 1975.

Höpel, Ingrid: *Emblem und Sinnbild. Vom Kunstbuch zum Erbauungsbuch*. Frankfurt a.M. 1987.

Hsia, R. Po-Chia and van Nierop, H.F.K. (eds.): *Calvinism and religious toleration in the Dutch Golden Age*. Cambridge 2001.

Huisman, Frank: 'Shaping the Medical Market. On the Construction of Quackery and Folk Medicine in Dutch Historiography'. *Medical History* 43. London 1999, pp. 359-375.

Hunt, John: *Irish medieval figure sculpture 1200-1600: a study of Irish tombs with notes on costumes and armour*. 2 vols. Dublin 1974.

I

St. Ignatius of Loyola: *Personal Writings*. Joseph A. Munitiz and Philip Endean (transl.). London 1996.

S. Ignatii de Loyola epistolae et instructiones. t. 10, MHSI. Rome 1968.

S. Ignatii de Loyola epistolae et instructiones. t. 12, MHSI. Rome 1968.

Imagination des Unsichtbaren. 1200 Jahre Bildener Kunst im Bistum Münster, 2 vols. Münster 1993.

J

Jones, Mark: *The Art of the Medal*. London 1979.

Jubilum Societatis Jesu seculare ob theologiam mysticam a fundatore suo Ignatio ejusque Sociis primo conditae Societatis seculo excultam et illustratam. Cologne 1640. Reprinted in: *Collection de la Bibliothèque des Exercises de Saint Ignace 77-78*. Engien, Paris 1922.

Julian of Norwich: *Revelations of Divine Love*. Harmondsworth 1966.

Jungmann, Joseph A.: *The Mass of the Roman Rite: Its Origin and Development (Missa Solemnis)*. Francis A. Brunner (transl.). Dublin 1986.

Jørgensen, Hans Henrik Lohfert: *I kroppens spejl. Krop og syn i senmiddelalderens danske kalkmalerier*. Århus 2004.

K

Kartsonis, Anna D.: *Anastasis. The Making of an Image*. Princeton 1986.

Kaufman, Peter Iver: 'Prophesying again'. *Church History. Studies in Christianity and Culture* 68:2. New Haven and Tallahassee 1999, pp. 337-358.

Kemp, Cornelia: *Angewandte Emblematik in süddeutschen Barockkirchen*. Berlin and München 1981.

Köster, Kurt: 'Mittelalterliche Pilgerzeichen'. *Wallfahrt kennt keine Grenzen. Themen zu einer Ausstellung des Bayerischen Nationalmuseums und des Adalbert Stifter Vereins, München*. Lenz Kriss-Rettenbeck and Gerda Möhler (eds.). München 1984.

Krailsheimer, Alban John: *Armand-Jean de Rancé: Abbot of La Trappe. His Influence in the Cloister and the World*. Oxford 1974.

Krailsheimer, Alban John: *Rancé and the Trappist Legacy*. Kalamazoo 1985.

Kretzmann, Norman: 'Philosophy of mind'. *The Cambridge Companion to Aquinas*. Norman Kretzmann and Elenore Stump (eds.). Cambridge 1994.

Kretzmann, Norman and Stump, Eleonore (eds.): *The Cambridge Companion to Aquinas*. Cambridge 1994.

Kuncze, Leo: *Systematik der Weihemünzen: Eine ergänzende Studie für alle Freunde der Numismatik*. Raab 1885.

L

Langer, Susanne: *Philosophy in a New Key*. Cambridge Mass. 1942.

Laugerud, Henning: 'Mali Corvi Malum Ovum: Reformasjonstidens satiriske medaljer'. *Biblioteca Obskura. Festskrift til Torstein Arisholm på 30-årsdagen*. Laugerud, Korslund and Emberland (eds.). Bergen 1996.

Laugerud, Henning: *Det Hagioskopiske Blikk. Bilder, syn og erkjennelse i høy-og senmiddelalder*. Avhandling for graden doctor artium, Institutt for Kunsthistorie, Det historisk-filosofiske fakultet, Universitetet i Bergen. Bergen 2005 (unpublished).

Lawrence, C.H: *Medieval Monasticism: Forms of Religious Life in Western Europe in the Middle Ages*. Harlow 2001 (1984).

Leclerc, Eloï: *La nuit est ma lumière: Matthias Grünewald*. Paris 1994.

Legenda Aurea. Readings on the Saints. William Granger Ryan (transl.). Princeton NJ 1993.

legenda aurea sanctorum, sive Lombardica historia from 1480, 1481, 1482, 1483 and 1478. *Verteilte Digitale Inkunabelbibliothek:* inkunabeln.ub.uni-koeln.de/

Legenda Aurea. Medieval Sourcebook Online: 'The Passion of the Lord'. www.fordham.edu/Halsall/basis/goldenlegend/GL-vol1-passionofourlLord.%20html

Lekai, Louis: *Cistercians: Ideals and Reality*. Kent 1977.

Lekai, Louis: *The Rise of the Cistercian Strict Observance in Seventeenth Century France*. Washington D.C. 1968.

Lentes, Thomas: 'Der mediale Status des Bildes. Bildlichkeit bei Heinrich Seuse – statt einer Einleitung'. *Kultbild. Ästhetik des Unsichtbaren. Bildtheorie und Bildgebrauch in der Vormoderne*. David Ganz and Thomas Lentes (eds.). Berlin 2004, pp. 13-73.

Emperor Leopold I/Count Caldana: *Il Sagrifizio d'Abramo* (1660). Musical score (manuscript). Musiksammlung, Österreichische Nationalbibliothek.

Emperor Leopold I/Johan Albrecht Ruedolf: *Die Erlösung des Menschlichen Geschlechts In der Figur des aus Egipten geführten Volcks Israel* (1679). Musical score (manuscript). Musiksammlung, Österreichische Nationalbibliothek.

Emperor Leopold I/Johan Albrecht Ruedolf: *Sig des Leÿdens Christi über die Sinnlichkeit* (1682). Musical score (manuscript). Musiksammlung, Österreichische Nationalbibliothek.

Leslie, Shane: *St Patrick's Purgatory: a record from history and literature*. London 1932.

Lewis, Flora: 'Rewarding devotion: indulgences and the promotion of images'. *The Church and the Arts*. Diana Wood (ed.). Oxford 1992, pp. 179-94.

van Lieburg, Fred: 'Preachers between inspiration and instruction: Dutch Reformed ministers without academic education (sixteenth-eighteenth centuries)'. *Dutch Review of Church History* 83. Clemens, Theo and Janse, Wim (eds.): *The Pastor Bonus. Papers read at the British-Dutch Colloquium at Utrecht, 18-21 September 2002*. Leiden and Boston 2004, pp. 166-190.

van Lieburg, Fred: 'Pasteurs calvinistes et prédicateurs laïcs piétistes. De l'anticléricalisme dans l'Église Réformée néerlandaise, 1550-1750'. *L'anticléricalisme intra-protestant en Europe continentale (XVIIe-XVIIIe siècles)*. Yves Krumenacker (ed.). Lyon 2003, pp. 103-125.

Libro de la vida, 6-8, *Obras completas*. Enrique Llamas, Teofanes Egido, D. De Pablo Maroto e.a., director Alberto Barrientos (eds and transl.). Madrid 1976.

Lindbeck, George A.: *The Nature of Doctrine: Religion and Theology in a Postliberal Age*. Philadelphia 1984.

Lindberg, David C.: *Theories of Vision from Al-Kindi to Kepler*. Chicago 1976.

Lipphardt, Walther (ed.): *Lateinische Osterfeiern und Osterspiele*, 9 vols. Berlin 1975-90.

Lipsius, Justus: *Physiologiae stoicorum*. Antwerp 1604.

M

MacDonald, Scott: 'Theory of knowledge'. *The Cambridge Companion to Aquinas*. Norman Kretzmann and Elenore Stump (eds.). Cambridge 1994.

Magri, Domenico: *Hierolexicon sive Sacrum Dictionarium in quo Ecclesiasticæ voces, earumque Etymologiae, Origines, Symbola, Cæremoniæ, Dubia, Barbara Vocabula, atque Sac.Scripturæ & SS.PP.Phrases Obscuræ elucidantur*. Rome 1677, www.uni-mannheim.de/mateo/camenaref/magri/magri1/books/magrihierolexicon_13.html

Malinowski, Bronislaw: 'Magic, Science and Religion'. *Science, Religion and Reality*. J.A.Needham (ed.). London 1925.

Mâle, Émile: *L'art religieux de la fin du moyen âge en France*. 7th ed. Paris 1995.

Marquard, Reiner: *Karl Barth und der Isenheimer Altar (Arbeiten zur Theologie)*. Stuttgart 1995.

Marland, H. and van Lieburg, M. J.: 'Midwife regulation, education and practice in the Netherlands during the nineteenth century'. *Medical History* 33. London 1989, pp. 296-317.

Marland, Hilary and Pelling, Margaret (eds.): *The task of healing. Medicine, religion and gender in England and the Netherlands 1450-1800*. Rotterdam 1996.

Mauquoy-Hendrickx, Marie: *Les estampes des Wierix. Catalogue raisonné*, vol. I, II, III.1-2. Bruxelles 1978-83.

McGuire, Brian (ed.): *Trivialliteratur og samfund i latinsk middelalder*. Copenhagen 1982.

McKenna, Lambert (ed.): *Dán Dé*. Dublin 1922.

McKenna, Lambert (ed.): *Aithdioghluim Dána*, 2 vols. Dublin 1939-40.

McKenna, Lambert (ed.): *The book of Magauran*. Dublin 1947.

McKenna, Lambert (ed.): 'Christ our saviour'. *Studies*. 1949.

McLeod, Hugh: *Religion and the people of Western Europe 1789-1989*. Oxford and New York 1997.

Meiss, Millard: *Painting in Florence and Siena after the Black Death. The Arts, Religion, and Society in the Mid-Fourteenth Century*. Princeton 1978 (1951).

Mellinkoff, Ruth: *The Devil at Isenheim. Reflections of Popular Belief in Grünewald's Altarpiece*. Berkeley 1988.

Meyendorff, John: *Byzantine Theology. Historical Trends and Doctrinal Themes*. New York 1974.

Miller, John D.: *Beads and Prayers. The Rosary in History and Devotion*. London 2001.

Minato, Nicolo: *La Vita nella morte. Rappresentatione sacra al SSmo sepolcro di Christo, nella Cesarea cappella della S.C.R. Maestà dell'Imperatore Leopoldo. La sera del Venerdì Santo. Posta in musica da Antonio Draghi*. Vienna 1688.

Mitchiner, Michael: *Medieval Pilgrim and Secular Badges*. London 1986.

Mitchiner, Michael: *Jetons, Medalets & Tokens, vol. 1: The Medieval Period and Nuremberg*. London 1988.

Mizruchi, Susan L. (ed.): *Religion and Cultural Studies*. Princeton and Oxford 2001.

Mödersheim, Sabine: *Domini Doctrina Coronat: Die geistliche Emblematikk Daniel Cramers (1568-1637)*. Frankfurt a.M. 1994.

Moltmann, Jürgen: *The Way of Jesus Christ. Christology in Messianic Dimensions*. London 1990.

Moltmann, Jürgen: *The Coming of God: Christian Eschatology*. London 1996

Morton, Karena: 'A spectacular revelation: medieval wall paintings at Ardamullivan'. *Irish Arts Review* 18. Dublin 2002, pp. 105-12.

Morton, Karena: 'Personal devotion or self promotion? Aspects of image and meaning in Irish medieval wall paintings'. *Art and devotion in late medieval Ireland*. Rachel Moss, Colman Ó Clabaigh and Salvador Ryan (eds.).

Moss, R.: 'Permanent expressions of piety: the secular and the sacred in later medieval stone sculpture'. *Art and devotion in late medieval Ireland*. Rachel Moss, Colman Ó Clabaigh and Salvador Ryan (eds.).

Mozart, Wolfgang Amadeus: *Grabmusik K 42*. Franz Giegling (ed.): *W.A. Mozart: Grabmusik KV 42*. Neue Mozart Ausgabe, Geistliche Gesangswerke, Werkgruppe 4, Band 4. Partitur, BA 4507. Kassel 1957.

Multatuli [pseudonym for Eduard Douwes Dekker]: *De geschiedenis van Woutertje Pieterse*. N. A. Donkersloot (ed.). Amsterdam 1938.

Mussafia, Adolfo: 'Studien zur Mittelalterlichen Marienlegenden. I.' *Sitzungsberichte der Phil.-Hist. Classe der Kaiserliche Akademie der Wissenschaften*, b. 113. Wien 1886, pp. 917-994.

N

New Advent: www.newadvent.com/

Nielsen, Martin Karl: *Middelalderens danske bønnebøger*, 5 vols. Copenhagen 1946.

de Niet, Johan: 'Comforting the sick: confessional cure of souls and pietist comfort in the Dutch Republic'. *Confessionalism and Pietism. Religious reform in early modern Europe and North America*. Fred van Lieburg (ed.). Mainz 2006, pp. 197-212.

Nyssen, Wilhelm: *Choral des Glaubens. Meditationen zum Isenheimer Altar*. Freiburg im Breisgau 1983.

O

Ó Cianáin, Tadgh: *The flight of the earls (1607)* (ed.) Paul Walsh [ref. p. 114]. Dublin 1916.

Oexle, Otto G.: 'Memoria, Memorialüberliefung'. *Lexikon des Mittelalters, vol. VI*. München 2002, pp. 510-512.

Oexle, Otto G.: 'Memoria in der Gesellschaft und in der Kultur des Mittelalters'. Heinzle J. (ed.): *Modernes Mittelalter. Neue Bilder einer populären Epoche*. Frankfurt a. M. 1999, pp. 297-323.

O'Farrell, Fergus: 'Our Lord's pity in Ennis friary'. *North Munster Antiquarian Journal* 22, Limerick1980.

O'Farrell, Fergus: 'Passion symbols in Irish church carvings'. *Old Kilkenny Review* 2:5. Kilkenny 1988, pp. 535-41.

Ó Maonaigh, Cainneach (ed.): *Smaointe beatha Chríost: innsint Ghaeilge a chuir Tomás Gruamdha Ó Bruacháin (fl.1450) ar an Meditationes Vitae Christi*. Dublin 1944.

Ortigues, Edmund: *Religions du livre et religions de la culture*. Paris 1981.

P

Pachinger, Anton M.: *Wallfahrts- und Weihemünzen des Erzhertogtums ob der Enns*. Linz 1904.

Pachinger, Anton M.: *Wallfahrts-, Bruderschafts- und Gnadenmedaillen des Herzogtums Salzburg*. Wien 1908.

Padberg, John W.: *The Constitutions of the Society of Jesus and Their Complementary Norms. A Complete English Translation of the Offical Latin Texts.* Jesuit Primary Sources in English Translation. 15. St. Louis MO 1996.

Panofsky, Erwin (ed. & transl.): *Abbot Suger on the Abbey Church of St.-Denis and its art treasures.* Princeton NJ 1979 (1946).

Pareyson, Luigi: *Ontologia della libertà. Il male e la sofferenza.* Torino 1995.

Peers, E. Allison (ed.): *The Life of Teresa of Jesus.* New York 1960.

Pedersen, Christiern: *Bog Om Messen.* Published by Brandt and Fenger: *Christiern Pedersens Danske Skrifter.* Copenhagen 1851.

Perniola, Mario: *Ritual Thinking. Sexuality, Death, World.* New Yok 2001.

Perniola, Mario: *Del sentire cattolico. La forma culturale di una religione universale.* Bologna 2001.

Perniola, Mario: 'La merce umana'. *Agalma* 1. June. Rome 2000.

Petersen, Nils Holger: 'Søren Kierkegaard's Aestheticist and Mozart's Don Giovanni'. *Interarts Studies – New Perspectives.* Ulla-Britta Lagerroth, Hans Lund, and Erik Hedling (eds.). Amsterdam 1997, pp. 167-76.

Petersen, Nils Holger: 'Intermedial Strategy and Spirituality in the Emerging Opera: Gagliano's *La Dafne* and Confraternity Devotion'. *Cultural Functions of Interart Poetics and Practice.* Ulla-Britta Lagerroth and Erik Hedling (eds.). Amsterdam 2002, pp. 75-86.

Petersen, Nils Holger: 'Time and Divine Providence in Mozart's Music'. *Voicing the Ineffable.* Siglind Bruhn (ed.). Hillsdale, New York 2002, pp. 265-86.

Petersen, Nils Holger: 'The Representational Liturgy of the *Regularis Concordia*'. *The White Mantle of Churches: Architecture, Liturgy, and Art Around the Millenium.* Nigel Hiscock (ed.). Turnhout 2003, pp. 107-17.

Petersen, Nils Holger: 'Renaissance Rituals in a Florentine Lay Confraternity: *Compagnia dell'arcangelo Raffaello*'. *Analecta Romana Instituti Danici.* Rome 2004, pp. 153-60.

Petersen, Nils Holger: 'The *Trump of God*: Musical Representations of Divine Judgment in Mozart Works, 1767-1791'. *Transfiguration: Nordic Yearbook for Religion and the Arts.* Copenhagen 2006.

Pettit, Norman: *The Heart Prepared: Grace and Conversion in Puritan Spiritual Life.* New Haven and London 1966.

Pinelli, Luca: *De chracht ende misterie de h. Misse met verklaringhe der selve.* Antwerp 1620.

Plathe, Sissel F. and Bruun, Jens (eds.): *Middelalderlige altetavler i Haderslev stift.* Herning 2003.

Pontifical Council for Culture: *Towards a Pastoral Approach to Culture.* Vatican 1999.

Pranger, Burcht: 'Images of Iron: Ignatius of Loyola and Joyce'. *Religion and Media.* Hent de Vries (ed.). Palo Alto CA 2001.

Praz, Mario: *Studies in Seventeenth-Century Imagery.* Rome 1964.

Pratiqve de l'amour de Dieu pour toutes sortes des personnes. Paris 1672.

Pseudo-Dionysius: *The Complete Works.* New York 1987.

Q

Quenot, Michel: *The Resurrection and the Icon.* New York 1997.

Quint, Josef (ed.): *Meister Eckharts Buch der göttlichen Tröstung und von dem edlen Menschen (Liber Benedictus).* Berlin 1952.

R

RB 1980: The Rule of St. Benedict. Timothy Fry et al. (ed. and transl.). Collegeville MN 1981.

Radcliffe-Brown, Alfred R.: *Structure and Function in Primitive Society*. London 1952.

Rahner, Hugo: 'Die Vision des heiligen Ignatius in der Kapelle von La Storta'. *Zeitschrift für Aszese und Mystik* 10:4. Innsbruck 1935.

de Rancé, Armand-Jean: *De la sainteté et des devoirs de la vie monastique*, 2 vols. Paris 1683.

Raymond of Capua: *The life of Catherine of Siena*. Conleth Kearns, OP (transl.). Washington D.C. 1994.

de Ribadeneira, Pedro: *Vita Ignatii Loyolae*, MHSI 93. Rome 1965.

Roe, Helen M.: 'Instruments of the Passion: notes towards a survey of their illustration and distribution in Ireland'. *Old Kilkenny Review* 2:5. Kilkenny 1988, pp. 527-34.

van Rooden, Peter: 'History, the Nation, and Religion: The Transformations of the Dutch Religious Past'. *Nation and Religion: Perspectives on Europe and Asia*. Peter van der Veer and Hartmut Lehmann (eds.). Princeton 1999, pp. 96-111.

de Rossi, Giovanni Battista: 'Le medaglie di devozione dei primi sei o sette secoli della chiesa'. *Bullettino di Archeologia Cristiana*, Anno VII:3 & 4. Rome 1869.

Rouyer, Jules and Hucher, Eugène: *Histoire du jeton au moyen age*. Paris 1858.

Rouse, Richard H. and Rouse, Mary A.: *Manuscripts and their Makers. Commercial book producers in Medieval Paris 1200-1500*. Turnhout 2000.

Rubin, Miri: *Corpus Christi. The Eucharist in Late Medieval Culture*. Cambridge 1994.

Ruusbroec, Jan van: *Opera Omnia 1*. Corpus Christianorum Continuatio Mediaevalis. Turnhout 1989.

Ruusbroec, Jan van: *Opera Omnia 5*. Corpus Christianorum Continuatio Mediaevalis. 105. Turnhout 2006.

Ruusbroec, Jan van: *Opera Omnia 6*. Corpus Christianorum Continuatio Mediaevalis. 106. Turnhout 2006.

Ruusbroec, Jan van: *Opera Omnia 7A*. Corpus Christianorum Continuatio Mediaevalis. 107A. Turnhout 2000.

Ruusbroec, Jan van: *Opera Omnia 10*. Corpus Christianorum Continuatio Mediaevalis. 110. Turnhout 1991.

Ryan, Salvador: *Popular religion in Gaelic Ireland, 1445-1645*. PhD thesis, National University of Ireland Maynooth 2002, 2 vols. (unpublished).

Ryan, Salvador: 'Reign of blood: devotion to the wounds of Christ in late medieval Gaelic Ireland'. *Irish history: a research yearbook*. Joost Augusteijn and May Ann Lyons (eds.). Dublin 2002, pp. 137-49.

Ryan, Salvador: 'A slighted source: rehabilitating Irish bardic religious poetry in historical discourse'. *Cambrian Medieval Celtic Studies* 48, Winter. Wales 2004, pp. 75-99.

Ryan, Salvador: 'Windows on late medieval devotional practice: Máire Ní Máilles's "Book of Piety" (1513) and the world behind the texts'. *Art and devotion in late medieval Ireland*. Rachel Moss, Colman Ó Clabaigh and Salvador Ryan (eds.). Dublin 2006.

S

Sadie, Stanley: *Mozart: The Early Years, 1756-1781*. New York 2006.

Sandler, Lucy Freeman: *Omne bonum. A fourteenth-century encyclopedia of universal knowledge*, 2. vols. London 1996.

Schiller, Gertrud: *Iconography of Christian art*. Trans. J. Seligman, 2 vols. London 1972.

Schneiders, Sandra M.: 'The Study of Christian Spirituality. Contours and Dynamics of a Discipline'. *Studies in Spirituality* 8. Leuven 1998, pp. 38-57.

Scholz, Bernhard: 'Het hart als "res significans" en als "res picta". Benedictus van Haeftens "Schola Cordis" (Antwerpen 1629)'. *Spiegel der letteren. Tijdschr. v. nederlandse literatuurgesch* nr. 3. Leuven 1991, pp. 115-147.

Scholz, Bernhard F.: 'Emblem und Emblempoetik'. *Wuppertaler Schriften 3*. Berlin 2002.

Schulz, Hans J.: 'Die Anastasis-Ikone als Erlösungsaussage und Spiegel des sakramentalen Christusmysteriums'. *Der Christliche Osten 36 (1981)*, pp. 3-12, 39-46.

Schulz, Hans J.: 'Die "Höllenfahrt" als "Anastasis"'. *Zeitschrift für Katholische Theologie 81 (1959)*, pp. 1-66.

Schwarz, Reinhard: *Vorgeschichte der reformatorischen Busstheologie*. Berlin 1968.

von Simson, Otto: *The Gothic Cathedral. Origins of Gothic Architecture and the Medieval Concept of Order*. Princeton 1988 (1954).

Smither, Howard E.: *A History of the Oratorio*, vols. I and III. Chapel Hill 1987-2000.

Sonnenwend, das ist, von Gleichförmigkeit deß Menschlichen Willens mit dem Willen Gottes: In fünff Buecher abgetheilt. München 1627.

Staal, Frits: *Rules without meaning*. New York, Bern, Frankfurt a.M. and Paris 1989.

Stambowsky, Phillip: *The Depictive Image. Metaphor and Literary Experience*. Amherst 1988.

Steonius, Nicolaus: *De musculis et glandulis observationum specimen*. Copenhagen, Amsterdam 1664.

Streider, Peter: *Tafelmalerei in Nürnberg 1350-1550*. Nürnberg 1993.

Surin, Jean-Joseph: *Guide spirituel pour la perfection*. Christus 12. Paris 1963.

Surin, Jean-Joseph: *Triomphe de l'amour divin sur les puissances de l'Enfer et Science expérimentale des chose de l'autre vie*. Collection Atopia. Grenoble 1990.

Surin, Jean-Joseph: *Questions importantes à la vie spirituelle. Sur l'amour de Dieu*. Aloys Potter & Louis Mariès (eds.). Paris 1930.

T

Tambiah, Stanley J.: *Culture, thought and social action: an anthropological perspective*. Cambridge Mass. 1985.

Terrin, Aldo Natale: *Il rito. Antropologia e fenomenologia della ritualità*. Brescia 1999.

The Aquinas Prayer Book. Manchester and New Hampshire 2000.

The Book of Margery Kempe. Harmondsworth 1994.

The Concise Oxford Dictionary of Current English, 8th ed. Oxford 1990.

The 'Little Flowers,' 'Life and 'Mirror' of St. Francis'. Ernest Rhys (ed.). London 1912.

The Material History of American Religion Project: www.materialreligion.org/documents/aug98doc.html

The Order of Saint Benedict: www.osb.org/gen/medal.html

Thévenot, Luc Boltanski-Laurent: *De la justification. Les économies de la grandeur*. Paris 1992.

Thomas a Kempis: *De Imitatione Christi*. Michael J. Pohl (ed.). Opera Omnia 2. Freiburg 1904.

St. Thomas of Aquino: *Summa Theologica*, 5 vols. Allen Texas 1981 (1911).

St. Thomas Aquinas Summa Theologica. The Fathers of the English Dominican Province (ed. and transl.). 1920. Online edition www.newadvent.org/summa/

St. Thomas of Aquino: *Truth*, 3 vols. (*Quaestiones disputatae de veritate*.) Indianapolis and Cambridge 1994 (1954).

Thomas of Celano: *Saint Francis of Assisi. First and Second Life of St. Francis*. Placid Hermann OFM (ed. and transl.). Chicago 1988 (1963).

Tomasic, Thomas Michael: 'William of Saint-Thierry against Peter Abaelard: A Dispute on the Meaning of Being a Person'. *Analecta Cisterciensia* 28. Rome 1972, pp. 3-76.

Tuhkanen, Tuija: 'Retorisk analys i bildtolkning. – att läse donatorernas intentioner i bilderna'. *Tegn, symbol og tolkning. Om forståelse og fortolkning av middelalderens bilder*. Gunnar Danbolt, Henning Laugerud and Lena Liepe (eds.). Copenhagen 2003, pp. 229-242.

Turner, Victor W.: *The Ritual Process. Structure and Anti-Structure*. Chicago 1969.

V

Varnhagen, Herman: *Zur Geschichte der Legende der Katharina von Alexandrien*. Erlangen 1891.

Vosmaer, Jacob: *Het leven en de wandelingen van Meester Maarten Vroeg*. J. Wagelaar (ed.). Culemborg 1978.

W

Waaijman, Kees: 'Transformation. A Key Word in Spirituality'. *Studies in spirituality*. 8. Leuven 1998, pp. 5-36.

de Waardt, Hans: 'Breaking the boundaries: irregular healers in eighteenth-century Holland'. *Illness and healing alternatives in Western Europe*. Marijke Gijswijt-Hofstra, Hilary Marland and Hans de Waardt (eds.). London and New York 1997, pp. 141-160.

Waddell, Chrysogonus: 'The Cistercian Dimension of the Reform of La Trappe'. *Cistercians in the Late Middle Ages*. Rozanne Elder (ed.). Kalamazoo 1981, pp. 102-161.

Waddell, Chrysogonus (ed.): *Narrative and Legislative Texts from Early Cîteaux*. Cîteaux 1999.

Ware, Kallistos: 'Dare We Hope for the Salvation of All? Origen, St Gregory of Nyssa and St Isaac the Syrian'. *The Inner Kingdom* (The Collected Works, 1). Crestwood N.Y. 2000.

Warncke, Carsten-Peter: *Symbol, Emblem, Allegorie. Die zweite Sprache der Bilder*. Köln 2005.

Watts, Alan: *Myth and Ritual in Christianity*. London 1983 (1954).

Wiersinga, Herman: *Geloven bij daglicht. Verlies en toekomst van een traditie*. Baarn 1992.

von Wilckens, Leonid: 'Die Kleidung des Pilger'. *Wallfahrt kennt keine Grenzen. Themen zu einer Ausstellung des Bayerischen Nationalmuseums und des Adalbert Stifter Vereins, München*. Lenz Kriss-Rettenbeck and Gerda Möhler (eds.). München 1984.

William of Saint-Thierry: *Epistula ad Fratres de Monte-Dei*. J. Déchanet (ed. and transl.). *Guillaume de Saint-Thierry, Lettre aux Frères du Mont-Dieu*. Paris 1975.

Winkelbauer, Thomas: *Ständefreiheit und Fürstenmacht: Länder und Untertanen des Hauses Habsburg im Konfessionellen Zeitalter*. Wolfram von Herwig (ed.): *Teil 2, Österreichische Geschichte, 1522-1699*. Wien 2003.

Woolf, Rosemary: 'Doctrinal influences on the Dream of the Rood'. *Medium Aevum* 27. Oxford 1958, pp. 137-53.

Woolf, Rosemary: 'The theme of Christ the lover-knight in medieval English literature'. *Review of English Studies* 13. Oxford 1962.

Woolf, Rosemary: *The English religious lyric in the Middle Ages*. Oxford 1968.

Z

Zabala, Santiago (ed.): *The Future of Religion*. New York 2005.

Ø

Østrem, Eyolf and Petersen, Nils Holger: 'The Singing of *Laude* and Musical Sensibilities in Early Seventeenth-Century Confraternity Devotion. Part I'. *Journal of Religious History* 28:3. 2004, pp. 276-97.

Østrem, Eyolf and Petersen, Nils Holger: 'The Singing of *Laude* and Musical Sensibilities in Early Seventeenth-Century Confraternity Devotion. Part II'. *Journal of Religious History* 29:2. 2005, pp. 163-76.

Notes on contributors

Henrik von Achen. Dr. art. Professor in art history at the University of Bergen, Bergen Museum (Norway). Curatorial responsibility for the collections of religious art, and collections of coins and medals. Research interests are late medieval art and society, instruments of devotion and Christian iconography. His publications include: The "Passion Clock" - a Lutheran "Way of the Cross". Reflections on a popular Motif in Early 18th Century Scandinavian Religious Imagery'. *Genre and Ritual. The Cultural Heritage of Medieval Rituals.* Mette Birkedal Bruun and Niels Holger Petersen et al (eds.). Copenhagen 2005. 'The Sinner's Contemplation'. *Images of Cult and Devotion.* Søren Kaspersen (ed.). Copenhagen 2004 and 'Human heart and Sacred Heart: reining in religious individualism. The heart figure in 17th century devotional piety and the emergence of the cult of the Sacred Heart'. *Categories of Sacredness in Europe, 1500-1800.* Arne Bugge Amundsen and Henning Laugerud (eds.). Oslo 2003.

Mette Birkedal Bruun. PhD. Research fellow, Centre for the Study of the Cultural Heritage of Medieval Rituals, University of Copenhagen. Works on monastic memory and reform as well as spatial aspects of text and ritual. Her publications include: 'The Cistercian Rethinking of the Desert'. *Cîteaux* 53 (2002); *The Appearances of Medieval Rituals: The Play of Construction and Modification.* Niels Holger Petersen and Mette Birkedal Bruun et al (eds.). (2004) and *Parables: Bernard of Clairvaux's Mapping of Spiritual Topography* Leiden 2007.

Peter De Mey. Dr. theol. Professor of systematic theology at the Catholic University of Leuven (Belgium) and director of the Centre for Ecumenical Research of the Leuven Faculty of Theology. One of his research interests is theology and the arts. His publications include: Peter De Mey & Katelijne Schiltz, 'The Dialogue between Theology and Music: The Theological Significance of the War Requiem by Benjamin Britten'. *Transfiguration: Nordic Journal of Christianity and the Arts*, Volume 6. Issue 2 (2006). Jacques Haers & Peter De Mey (eds.): *Theology & Conversation: Developing a Relational Theology* (2003). Peter De Mey, Jacques Haers & Jozef Lamberts (eds.): *The Mission to Proclaim and to Celebrate Christian Existence* (2005).

Rob Faesen. Professor of Medieval Dutch Mystical Litterature at the Catholic University of Leuven (Belgium) and member of the Ruusbroec Society (University of Antwerp, Belgium). In Leuven, he holds the Jesuitica and Ignatiana Chair. In 2004 he held the MacLean Chair in the College of Arts and Sciences of Saint Joseph's University, Philadelphia (USA). His publications include the critical edition of Jan van Ruusbroec, *Van Seven Trappen [Seven Rungs]*, *Corpus Christianorum Continuatio Mediaevalis 109* (2003). He is also editor of Albert Deblaere (1916-1994), *Essays on Mystical Litterature, Bibliotheca Ephemeridum Theologicarum Lovaniensium 177* (2004).

Henning Laugerud. Dr. art. Senior Lecturer at the Department of Cultural Studies and Oriental Languages, Faculty of Humanities, University of Oslo (Norway). His research interests include the medieval and early modern period. Art- and cultural-history, visual studies, rhetoric and theories of interpretation. His publications include: *Tegn, symbol og tolkning. Om forståelse og fortolkning av middelalderens bilder [Sign, Symbol and Interpretation. On understanding and interpretation of Medieval Images]*. Ed. together with Gunnar Danbolt and Lena Liepe (2003). 'Some remarks on the Sacredness or the Sanctity of Images according to the Council of Trent and St. Thomas Aquinas'. *Categories of Sacredness in Europe, 1500-1800*. Arne Bugge Amundsen and Henning Laugerud (eds.) (2003). *Norsk fritenkerhistorie 1500-1800 [The History of Norwegian Free-thinking 1500-1800]* with Arne Bugge Amundsen (2001).

Fred van Lieburg. Dr. Professor of Protestant History at the VU University in Amsterdam and co-director of ReLiC, the VU Centre for Dutch Religious History. He is interested in the history of Protestant clergy, lay religion, oral tradition and other cultural topics. His publications include the handbook *Nederlandse religiegeschiedenis (Dutch religious history)* with Joris van Eijnatten (2005, second edition 2006). *Living for God. Eighteenth-Century Dutch Pietist Autobiography* (2006), and he has edited *Confessionalism and Pietism. Religious Reform in Early Modern Europe* (2006).

Mario Perniola. Professor of Aesthetics and former director of the Department of Philosophy at the University of Rome 'Tor Vergata' (Italy). Visiting Professor in many universities and research centres in France, Denmark, Brazil, Japan, Canada and USA. He is the author of several books of philosophy and aesthetics translated into many languages. He has edited the journals *Agaragar* (1971-3), *Clinamen* (1988-92), *Estetica News* (1988-95) and *Ágalma. Rivista di studi culturali e di estetica* (since 2000). His publications include: *The Sex-appeal of the Inorganic* (2004), *The Art and Its Shadow* (2004), *Del sentire cattolico* (2001) and *Ritual Thinking. Sexuality, Death, World* (2000).

Nils Holger Petersen. M.Sc. and PhD. Associate Professor at the Theological Faculty of the University of Copenhagen, Denmark, and the leader of the Danish National Research Foundation Centre for the Study of the Cultural Heritage of Medieval Rituals. His research interests are medieval liturgy and drama, medievalism in opera, and topics of cultural history, theology, and music. His publications include: *The Appearances of Medieval Rituals: The Play of Construction and Modification* edited with Mette Birkedal Bruun et al (2004) and with Eyolf Østrem: *Medieval Ritual and Early Modern Music: The Devotional Practice of Lauda Singing in Late-Renaissance Italy*. (forthcoming).

Salvador Ryan, PhD. Academic Coordinator at St Patrick's College, Thurles, County Tipperary (Ireland), where he also lectures in Church History. His main research interests are in the area of popular religion and ritual in late medieval and early modern Ireland, Irish catechetical works produced on the Continent and the religious works of Irish bardic poets. His publications include: 'Exchanging blood for wine: Envisaging Heaven in Irish bardic religious poetry'. *Envisaging Heaven in the Middle Ages*. Carolyn

Muessig and Ad Putter (eds.) (2006); Co-editor (with Rachel Moss and Colmán Ó Clabaigh OSB) of *Art and devotion in late medieval Ireland* (2006) and 'From late medieval piety to Tridentine pietism? The case of 17th century Ireland'. *Confessionalism and Pietism: religious reform in the Early Modern period, Veröfentlichungen des Instituts für Europäische Geschichte.* Fred van Lieburg (ed.) (2006).

Eli Heldaas Seland. Cand.philol. PhD. student at the University of Bergen, Bergen Museum (Norway), Cultural History Collections. The preliminary title of the project is: *The Folk Song of Sculpture or Pocket Piety: Religious Medals of the Nineteenth Century.* Fields of interest are Medals, Christian art, iconography, narratology and visual culture.

Laura Katrine Skinnebach. MA in History and Communication from Roskilde University Centre in Denmark. PhD. student at the University of Bergen, Bergen Museum (Norway). The preliminary title of the project is *Images and Devotional Practises in Late Medieval Northern Europe.* Main interests are the study of practices and how they relate to instruments of devotion in particular images and the space in which they take place.